AMERICAN RIGHTS

The Constitution in Action

THE MACMILLAN COMPANY
NEW YORK · CHICAGO
DALLAS · ATLANTA · SAN FRANCISCO
LONDON · MANILA

IN CANADA
BRETT-MACMILLAN LTD.
GALT, ONTARIO

AMERICAN RIGHTS

The Constitution in Action

WALTER GELLHORN

Betts Professor of Law
Columbia University

THE MACMILLAN COMPANY
New York · 1960

First Printing

Printed in the United States of America

The Macmillan Company, New York
Brett-Macmillan Ltd., Galt, Ontario
Library of Congress catalog card number: 60-5408

CONTENTS

AMERICAN RIGHTS

The Constitution in Action

INTRODUCTION

Everybody likes the Constitution. That is a central fact of American political life. Nobody admits wishing to undermine the fundamental document of our government. Those who bomb schoolhouses because a Negro child has been allowed within their doors do so in the stated belief that they are upholding the sacred Constitution. Even the Communists indignantly deny they are subverters. At times they seek to wrap themselves in the mantle of Jefferson as pure defenders of democracy's basic tenets. Political figures can freely denounce the Supreme Court without risking their popularity; but they must take care at the same time to laud the Constitution, and to blame the Court for having distorted its true meaning.

Despite the almost unanimous adulation of the Constitution—or, possibly, because of this adulation—little attention is given to the details of its application to specific cases. Litigation is the lawyer's business. The nonlawyer tends to think it a very dull business, and probably too technical to be grasped, anyway. Still, if the Constitution is to be meaningful to Americans, they must know what impact it has on problems of contemporary importance, and must cease regarding it abstractly (and somewhat simple-mindedly) as A Good Thing.

The Supreme Court, at any rate, cannot regard the Constitution abstractly. The Court cannot, for example, express sentiments about the validity of a statute except as that issue has been raised in an actual case or controversy, and is thus subject to being examined in a precise context. Only by litigation, then, can be brought into play the highly important judicial power to invalidate a legislative enactment. And only by the exercise of this power of judicial

1

review do American courts give content to broad constitutional phrases that were written without foreknowledge of the myriad circumstances to which they now have pertinence.

The courts of most countries regard themselves as duty bound to apply statutory enactments without inquiring into their harmony with the Constitution. Of course the legislature is obligated to comply with constitutional prescriptions and prohibitions. But it is not the judges' job to inquire into whether that obligation has been fulfilled. Just as an American policeman or official seeks to enforce the laws the legislature adopts without speculating concerning their validity, so might our own judges have left to the legislators the responsibility for defining and observing constitutional boundaries. Since 1803, however, judges in the United States have been held to possess not only the power, but also the positive duty, to pass upon the constitutionality of statutes and other governmental actions.[1] Japan, West Germany, India, Canada, Italy, Argentina, Australia, France, and Greece have in one degree or another adopted this distinctly American contribution to political science;[2] but many nations with strong traditions of constitutional observance still function without any judicial oversight.

The American theory on this point may be very simply formulated. The Constitution itself is a law. In fact, according to Article VI of the Constitution, it and the statutes "made in pursuance thereof" and the treaties made by the United States are collectively "the supreme law of the land." When a judge, whether of high or low degree, is asked to apply a state or federal statute, the statute may possibly conflict with some provision of the Constitution. In order to decide the case before him, the judge must choose which of two conflicting laws he will enforce—the law stated in the statute or the law stated in the Constitution. Since the latter is by hypothesis the law superior to all others, the judge must disregard the statute if it runs counter to the constitutional command. If the judge were required to give effect to any law the members of the legislature had adopted, he might be confronted with the unpleasant necessity of deciding cases on the basis of what he regarded as a defective statute.

As has been said above, judges in this country have no general supervisory power over government to see that the Constitution is always observed. They deal only with *cases*—in other words, with adversary proceedings in which one party relies on a governmental action as the basis of his claim or his defense, and the other party says that the governmental action should be held invalid because it disregards the Constitution. The issues that come before the courts grow out of concrete disputes. The judges do not decide, as a body of high level legal advisers, whether a legislative enactment might be said in some circumstances to have ignored constitutional limits. Rather, they decide a ripened controversy in which one side or the other says that its constitutional rights have been impaired, here and now, in a clearly identifiable way.

Judges—even Justices of the Supreme Court of the United States —are human beings, not oracles. Hence they are as fallible as the human beings who compose the legislative and executive branches of government. Nevertheless, the relative independence of their tenure makes them less likely than the others to be "influenced by diverting pressure," in Judge Learned Hand's somewhat euphemistic phrase.[3] Being somewhat removed from the pulls and tugs of partisan politics and being at least partially immunized against momentary passions and panics,* the courts are able to speak not, to be sure, as disembodied spirits, but as still fairly cool evaluators of constitutional controversies.

Yet, even though judges are in a relatively detached position

---

* In *The Bill of Rights* (1958), at p. 69, Judge Hand speaks about the judicial review of governmental restraints upon free speech: "The most important issues here arise when a majority of the voters are hostile, often bitterly hostile, to the dissidents against whom the statute is directed; and legislatures are more likely than courts to repress what ought to be free. It is true that the periods of passion or panic are ordinarily not very long, and that they are usually succeeded by a serener and more tolerant temper; but . . . serious damage may have been done that cannot be undone, and no restitution is ordinarily possible for the individuals who have suffered. This is a substantial and important advantage of wide judicial review."

and even though their official utterances are usually couched in
terms of impersonal principle rather than personal preferences, a
large personal element does enter into constitutional judgment.
In theory the judges devote themselves to the purely intellectual
task of comparing a statutory text with a constitutional text, to
see whether they are in conflict.[4] Few important constitutional
provisions, however, are so indisputably clear that all the judge
must do is to match their words against a challenged statute, as
though one were matching the colors of two samples of silk.

Consider, for example, the words of the Fifth and Fourteenth
Amendments that forbid either Congress or the state legislatures to
deprive any "person" of "life, liberty, or property without due process of law." The courts, as we have seen, are empowered and obligated to set aside any statute that, when suitably challenged, is found
to conflict with this basic law. To declare the existence of this
judicial duty is easy. To execute the duty is extremely difficult.

What, exactly, is a "person"? After a hard wrestle with the
question, the courts decided that a corporation is a person, for
present purposes. What about a labor union or some other voluntary
organization that seems to have a strong identity of its own, but
is not incorporated? Answers to questions of that type cannot be
discovered in the constitutional text that supposedly provides the
guide.

What is "liberty"? Liberty has been undoubtedly limited if a
person has been imprisoned. What if a person has merely been
restricted in what he would like to do? Would a law that fixed
the number of persons who could become lawyers be a deprivation
of the liberty of someone who was otherwise eligible to be a member of the bar, but who was over-quota? Would liberty be impaired
if loud-speakers were installed in all factories working on military
supply contracts, to blare forth governmental messages which the
persons who worked in the factories would have to hear whether
or not they approved? "Liberty" can scarcely mean an absolutely
unbridled freedom. We could not live together in our complex

modern civilization if it did. But what, exactly, are the constitutionally allowable limits?

And what about the "due process of law" that must attend any deprivation of life or liberty or property? This phrasing has come to be read as though it said, in essence, that life, liberty, or property cannot be taken away except in accordance with a procedure that is fair, and for reasons that might to a fair-minded man seem just. Does this not mean that, in the end, the judges through the process of constitutional litigation must decide whether the legislative action satisfies at least minimum standards of fairness and wisdom? The tests being so imprecise, how can judges decide cases without consulting to some extent their own conceptions of what is seemly and prudent? No matter how doggedly we may pretend that judges merely ascertain the meaning of words embodied in a constitutional text, a court can rarely discharge its review function without consciously or unconsciously indulging its own value judgments.

Thus the Supreme Court's decisions are necessarily influenced by the personalities of the Justices who happen to be serving at any period. It would be quite wrong to think otherwise. Nonetheless, the public at large does widely and justifiably believe that judges do seek to subordinate their own prejudices or convictions, that they do try hard to maintain a stable set of rules, that they do generally succeed in considering issues of constitutional law dispassionately rather than with an eye to any party's or group's advantage. Above all, there is a strong and pervasive sentiment in America that all men's rights are fortified when an individual can challenge the validity of governmental acts affecting him, and can have his challenge heard by a court. There is an old saw that we no longer have a government of laws, but simply a government of lawyers. Still, lawyers who retain their humility and couple it with a passion for justice are useful men to have on the premises, as guardians against oppressions that flow from carelessness or beclouded legislative judgment.

The following chapters consider how the American Constitution has developed in practice. The Constitution devotes only 166 words to all the topics that are here discussed. The ways in which those words have been used are more meaningful than the words themselves, for they indicate not merely what has happened in the past, but also shed light on the emerging problems of the future.

Chapter 1

HABEAS CORPUS
AND JUST PROCEDURES

Habeas Corpus has been an important element of American Law from the very beginnings of the United States, for it is embodied in Article I of the original Constitution:

The Privilege of the Writ of Habeas Corpus shall not be suspended, unless when in cases of Rebellion or Invasion the public safety may require it.

On the face of it, habeas corpus seems to be one of those dry-as-dust procedural matters, dear to the hearts of lawyers but not very exciting for others. What is it, after all, but a judicial direction to a person who has custody of another to produce his prisoner before the court and explain why he is being detained?

In purely descriptive terms, that is exactly what habeas corpus is. But, as is so often the case with procedural devices, this simple little lawyer's maneuver is an unassuming mask behind which may be found matters of great substance. The late Professor Chafee, perhaps America's outstanding scholar in the field of civil liberties, thought without any doubt at all that it is "the most important human rights provision in the Constitution." Censorship, he explained, can be evaded; efforts to suppress ideas by prosecuting those who express them may perhaps be defeated. But a prison wall is a tangible reality, an existing fact. Only habeas corpus, he maintained, has the power to penetrate that wall. "When imprisonment is possible without explanation or redress," he added, "every form of liberty is impaired. A man in jail cannot go to church or discuss or publish or assemble or enjoy property or go to the polls." [1]

Such an enthusiastic comment must, of course, be regarded with prudent skepticism. There is, alas, no single magic measure that can be counted upon to produce justice without fail. The statutes and procedures that deal with habeas corpus are not always free from complexities. A person who challenges the legality of his detention must overcome very real difficulties of proof; and, quite apart from that, we must always remember that a man can be *legally* detained if he is held by virtue of the decision of a tribunal that had jurisdiction of the matter, even though the tribunal's decision may in actuality have rested on an error.[2] Honest mistakes in law administration can still occur. Moreover, since habeas corpus operates only to challenge unlawful imprisonment or other detention, we still have to be concerned about the sorts of things that can lead to a man's being lawfully detained. If the area of lawful detentions is unduly broadened, the significance of habeas corpus is correspondingly narrowed. So habeas corpus cannot be regarded as having some limitless virtue; nobody can afford to fall into a self-deluding dream that a constitutional provision of 1787 has created an unshatterable shield against oppression. Nevertheless, lawyers can justly take pride in the mechanism they have developed for challenging claims of the power to detain.

MILITARY CONTROL OVER CIVILIANS

In recent years the people of the United States have been unworried about domination of the nation's life by its own military. Elsewhere in the world this comfortable state of affairs has not existed. Habeas corpus has been a strong American weapon by which the rule of law has been guarded against threatened impositions of the rule of might. In the future it may continue to be a preserver of civilian supremacy.

A few experiences of the past may provide useful illustration.

The national and state constitutions alike provide that a person who is accused of wrongdoing shall be informed of the charges against him, and shall have a prompt and fair trial by a tribunal committed to the administration of justice according to the forms of law. Of what avail are those constitutional safeguards if they can be set aside by the military in times of stress? To what extent can martial law supplant the procedures normally regarded as prerequisite to a lawful detention?

During the tense and tragic years of the war between the States, the nation's traditions were at times among the casualties. With President Lincoln's consent the military authorities in some of the states in which sentiment was divided, arrested and detained individuals who were thought to be lending assistance to the rebellion against the established government. Men were held by the fiat of soldiers, rather than by the orderly determinations of judges. Those who were detained could not match force with force, in order to escape from an imprisonment for offenses of which they had not been duly convicted. But perhaps they could secure release from detention by utilizing the writ of habeas corpus, on the ground that the military had no right to abrogate the system of trials the Constitution had guaranteed.

Recall, in this connection, what the American Constitution says about habeas corpus: the privilege of the writ "shall not be suspended, unless when in cases of Rebellion or Invasion the public safety may require it." President Lincoln contended, in effect, that the existing rebellion had created conditions that necessitated the steps taken to protect the public safety. When the issue came before the Supreme Court, however, the Justices would not accept the view that the Army or the President or even the Congress could foreclose the question of whether the public safety *required* the suspension of the writ of habeas corpus. In this instance, the Supreme Court noted, the regular courts were still functioning to try criminal cases; if the Army thought that illegal acts were being committed by individuals in the community, the Army could see to it that the accused individuals were prosecuted in the courts according to law;

hence there was no necessity for the imposition of military decisions upon civilians, and the detention was therefore illegal.[3]

The judgment in that case, as one commentator has said, "is the pledge of the Supreme Court to the people of the United States that the constitutional right of freedom from arrest and punishment at the caprice of the executive branch of the Government, particularly the military, . . . can never be taken away so long as the courts are open and can function. There are no more important constitutional rights than those." *

Of course it would be wrong to conclude that only courts have power to give orders in America. There are no doubt moments of crisis in every society in which action must be taken quickly and forcefully. There is no time for calling a convention of judges to gather their reactions. Somebody has to be decisive—and then must carry out his decisions without delay. The head of the State— the President if the nation is involved, or the Governor if only one of the states is involved—must decide whether guns are needed to preserve the State's life. The significant thing, for purposes of the present discussion, is that the courts do not regard themselves as precluded from a later inquiry into the basic facts, after martial law has been declared because of alleged insurrection. If the courts were to be made subordinate to the military, the Supreme Court said in a case involving martial law in the state of Texas, "it is manifest that the fiat of a state governor, and not the Constitution of the United States, would be the supreme Law of the Land. . . ." While the Governor does have to decide whether or not to bring troops into action, "what are the allowable limits of military discretion, and whether or not they have been overstepped in a particular case, are judicial questions." [4]

In other words, as a leading authority on martial law has con-

* John P. Frank, "*Ex Parte Milligan* v. *The Five Companies:* Martial Law in Hawaii," 44 *Columbia Law Rev.* 639 (1944). Candor compels the additional remark, however, that the judicial protection against capricious arrest sometimes comes rather tardily. The *Milligan* case, for example, was decided by the Supreme Court after the Civil War was over; meanwhile, Milligan's rights were being effectively interfered with by the military. Delay is unfortunately typical of legal proceedings; they take time to get started, and they take time to complete.

cluded, the courts retain the power finally to determine "whether the invasion of interests normally protected was, under the circumstances, arbitrary and in excess of the occasion." [5] In making that determination, the courts will give respectful consideration to the executive judgment they are now asked to overturn, and will no doubt seek to evaluate the situation as it appeared when the judgment had to be exercised. Baseball enthusiasts know how delightfully easy it is to "second-guess" the manager after the game has been played; but the manager, unlike the spectator in the grandstand, has to make his decisions before the result is known. The Supreme Court does not irresponsibly indulge in second-guessing the chief executive who had a reasonable basis for fearing that disaster would occur if military measures were not promptly taken. In the end, however, *necessity* is the only basis upon which military might can properly supplant the rule of law, and the judges are not willing to let any military commander have the last word on that subject. The military power, the courts candidly recognize, is as broad as the danger it is to meet; still, when an individual seeks by habeas corpus to secure his release from military custody, the courts must be able to see that there was in fact a direct relationship between the danger and the step taken to meet it. There must be a "substantial basis for the conclusion" that the military determination was truly "a protective measure necessary to meet the threat." [6]

These general propositions were given an interesting application during World War II. Immediately after the Japanese bombing of Pearl Harbor on December 7, 1941, the civilian governor of Hawaii virtually abdicated his office by turning over his powers to the general in command of that territory. The general created the "Military Government of Hawaii," and decreed that offenders were henceforth to be tried in a somewhat summary manner in military courts. Soon afterward Hawaii was no longer in a forward area, for the zone of hostilities had moved much farther to the west. There was, in short, no real necessity for setting aside the normalities of civilian government. Needless to say, however, the military was not enthusiastic about giving up the power it had acquired. Persons accused of such crimes as embezzlement—things

that had nothing whatsoever to do with military operations—
continued to be tried before courts staffed by officers rather than
judges.

Then habeas corpus came into play. Some of the military's
prisoners began proceedings to test the legality of their detention.
At first the commanding general refused to pay any attention to the
inconspicuous and powerless little judge who had ordered him, the
mighty general, to justify his conduct. So the judge fined the general for contempt of court—and he fined him heavily, too. That
got some action. The judge would have encountered great difficulty
in collecting the fine if the general had remained adamant; the usual
method would be to order confinement in jail until the fine was
paid, but the judge would have had a hard time recruiting enough
troops to capture the general. Here is where a good tradition proved
to be a more potent weapon than the sword. Long ago the Supreme
Court, expressing the true sentiments of the United States, had
declared that "the military should always be kept in subjection to
the laws of the country to which it belongs, and that he is no
friend to the Republic who advocates the contrary. The established
principle of every free people is, that the Law shall alone govern;
and to it the military must always yield." [7] When the courageous
judge in Hawaii gave his order to the commanding general, the
order was heard in distant Washington. Emissaries hastened to the
scene to restore peace—not between Japan and the United States,
but between the general and the judge. Peace was restored, but it
was on the judge's rather than the general's terms. The prisoners
were produced in response to the writ of habeas corpus, and the
legality of their military detention was put to the test.

Ultimately, the Supreme Court agreed with the local judge that
the whole military proceeding was an impropriety and that the
prisoners should be released. Justice Murphy in a concurring opinion
wrote words that bear repeating: "From time immemorial despots
have used real or imagined threats to the public welfare as an excuse
for needlessly abrogating human rights. That excuse is no less unworthy of our traditions when used in this day of atomic warfare
or at a future time when some other type of warfare may be de-

vised. The . . . constitutional rights of an accused individual are too fundamental to be sacrificed merely through a reasonable fear of military assault. There must be some overpowering factor that makes a recognition of these rights incompatible with the public safety before we should consent to their temporary suspension." [8] In Hawaii at the time there was no such overpowering factor. The civil courts were capable of functioning in their usual manner to try criminals and to dispense justice. All that kept them from doing so was the superior force of the military authorities, rather than the immediate necessities of war. In those circumstances habeas corpus came to the rescue—and the rights of civilians were vindicated.

Nobody should naively suppose that the writ of habeas corpus is an impregnable barrier against government by bayonets. No piece of paper, no lawyer's ingenuity can supply the will to live as a free people. We ourselves have to generate that will; we ourselves must resolve not to exalt the warrior as the highest expression of the state. But so long as habeas corpus remains to be used by honorable judges upon the plea of the individual members of the nation, we possess a method for testing the legality of military impositions on the citizenry.* If the time ever comes when habeas corpus orders are ignored, we can conclude that power has been usurped and that the military are no longer the defenders of the institutions they profess to serve.

HABEAS CORPUS AND CRIMINAL PROCEDURE

The public is not keenly interested in the law of criminal procedure. The newspapers and the other mass media of information tend to stress the sensational and the bizarre. Matters of procedure

---

* In this connection, consider *United States ex rel. Toth* v. *Quarles,* 350 U.S. 11 (1956) (the military courts are not permitted to try a former soldier for a crime he had allegedly committed while a member of the armed forces; since he is no longer a member of the military, he is entitled to be tried by a civilian court according to established procedures); *Reid* v. *Covert,* 354 U.S. 1 (1957) (courts-martial do not have jurisdiction over civilian dependents of armed services personnel, to prosecute them in peacetime for the alleged murder of members of the armed services overseas; these cases involved wives who had killed their husbands, while assigned to foreign stations). And see Carl B. Swisher, *The Supreme Court in Modern Role* (1958), ch. IV, on military-civil relations.

seem dull to newspaper reporters—and, indeed, to almost everybody who is not a lawyer. This is true even though, as Justice
Frankfurter has remarked, "The history of liberty has largely been
the history of the observance of procedural safeguards." [9] Without
those safeguards, many of the values of democratic society would be
destroyed. "The quality of a nation's civilization," an able judge
recently declared, "can be largely measured by the methods it uses
in the enforcement of its criminal law." [10] Even so, most people
become interested in procedural problems only when, as sometimes
happens, a seemingly guilty person escapes his doom because of
what appears to be a "mere technicality." When that happens, there
may be a little flurry of excitement—usually about the wrong things.

The Constitution of the United States sets forth in some detail the
rights of persons accused of crime. Yet, despite what impress me as
admirable constitutional provisions, I venture to suggest that the
intended protections might on some occasions fall far short of their
goal if they were not buttressed by the writ of habeas corpus, or, as
it has sometimes been admiringly called, "the freedom writ."

First of all, recall again what habeas corpus is. It is, to begin with,
an independent civil proceeding against the jailer or other detainer
of the person in whose behalf the writ is sought. A person must be
in actual custody in order to be entitled to the writ. Notice that
the operative word is "custody" rather than "imprisonment," for
the writ would be appropriate in such cases as an allegedly improper commitment to a mental hospital, or a detention of an alien
with a view to deporting him, or an induction of a person into the
military forces, or, indeed, in any purely private detention, such as
that of a child by an adult. Upon an appropriate court's receiving a
petition, the court issues a command that the prisoner be produced
before it, unless the petition itself discloses that the petitioner is
properly held in detention or unless only questions of law rather
than issues of fact are raised. In the latter situation, the court need
not require that the prisoner be produced in person, but instead it
may issue an order to the custodian to show cause why the
petitioner should be detained further. In other words, the reasons

for the detention can in some cases be explored without receiving the petitioner's testimony or requiring his presence.[11] Habeas corpus is not available until all other suitable administrative or judicial remedies have been exhausted.[12] The purpose of the writ is not to disturb the orderly course of proceedings, but to afford a final opportunity to assure that the appearance of orderliness accords with the realities.

The American writ of habeas corpus is a descendant of earlier English statutes. These statutes had had as their declared purpose the guaranteeing that proper legal processes would be used. Critics of the old English models have maintained that they tended to encourage almost ritualistic observance of forms without much regard for the substantial fairness the forms were intended to nourish. Someone has said that the ancient English writ of habeas corpus assured only a "check-list freedom." The American counterpart was a big improvement over its predecessor. The big step forward in the United States was taken in 1867, when Congress enacted that the federal courts shall "have power to grant writs of habeas corpus in all cases where any person may be restrained of his or her liberty in violation of the constitution, or of any treaty or law of the United States. . . ." [13] This put the chief focus not on a preordained list of ingredients, but, rather, on claimed violations of fundamental fairness by either the state or the federal government. The federal court's responsibility when it receives an application for habeas corpus, the Supreme Court has said, is "to look beyond forms and inquire into the very substance of the matter, to the extent of deciding whether the prisoner has been deprived of his liberty without due process of law. . . ." [14]

Consider, for example, a case that arose a dozen years ago. A young man named Francis was tried for a capital offense in Louisiana and was sentenced to death by electrocution. His trial was fair and, if capital punishment is ever just, his sentence was just. On the day set for his execution, he was strapped in the electric chair, all the final measures were taken, and the switch was thrown. Through some gruesome accident, the current that passed through

Francis's body was insufficient to kill him. The electrical equipment needed repair. Francis was removed from the chair and was returned to his cell to await execution on another day. What would you have done in Francis's behalf if you had been his legal representative? Undoubtedly you would have thought of using habeas corpus in order to raise the question of whether poor Francis could be forced to undergo again the harrowing experience of being prepared for execution. There would at this point still be no complaint about the procedure that had led to his being convicted and sentenced in the first place. But the doomed man's spokesman might want to argue that a second exposure to the electric chair would disregard the constitutional prohibition of cruel and unusual punishments.

The Supreme Court, upon considering the problem, concluded by a majority vote that this constitutional provision would not save Francis.[15] The Court did, however, weigh very carefully whether the unusual circumstances of the case had produced a result "offensive to a decent respect for the dignity of man, and heedless of his freedom." If the Court had been persuaded that this had happened, habeas corpus would have provided the remedy.

A very recent case well illustrates the point. A Californian named Chessman was convicted of some revolting crimes and was sentenced to die. Appeal followed appeal, all to no avail. Chessman remained in his death cell, awaiting execution. As the date of his execution drew near, he filed a petition for a writ of habeas corpus contending that the stenographic transcript of the testimony taken in his trial was incorrect in important respects, and that for this reason the courts that had reviewed his conviction had not had a true record before them on which to act. The court stenographer who had taken notes during Chessman's trial had died before he had finished transcribing his notes. The job was completed by another stenographer, who had concededly encountered difficulty in deciphering some of his colleague's shorthand notations. Chessman had protested vainly and repeatedly. Now he tried once more, by habeas corpus. The Supreme Court held that he was entitled to an opportunity for a full hearing on the issue of whether the transcript was in fact complete and accurate. If not, he should have a new trial, because it would be unfair to allow a sentence to be carried out when the appellate court might possibly have been misinformed.*

There is nothing in the American constitution that explicitly reaches a case like this one. The Supreme Court relied on the broad language of the Fourteenth Amendment—"nor shall any State deprive any person of life, liberty, or property, without due process of law." Even at the eleventh hour the courts were ready and able to consider whether a man's life was to be taken without a fully fair procedure.

Or take the extraordinary case of a young rascal named Smith— at least, one hopes it is extraordinary. Smith was arrested, so he says, as a suspect in a minor burglary. He alleges that he agreed to plead guilty to a charge of unlawful entry, a lesser offense for which he might have anticipated being sent to the penitentiary for three years. The police and the prosecuting attorney hustled him off to court, where, without really understanding the nature of the charge against him, he pleaded guilty—and, to his great dismay, was promptly sentenced to imprisonment for twenty years. Subsequently, he now asserts, he discovered that he had been accused of a much more serious crime than the one as to which he had intended to admit his guilt. But Smith was poor and ignorant and, moreover, imprisoned. By the time he had found out what had happened to him, his opportunity for an appeal had long since expired. After eight years in the penitentiary he filed a petition for a writ of habeas corpus, and at last he was assured of a hearing on

* *Chessman* v. *Teets*, 354 U.S. 156 (1957). Justice Harlan, in the Court's majority opinion, wrote (p. 165) that it "needs to be repeated that the overriding responsibility of this Court is to the Constitution of the United States, no matter how late it may be that a violation of the Constitution is found to exist. This Court may not disregard the Constitution because an appeal in this case, as in others, has been made on the eve of execution. We must be deaf to all suggestions that a valid appeal to the Constitution, even by a guilty man, comes too late, because courts, including this Court, were not earlier able to enforce what the Constitution demands. The proponent before the Court is not the petitioner but the Constitution of the United States."

his very grave charges against the prosecutor and the policeman who, if Smith's account were true, would be the real villains in the drama.[16] An arrested person is entitled to be informed of the charges against him, and to have the privilege of consulting counsel, and to insist that cause for his detention be shown in open court. But these constitutional protections can sometimes be lost through carelessness or malice. We like to feel that local officials are rarely as wicked as were those involved in young Mr. Smith's case. If by ill chance some wrongdoer does come to hold an official position, it is comforting to think that habeas corpus might enable a victim to escape from his clutches.

This statement of three bad cases would be seriously misleading if it were taken as suggesting that improper convictions are usual in the United States. It is perfectly true that the federal district courts receive a large number of petitions for habeas corpus. In the year 1956, which was not abnormal, 660 petitions were filed, all of them alleging that grave wrongs had been done to a person in custody. But, as Professor Pollak has recently shown, "the percentage of applications in which relief was granted was never large and has not risen. On the contrary—in 1946 (when applications were at about the 500 mark) only 2.8 of the applications had some measure of success, and by 1954 even that figure had shrunk to 1.3 per cent." [17] The great bulk of the applications are marked by such inadequacy that well over 90 per cent of them are disposed of without any hearing at all. It is arguable, of course, that some meritorious cases are overlooked because of the inability of a prisoner to present his problem in a persuasive manner. On the other hand, some judges rather gruffly believe that prison officials may encourage their prisoners to file applications for the writ, perhaps as a form of occupational therapy intended to distract them from engaging in "more mischievous pursuits." [18] One of the huge penitentiaries in the state of Illinois has been called "the world's largest law school." Prisoners are allowed to use the prison law library as well as to buy their own books. There are 4400 prisoners in that particular penitentiary, and among them they own 400 typewriters with which they manage to produce some 3000 legal documents each year. As one even-tempered judge commented not long ago, this may cause some extra work for the courts; "but prisoners whose energies are directed to getting out of the prison by judicial process are not so likely to be concentrating on other methods of getting out which may be less socially acceptable." [19]

Still, the small number of meritorious applications for habeas corpus in federal courts should not be viewed as diminishing the present importance of the writ. Before an application may be made to a federal court, all available state procedures must first have been utilized. An unknown, but probably significant, number of wrongs and errors are corrected by state judges, who thus reduce the number of serious cases that would otherwise have to be considered by federal courts. Furthermore, the availability of the writ is a major factor, if not actually the chief factor, in stimulating observance of correct standards in criminal proceedings. The emphasis habeas corpus places upon justice rather than on the mere forms of justice serves to remind American lawyers and law administrators that ideals must constantly be translated into action. If, as we hope is true, we Americans are slowly becoming civilized, the availability of habeas corpus provides us an instrument with which, from time to time, we can test whether our law enforcement practices are keeping abreast of our consciences.

Chapter 2

SOME ASPECTS OF FAIRNESS IN CRIMINAL PROCEDURES

THE RIGHT TO COUNSEL

Americans are brought up to believe that "every man is entitled to have his day in court." Courts being what they are, this conjures up a picture of representation by a trained legal adviser, who can surefootedly guide his client through the maze of technicalities in which he might otherwise become lost. A question remains, however, about who is to pay for the guide when the client himself cannot afford to engage one.

The Sixth Amendment to the United States Constitution provides that "In all criminal prosecutions, the accused shall enjoy the right . . . to have the Assistance of Counsel for his defence." After that provision had been in the Constitution for a hundred and fifty years, the Supreme Court *for the first time* held that this meant something more than that the accused could hire a lawyer if he had enough money. In 1938, in the case of *Johnson* v. *Zerbst*,[1] the Court concluded that a defendant must either have the assistance of counsel or must understandingly waive his right to such assistance; this means that a defendant who cannot afford to pay a fee may nevertheless insist that the court appoint a lawyer to represent him.

That is the situation in the federal courts today. It is not, however, a wholly satisfactory situation. The Government does not provide any payment at all for the court-appointed attorneys, who therefore serve at considerable sacrifice to themselves and perhaps to their clients. Former Attorney General Brownell thought that "voluntary acceptance of assignments as defense counsel, without compensation, is as outmoded as a volunteer fire department in modern society." * Moreover, there are many expenses other than counsel fees that must be met by a litigant. In order to call an ordinary witness in a federal court, for example, a litigant must be prepared to pay the witness traveling expenses, a daily fee of four dollars, and a daily subsistence allowance of eight dollars. If expert witnesses or searches for evidence are necessary, costs of course increase greatly. The late Jerome Frank, a great federal judge who had a penchant for speaking strong words, once exclaimed that "a man may be jailed for life, or even electrocuted, because he hasn't the money to discover a missing document necessary to win his case or to employ a competent hand-writing expert or psychiatrist. This is not democratic justice. It makes a farce of 'equality before the law,' one of the first principles of a democracy." [2] Still, as a recent *Columbia Law Review* study shows, some advances have been made in recent years in the federal courts, and there appears to be a mounting awareness that the reality of legal rights must be provided for those whose poverty stands in the way.[3]

Progress has been less clear in most of the state courts. Complexities arise in American law because fifty states continue a sort of dual existence in America, being a part of a union of states on the one hand while they remain separate sovereigns on the other. They are of course subject to the Constitution of the United States. Some provisions of the Constitution, however, are applicable directly to the federal government alone. That is true of the Sixth Amendment, the one that talks about the right to have counsel. So the Supreme Court's holding in *Johnson* v. *Zerbst* did not in-

* Herbert Brownell, Jr., "The Bill of Rights," 41 *Am. Bar Assn. Journal* 517, 521 (1955). Britain is ahead of the United States in this respect, for since 1949 indigents in that country have been allowed to select counsel from a list of attorneys who have agreed to serve and who receive compensation from the Government for the services they render. Legal Aid and Advice Act, 12 & 13 Geo. 6, c.51.

stantly answer the question of whether state governments as well as the federal government had to provide lawyers for poor defendants. If the state governments were required to do so, it would be because the Fourteenth Amendment forbids them to deprive anyone of life or liberty without *due process of law*.

Even before *Johnson* v. *Zerbst* the Supreme Court had held that the due process clause of the Fourteenth Amendment might require the provision of counsel for indigent defendants. In one well known case a group of ignorant and frightened boys were placed on trial for their lives, with only the most perfunctory sort of legal assistance. After they had been convicted, there was much indignation in some parts of the community, and money was raised for an appeal to the higher courts. Ultimately, the Supreme Court held that their conviction must be set aside because they had not been accorded due process. In many cases the right to be heard, said the Court, would be of little use if it did not include the right to be heard by counsel. "Even the intelligent and educated layman has small and sometimes no skill in the science of law. If charged with crime, he is incapable, generally, of determining for himself whether the indictment [the accusation] is good or bad. He is unfamiliar with the rules of evidence. Left without the aid of counsel he may be put on trial without a proper charge, and convicted upon incompetent evidence, or evidence irrelevant to the issue or otherwise inadmissible. He lacks both the skill and knowledge adequately to prepare his defense, even though he have a perfect one. He requires the guiding hand of counsel at every stage in the proceedings against him." [4]

With this case to go along with *Johnson* v. *Zerbst*, one might have guessed that the Supreme Court would hold that all American defendants—whether in federal or in local cases—should receive the same degree of help. But the guess would have been wrong. In *Betts* v. *Brady* [5] the Court declared that due process required the aid of counsel in all capital cases—that is, all cases in which the death sentence might be imposed; as to all other sorts of cases, the obligation to provide a lawyer for the defendant "depends upon the offense and a determination of the defendant's ability, in the light of his age, education, and the like, to defend himself without counsel."

This rather fluid result has stirred considerable criticism within the judiciary itself. Some of the judges think that the rule should be inflexible. The variability of the requirement gives rise in America to a number of habeas corpus petitions by convicts who say that they did not have lawyers at their trials although they were incapable of defending themselves—and sometimes this sort of incidental litigation arises so long after the trials that it creates severe difficulties in law administration.* Moreover, there are many Americans who worry about the unfairness that may flow from the defendant's poverty; they recall the stinging words of the French satirist, Anatole France: "The law, in its magnificent equality, forbids the rich as well as the poor to sleep under bridges, to beg in the streets, and to steal bread." Fair-minded men want to achieve real rather than merely superficial equality. To some extent the inequity is being lessened; in some cities, for example, there is a voluntarily supported Legal Aid Society that provides free legal services for needy persons, and in some places provision is made for "public defenders," lawyers in the employ of the state whose talents are placed at the disposal of all who need them.[6]

Furthermore, the Supreme Court has recently announced two decisions that may lead to reexamining the right-to-counsel cases. The first case involved a procedural rule of the State of Illinois that a re-

* See, for example, *Palmer* v. *Ashe*, 342 U.S. 134 (1951) (a seemingly dull-witted defendant was not provided counsel; he successfully challenged his conviction in a habeas corpus proceeding commenced eighteen years afterward); *Pennsylvania ex rel. Herman* v. *Claudy*, 350 U.S. 116 (1956) (eight years after conviction); *Cash* v. *Culver*, 358 U.S. 633 (1959) ("an uneducated farm boy of 20" convicted of burglary and sentenced to a fifteen-year imprisonment, successfully challenged his conviction after four years behind bars). And see also *Uveges* v. *Pennsylvania*, 335 U.S. 437 (1948); *Bute* v. *Illinois*, 333 U.S. 640, 677 (1948); *Gibbs* v. *Burke*, 337 U.S. 773 (1949) (The State argues that the Supreme Court's somewhat wavering rule "leaves the state prosecuting authorities uncertain as to whether to offer counsel to all accused who are without adequate funds and under serious charges in state courts. We cannot offer a panacea for the difficulty. . . . The due process clause is not susceptible of reduction to a mathematical formula.")

view by an appellate court can be had only on a fully transcribed record of the trial court's proceedings. A record of a long trial, however, is an expensive document. What about the man who cannot afford to procure one? Shall he be deprived of the opportunity to take an appeal, while a richer man can have one? The Court has now held that the State must assure equal treatment; it must provide a transcript free to those who cannot pay for it. The second case involved an Ohio requirement that a docket fee of $20 be paid by each appellant to the state supreme court. A convicted felon complained that he had been deprived of opportunity to appeal because he could not raise the needed money. The Supreme Court has now upset the Ohio requirement, saying that the indigent and the wealthy alike must have access to the appellate court; "the imposition by the State of financial barriers restricting the availability of appellate review for indigent criminal defendants has no place in our heritage of Equal Justice Under Law." [7] There is a very close resemblance between these two cases and the right-to-counsel case. The lesson they seemingly teach is that the nature and effectiveness of procedural safeguards should never be allowed to hinge on the size of the defendant's pocketbook.

THE USE OF CONFESSIONS

In many countries today, and in most countries at some time in their past, prosecutions of alleged criminal offenders have often been founded on the defendants' own confessions, extorted from them during prolonged interrogations before trial. In modern times, and especially in western countries, two intellectual currents have combined to discourage the open use of torture as an instrumentality of law administration. First, the humanist belief in the worth and dignity of the individual has made physical brutality repugnant. Second, skepticism about the reliability of confessions has replaced the former uncritical conclusion that they were worthy of credence no matter how shockingly they might have been obtained. Forced confessions, it is now thought, are as likely to be false as to be true;

and even when they can be confirmed by extrinsic evidence, confessions obtained by oppressive methods are a danger to society. Too short a step lies between police lawlessness and the full-fledged police state, in which the police become a law unto themselves and terror becomes a calculatingly used tool of government.

America, like other lands, still has some policemen who believe that the end justifies the means. If the end has been to gain a conviction, they have been willing to use the means of extracting a confession instead of the more laborious discovery of evidence. Until recent years the judges of American courts tended to avoid coming to grips with this problem. For a long time everybody suspected that police often indulged in abusive methods to gain confessions; [8] in a very few instances an officer would be prosecuted for having gone to extremes of violence, and even more infrequently a victim of prolonged interrogation would bring an action for damages. Not until 1936, however, did the Supreme Court of the United States find opportunity for the flat declaration that a coerced confession could not be used as evidence; [9] before then, the weight to be given to a confession was one of the questions that was left to the fact-finders in each case. Then finally, in the 1936 case, the Court woke up to the realization that the most effective way to guard against official oppression was to forbid the use of its fruits.

This relatively minor point may serve as a reminder that our forefathers have not invariably been all-wise or vigilantly sensitive about law administration. We tend much too often to excuse some silly or even vicious practice on the ground that it has existed for a long, long time. Instead, we ought to look at ancient practices with a wary and critical eye. Someone has said that traditions are like snakes; the longer they grow, the more dangerous they become. No doubt that is an overstatement. But there is a seed of truth in it. Consider, for example, a practice in ancient England, from which America derived so much of its law. There, if an accused person refused to answer to a charge, he was "pressed"—quite literally, he was pressed under heavy weights, until he either grew less stubborn or was crushed to death. This atrocious torture in the name of the law lasted for four hundred and fifty years, from the end of the thirteenth to the middle of the eighteenth century. Eventually, somebody achieved the reform of simply assuming that an accused person who remained silent had, in effect, denied his guilt; and trials thereafter proceeded on that basis without the "pressing" of olden days. As Glanville Williams has said in describing this matter, "One hardly knows whether to marvel more at the appalling cruelty of our ancestors or at their baffling lethargy, in failing for so long a time to avoid horrible cruelty by a simple legislative change." [10] It is worth remembering that many of the good things in American law—like the revolt against police brutality—are not things that came to us from our ancestors, but are of recent origin, having been stimulated by reformers who were not afraid to challenge imperfections no matter how well intrenched they had become.

At any rate, since 1936 the Supreme Court has most forcefully and repeatedly stated that a conviction must be upset if based on a confession gained by oppression. No showing of violence is needed. "There is torture of the mind as well as the body; the will is as much affected by fear as by force." [11] Hence, for example, a confession made to a police psychiatrist has been found inadmissible because the surrounding circumstances disclosed that the accused had been under sustained pressure that robbed his confession of its voluntary character.[12]

The most important development in the federal courts has been the rule that delay in taking an arrested person before a judicial authority will in itself invalidate any confession made during that delay. This rule was first announced in 1943 in *McNabb* v. *United States*,[13] a well known case involving some brothers who were suspected of having shot a federal officer. They were held for periods ranging from about fourteen hours to three days, during which they were allowed to see nobody but their captors. One of the brothers was questioned for five or six hours, but apparently without threats or violence. In the end, confessions were made. The Court said that they could not be used as evidence. The requirement that arrested persons be taken before a magistrate without delay is intended to check the reprehensible practices called "the third degree"—police aggression or intimidation against a person in custody. If the requirement is disregarded, there is an opportunity for third-degree methods before the accused is fully informed concerning his rights. The way to destroy that opportunity, the Court asserted, was simply to reject the confessions even though there was no evidence that there had in this particular case been any specific coercion, either physical or psychological.[14]

That is the rule in the federal courts. In the state courts the test of admissibility continues to be whether the confession was voluntary or was coerced.[15]

Acceptance of the notion that a man may be robbed of his will even though he has not been physically attacked may soon bring the federal and the state positions together. At the very least, it is now clear that a prolonged detention away from the protections that judicial supervision would presumably provide, can constitute pressure that weakens an accused's resistance and can properly be recognized as coercion.[16]

Moreover, purely in terms of efficiency rather than of justice, the modern world requires police methods that do not rely too heavily upon the grilling of suspects in order to wring confessions from their lips. Police who can unravel the mysteries of crimes only if the criminals will tell all, are likely to miss much that more up-to-date methods might disclose.

In any event, courts that are dedicated to the attainment of justice will carry heavy responsibility for discouraging unfair methods, whether or not they appear to be expedient in some circumstances. Disregard of individual rights by the use of crude procedures is not a sound means of securing the reign of law and order. As Professor Hogan and Father Snee of Georgetown University have said in a recent penetrating study, this is the root of the Supreme Court's decisions in this area. "Trials which are the outgrowth or fruit of the Government's illegality debase the processes of justice. They cannot be countenanced in any nation which expects its citizens to esteem those processes. It is important that the trial demonstrate the guilt of the accused, but it is important also that it not disclose the criminality of the accuser." [17]

SEARCH AND SEIZURE

The United States Constitution and the state constitutions as well contain fundamentally similar provisions to protect against un-heralded police invasions of private homes and offices. The federal constitution, in the Fourth Amendment, reflects the general tone. The people, the Constitution says, are to be secure "against un-reasonable searches and seizures" of their "persons, houses, papers, and effects." Warrants to authorize a search are to be issued only "upon probable cause," and they must particularly describe "the place to be searched, and the persons or things to be seized."

Of course this does not mean that a warrant has to be obtained before an arrested person may be searched. Immediate search is a necessary incident of the arrest, to protect the arresting officer against being attacked with concealed weapons, to deprive the prisoner of means of escaping, and to prevent the destruction of evidence the arrested person may possess. Similarly, vehicles and vessels may be searched without a warrant issued by a judge if there is probable cause to think a search is justified, because they can be too easily moved away during the time a warrant is being obtained.[18]

But in the absence of some such compelling necessity, a judicial officer stands between the police and the individual. As the United States Supreme Court has stated, "This was not done to shield criminals nor to make the home a safe haven for illegal activities. It was done so that an objective mind might weigh the need to invade that privacy in order to enforce the law. The right of privacy was deemed too precious to entrust to the discretion of those whose job is the detection of crime and the arrest of criminals. Power is a heady thing; and history shows that the police acting on their own cannot be trusted. And so the Constitution requires a magistrate to pass on the desires of the police before they violate the privacy of the home." [19] An able American law professor has summarized the matter by saying, "An officer ought to search only if he has good reason grounded in information which can persuade a non-policeman of the reason." [20]

General statements of this sort reflect a commendable attitude, but they do not dictate the answer to specific cases. How "necessary" does a search have to be before it is sufficiently necessary to overcome the need for obtaining a search warrant? We have said, for example, that an arrested person may be searched. It is an easy and logical step, then, to conclude that officers may also search things that are within the immediate physical control of the prisoner. If a suspected murderer were arrested while seated at his desk, a prudent officer might reasonably look in the desk drawer to make sure that it did not contain a pistol; and if a man were arrested for having broken into somebody's house, it might not be unreasonable for the arresting officer to look into the suitcase the burglar happened to be carrying in his hand.

But what about the following case, presented to the judges a few years ago? A dealer in rare stamps that were bought by stamp collectors, had sold some forgeries. A warrant for his arrest was obtained. Officers went to his one-room place of business. There they arrested him and then, without a search warrant, searched his desk, safe, and file cabinets. The officers seized 573 forged stamps they found in those places. Was this search and seizure reasonably incident to the arrest, or was the Constitution violated? The Supreme Court was of divided opinion, but the majority held that the search was lawful because it was linked with a valid arrest, involved a business room that was open to the public, the searched room was small and was under the prisoner's immediate and complete control, and the search went no farther than the room that was itself used for the unlawful activities giving rise to the arrest. Moreover, the Court emphasized that this was not a general exploratory search to see if evidence of some unspecified crime might be turned up—unfocussed search of that type would have been bad with or without a warrant; the search in this case was as specific as it could be, being limited to a hunt for forged stamps whose possession was itself a crime.[21]

Why was there any disagreement in a case like this, involving as it did a shabby little cheater about whom nobody should really care very much? Justice Frankfurter answered that question in his dissenting opinion. History teaches us, he said, that the safeguards of liberty have very frequently been outgrowths of "controversies involving not very nice people." We cannot allow our vision to be beclouded by the identity of a particular defendant; we have to deal with the great themes expressed by the Constitution, rather than with the man whose case has presented the occasion for thinking about those themes. When the dissenting justices approached the matter in this way, they feared that the Court was weakening the requirement of *absolute necessity* as the only permissible exception to the general rule of search warrants.*

Departure from the *absolute necessity* requirement has introduced an element of uncertainty into American law. But there is no tendency to hold that an arrest gives the police *carte blanche* to search and seize. Just recently, for example, the Supreme Court considered the case of some individuals who had been arrested for harboring a fugitive from justice; they had been hiding a convicted person at a secluded cabin in the California mountains. The arresting officers had had the cabin under surveillance for twenty-four hours before they made the arrests. After the arrests, the police agents searched their prisoners. Then they transported the entire contents of the cabin—everything from ladies' underwear to musical recordings, from toothbrushes to toilet paper—to the offices of the Federal Bureau of Investigation in San Francisco, two hundred miles away. Some of the items thus seized were later used in evi-

---

* This had previously been the declared view of the Court. *Trupiano* v. *United States,* 334 U.S. 699 (1948), had held that a search warrant *must* be obtained if practicable. In the case now under discussion the arresting officers had had time to obtain a search warrant, and there was no excuse for not getting one. The decision in the present case overrules *Trupiano* v. *United States* to the extent that it fails to take into account "the reasonableness of the search after a lawful arrest."

dence. The Court held this to be wholly improper, and reversed the guilty verdicts.[22]

This is a matter of great importance. If the mere fact of an arrest were to legalize any subsequent search, the constitutional protection would soon become a sham. Police would find it much too easy to enter premises in order to make an arrest for some petty offense— or even on some wholly spurious charge—and thus confer upon themselves the right to rummage through the arrested person's papers and possessions. This is exactly what American constitutional provisions were intended to prevent.

Now, how can we most effectively police the police, to make sure they will not overstep the line between legal and illegal searches? For a long time the federal courts have ruled very simply that illegally seized evidence must be excluded from a trial. This reflects the extremely practical judgment that the constitutional immunity against police invasion would otherwise be nullified; illegal searches are most sharply discouraged by eliminating the utility of lawlessness.[23]

Once again, however, the American courts have had to face the problem of federal and state relations. Are the state courts required to adopt the same exclusionary rule of evidence as is enforced in the federal courts? To put the question differently, could the states forbid illegal searches (as all of the states do), but at the same time allow the fruits of any illegal search to be used in evidence?

In *Wolf* v. *Colorado* [24] decided in 1949, the Supreme Court said that this was a matter within each state's discretion. No state can authorize an illegal search of a man's papers or effects, said the Court; but each state may choose for itself how the right of privacy is to be enforced. If a state wants to rely on the deterrent effect of criminal proceedings against lawless police officers, it may do so. If it wants to rely on civil proceedings brought by individuals against the officers who have trespassed against them, that is for the state to say. Actually, of course, the wrongdoing policemen are not likely to be arrested by their colleagues; and, while there are recorded instances of substantial verdicts in behalf of outraged citizens, the chances of recovery in a law suit are not very good.[25]

At the time of the *Wolf* decision, sixteen of the then existing forty-eight states had already adopted the federal exclusionary rule, and since then five other states have adopted it. Moreover, the newly admitted states of Alaska and Hawaii had perforce followed the federal practice during their days as territories, and will presumably adhere to it in the future. The California Supreme Court in 1955 was very specific in condemning police in that state for repeatedly acting lawlessly while they were supposedly enforcing the law; the Court said that it would no longer allow itself to participate in this wrongdoing by receiving as evidence the articles and papers the police had seized after illegal searches.[26] Twenty-seven of the state courts, however, were in 1959 still failing to exercise an effective restraint upon wrongful seizures of evidence.

This is perhaps not quite so serious as it seems at first, for two reasons. The first reason is that the most dangerous threats to the general liberties of the people are likely to come from the national (the central) government, rather than from the states where excesses in law enforcement may arouse a storm of local political protest; and since the courts do exclude evidence in federal prosecutions if it was illegally seized, there is an effective protection at perhaps the point of greatest need.[27] The second reason is that the due process clause may still operate to bar the use of evidence that was acquired by particularly atrocious means.

This possibility is well illustrated by the 1952 case of *Rochin* v. *California*.[28] Police officers broke into Rochin's room, believing that he was a peddler of narcotics. They saw him pick up some capsules from a table by his bed, and swallow them. First they tried to shake them out of his mouth and throat. Failing in that, they handcuffed him, rushed him to a hospital, and persuaded a doctor to force an emetic solution through a tube into Rochin's stomach. This "stomach pumping" caused Rochin to vomit, and in the vomited matter were found two capsules containing morphine. Rochin was prosecuted in the California courts, which at that time still allowed illegally seized evidence to be used. After his conviction, Rochin sought review by the Supreme Court of the United States on the ground that the state had not conducted the criminal proceedings against him in accordance with the demands of due process. The Supreme Court agreed, though the judges arrived at their conclusions by different paths.

Justice Frankfurter, writing the majority opinion, said that the conduct of the police in this instance "shocks the conscience. Illegally breaking into the privacy of the petitioner [Rochin], the struggle to open his mouth and remove what was there, the forcible extraction of his stomach's contents—this course of proceeding by agents of government to obtain evidence is bound to offend even hardened sensibilities." States, he added, must in their criminal prosecutions "respect certain decencies of civilized conduct. Due process of law, as a historic and generative principle, precludes defining, and thereby confining, these standards of conduct more precisely than to say that convictions cannot be brought about by methods that offend 'a sense of justice.'" To tolerate the police action in the present case, he asserted, "would be to afford brutality the cloak of law. Nothing would be more calculated to discredit law and thereby to brutalize the temper of a society."

Some of the judges, while they agreed that the morphine capsules should not be used as evidence, thought that this rather misty sort of talk left too much to the personal reactions of the judges. Their doubts have been somewhat strengthened by a very recent decision which deserves discussion here not because the result is highly important in itself, but because it well illustrates how American constitutional law is built up on a case-by-case basis rather than by a series of absolute pronouncements. American constitutional law is not a massive structure that is erected all at once, and then continues to stand unchanged; rather it resembles a coral reef that gains bulk from many small accretions, and changes shape through the tiny erosions of wind and wave.

Breithaupt v. *Abram* [29] involved a defendant charged with having driven a motorcar while intoxicated. Still unconscious from an accident in which his car had been involved, he was removed to a hospital where a sample of his blood was taken for tests which showed a high alcohol content. After he had been convicted, he sought his release by habeas corpus, contending that the use of the involuntary blood test had deprived him of his liberty without due process of law. Of course he relied on Rochin's case that has just been discussed. Breithaupt argued that taking his blood was just as bad as making Rochin vomit. But a majority of the judges did not agree with his argument. They thought that there was nothing "brutal" about extracting a blood sample under the protective eye of a physician. "As against the right of an individual that his person be held inviolable, even against so slight an intrusion as is involved in applying a blood test of the kind to which millions of Americans submit as a matter of course nearly every day, must be set the interests of society in the scientific determination of intoxication, one of the great causes of the mortal hazards of the road." [30]

The dissenting judges were not content with this differentiation between the *Breithaupt* and *Rochin* cases. "Only personal reaction to the stomach pump and the blood test can distinguish them," Justice Black exclaimed rather crossly; this is "to build on shifting sands." Chief Justice Warren thought the Court should say flatly that "law enforcement officers in their efforts to obtain evidence from persons suspected of crime must stop short of bruising the body, breaking skin, puncturing tissue or extracting body fluids, whether they contemplate doing it by force or by stealth." Justice Douglas wrote: "If law enforcement were the chief value in our Constitutional scheme, then due process would shrivel and become of little value in protecting the rights of a citizen. But those who fashioned the Constitution put certain rights out of the reach of the police and preferred other rights over law enforcement." If "the decencies of a civilized state" are to be the test of whether the police have gone too far, he declared that he thought it repulsive "for the police to insert needles into an unconscious person in order to get the evidence necessary to convict him, whether they find the person unconscious, give him a pill which puts him to sleep, or use force to subdue him. The indignity to the individual is the same in one case as in the other, for in each is his body invaded and assaulted by the police who are supposed to be the citizen's protector."

Here again, then, we detect the clashing of values that underlies so much constitutional litigation. The conflict is not always one between good and evil, but, as in the cases just discussed, may be between good and good. Society does have an interest in law enforcement. Society also does have an interest in preserving the individual's privacy—which Justice Brandeis characterized many years ago as "the right to be let alone—the most comprehensive of rights and the right most valued by civilized men." [31]

In one closely related field of litigation, involving "electronics eavesdropping," the scales have been tipped heavily, perhaps much too heavily, on the side of law enforcement rather than on the side of privacy.

In 1928 the Supreme Court held that no unreasonable search was involved when the police tapped a suspect's telephone wires and listened to his conversations.[32] Of course the men who wrote the American Constitution knew nothing about telecommunications; even so, the spirit of their attempt to protect privacy might well have led the Court to a different conclusion from the one it reached. But, for good or ill, the constitutional question was answered negatively.

Congress, however, enacted a law in 1934 forbidding the use in court of evidence obtained through wire tapping. As far as the federal courts are concerned, even evidence that has been obtained indirectly as a result of wire tapping is not admissible.[33]

But wire tapping is old-fashioned in this day of electronic achievement. Devices have been invented that faithfully record distant whispers; and the conversations that can thus be overheard by stealth can be used as evidence.[34] Tiny radio telephone transmitting sets can be carried in an officer's pocket, and the words uttered by a suspect in conversation with the officer can be carried through the air, to be used against him afterward.[35] Overheard conversations can be used even when, as in one recent case, the Supreme

Court thought that the eavesdropping officers' conduct in placing a microphone in a suspect's bedroom "would be almost incredible if it were not admitted." [36]

Those who feel that the most important need of the day is to send criminals to jail will not be overly worried that the area of individual privacy is growing smaller, and that innocent communication is becoming increasingly subject to interception. On the other hand, the spirit of freedom can be crushed, the confidence of people in one another can be destroyed, the individual can be too readily deprived of his right to remain an individual, if truly strong barriers are not erected against searches and snoopings by unregulated police agents. Justice Jackson, who had occasion to be in Germany immediately at the end of the Hitler régime, declared soon afterward: "Uncontrolled search and seizure is one of the first and most effective weapons in the arsenal of every arbitrary government. And one need only briefly to have dwelt and worked among a people possessed of many admirable qualities but deprived of these rights to know that the human personality deteriorates and dignity and self-reliance disappear where homes, persons and possessions are subject at any hour to unheralded search and seizure by the police." [37]

THE PROSECUTOR AS THE SERVANT OF JUSTICE

The topics discussed previously in this chapter have drawn attention to various procedural matters bearing upon fairness toward a person believed to be involved in a crime. This concentration upon the rights of supposed criminals is not meant to cause forgetfulness of the whole community's rights. There is indeed a strong social interest in preserving civil liberties by protecting accused persons against abuse. There is at the same time a strong social interest in discouraging criminality by catching and convicting wrongdoers. The community, which, after all, is merely an aggregation of individuals, wants to be sure that its individual members are not victimized by overzealous officials; but it also wants to be sure that they are not victimized by overzealous criminals.

The two social objectives of justice and efficiency are entirely compatible. On occasion, no doubt, the guardians of law and order may have to work harder to achieve results by lawful means than would be required of them if they were themselves to break the law. As an Indian civil servant remarked three-quarters of a century ago, there is a great deal of laziness involved in the short cuts that are sometimes taken in the quest for proof of guilt. "It is far pleasanter," he said, "to sit comfortably in the shade rubbing red pepper into a poor devil's eyes than to go about in the sun hunting up evidence." [38]

In every American jurisdiction the public prosecutor is of great importance in setting the tone. The best devised system of criminal procedure can be subverted by prosecuting attorneys who do not regard themselves as the dedicated servants of justice.[39]

In most jurisdictions—the cities or other units of government in which prosecutors hold office—the volume of cases far outstrips the available personnel to bring all cases to trial. Clearly, the prosecutor has a vast power, and a power that in America is virtually uncontrollable, to decide which cases should be pressed toward decision. His responsibility is, of course, to select those in which prosecution is most clearly warranted by the seriousness of the offense or by the existence of strongly persuasive evidence or by the character of the defendant. But there is still an inescapable danger, as a famous Attorney General of the United States once remarked, that he may "pick people that he thinks he should get, rather than pick cases that need to be prosecuted." [40]

Because he is overburdened with cases, a busy prosecutor tends to allow many defendants to plead guilty to some crime less serious than the one of which they have been accused. This eliminates the necessity for a trial. A "bargain plea" of this sort is often very satisfactory to the defendant, who gains a less severe punishment; and it is perfectly proper when the volume of pending court cases, the existence of mitigating circumstances (such as, for example, the defendant's good record in the past), or the difficulties of proof of the original charge argue against taking the case to court.

Here, too, however, there are dangers about which everyone must be keenly aware. First, there is a chance for favoritism if not downright corruption in arranging these bargain pleas. Second, there is a chance that undue pressures can be placed on a defendant to make him plead guilty, just to bring an end to his uncertainty.

The possibility of coerced confessions during prolonged detention has already been discussed. To that we must add that when a defendant's trial is unduly postponed, he may in effect lose his right to defend himself "without jeopardizing his job [and] his family ties." [41]

Of course there are occasions when a delay in bringing a case to hearing is justifiable, as, for example, when a necessary witness is ill. But abuses of discretion can readily develop. In extreme cases the courts have had justification for actually dismissing the accusation against an accused person, on the grounds of failure to prosecute after a person had been kept under the shadow of charges for unreasonably long periods of time.

Despite all efforts to forestall the grosser forms of injustice, we must be mindful that the defendant in a criminal proceeding remains at a marked disadvantage as compared with the prosecutor. In the United States, differently from some other countries, the defendant has no police force or vast public resources to help him gather the evidence he needs; * nor does he have either the prestige or the power that the prosecutor enjoys and that help him gain cooperation in the community. One must not become tearfully sentimental about the plight of the poor defendant. Often he deserves no better than he gets—and perhaps he deserves even worse. Still, in a civilized society, the prosecutor does bear a responsibility for doing more than winning cases. A series of successful prosecutions may

* "By contrast, in certain Scandinavian countries it has been the practice for over half a century for the government to provide every criminal defendant with a defense attorney of his choice and to place the police department at his service. Furthermore, the government will pay for all 'necessary investigations, including searches for witnesses, and documents and analyses by handwriting, medical or chemical experts.' Even in the civil area, many investigations in Scandinavian countries are financed by the government." "Aid for Indigent Defendants in the Federal Courts," 58 *Columbia Law Rev.* 832, 837n.

build up a district attorney's reputation; but overzealousness may in the end destroy more than it builds. Nearly a century ago Lord Cockburn, the then Lord Chief Justice of England, reminded the advocate in the courtroom that "the arms which he wields are to be the arms of the warrior and not of the assassin." [42] More recently, and in similar vein, the Supreme Court of the United States reversed a conviction and ordered a new trial because the prosecutor had "overstepped the bounds of that propriety and fairness which should characterize the conduct of such an officer." In that instance the prosecutor had bullied witnesses during the trial, and had presented arguments that the Court deemed "undignified and intemperate, containing improper insinuations and assertions calculated to mislead. . . ." All of this, said Justice Sutherland, speaking for the entire Court, disregarded the fact that the government's interest in a criminal prosecution "is not that it shall win a case, but that justice shall be done." The official who is responsible for bringing a matter to trial "may prosecute with earnestness and vigor—indeed, he should do so. *But, while he may strike hard blows, he is not at liberty to strike foul ones.* It is as much his duty to refrain from improper methods calculated to produce a wrongful conviction as it is to use every legitimate means to bring about a just one." [43] The line between hard blows and foul blows may not always be easy to draw, but both the courts and the responsible public officials will have a legitimate interest in seeing that its existence is never disregarded.* Prosecuting attorneys must be committed to being servants of justice in fact as well as in name.

An especially difficult problem arises in connection with newspaper, radio, and television publicity about cases that are still await-

---

* In what one hopes are very rare instances, a prosecutor may sink to the depths of using testimony or evidence he knows to be false, or to suppress evidence he knows will help the defense. When this outrageous misconduct has come to light, American courts have not hesitated to recognize that the writ of habeas corpus may properly be used to free the victims of the prosecutor's wrongdoing. See, for example, *Ex parte Hawk*, 321 U.S. 114, 115–116 (1944); *Mooney* v. *Holohan*, 294 U.S. 103 (1935); *Alcorta* v. *Texas*, 355 U.S. 28 (1957); and see *Bales* v. *Lainson*, 244 F. 2d 495 (8th Cir., 1957); *Napue* v. *Illinois*, 360 U.S. 264 (1959).

ing decision. There have been a number of unedifying instances in the United States of pretrial announcements or "leaks" to the press, calculated to inflame public feeling against a defendant and thus to jeopardize the fairness of his trial. This has happened particularly in connection with atrocious sex crimes or murders, which receive disproportionately heavy attention from the more sensational newspapers; and it has occurred, too, in cases involving espionage or some other activity about which there was already an acute sensitivity. In Britain, as is well known, discussion of cases that are as yet undecided is very strictly limited. Newspaper editors have been heavily fined and even imprisoned for publishing stories about the evidence that may later be introduced, or speculating about the guilt or innocence of the accused. This has been deemed to be contempt of court, and has been punished accordingly.[44] In the United States, by contrast, the press and the other communications media are largely unhampered in what they print about pending cases. The interest in safeguarding the defendant against any conceivable interference with the objectivity and dispassionateness of his trial is offset by the interest in safeguarding the press against governmental interference with news reporting. While the United States Supreme Court has not yet passed upon the validity of efforts to restrict the newspapers in this respect, those efforts have in any event made very little headway.[45] The bar associations are now seeking to curb any statements by a lawyer concerning pending or anticipated litigation, as a matter of professional self-discipline. Whether they will succeed is not yet clear. The problem in one form or another exists, and must be overcome, in every nation that has a literate population and widely disseminated press.

Chapter 3

THE FREEDOM
TO SPEAK FREELY

The freedom to speak is highly valued in all societies that maintain a democratic structure. Governmentally imposed constrictions of thought and conscience are obviously inconsistent with popular control of the government. And since thinking without communication is profitless, freedom of expression must be protected in order to make freedom of thought a reality. In extraordinarily precise and unqualified language the American Constitution seeks to provide that protection, in the First Amendment: "Congress shall make no law . . . abridging the freedom of speech. . . ." This same prohibition is operative against the states, which, as a result of judicial interpretation of the Fourteenth Amendment, have been forbidden to place unreasonable restraints on speech.

In these days of international tensions and conflicting ideologies, freedom of speech is sometimes considered in too narrow a context. Too often it is seen merely as an aspect of the problem of forestalling subversive movements that insist on their own freedom to speak, but would undoubtedly like to prevent speech by anyone else. That particular problem does truly have important dimensions; it will be discussed later in these pages. Before dealing with that big issue, so closely intertwined with issues of international intrigue and national survival, I propose, however, to turn attention to one or two smaller areas in which the law and philosophy of free speech may be examined perhaps more comfortably.

The chance to express oneself without restraint is no doubt personally enjoyable. Since the production of happiness for one and all is a desirable goal of government, free speech could perhaps be plausibly justified simply as a means to the end of individual fulfillment. But the hard fact remains that one man's enjoyment may prove to be another man's sorrow; the competition of values therefore requires the making of choices on some level other than that of undiluted self-indulgence. Thus, for example, the homeward bound reveler who wishes to exercise his freedom by delivering a boisterous speech that awakens all his neighbors, must be controlled rather than encouraged, no matter how happy he might be if he were allowed to complete his lecture to the night spirits. We live not solely as individuals, but as parts of a community. Community values rather than individual values are the chief molders of the concept of free speech.

Two main social justifications for preserving and, indeed, stimulating free expression should be recognized.

The first of these, as already suggested, is inextricably a part of our political philosophy. We base our whole governmental structure on the belief that government is not master, but servant. We maintain that citizens have not only a right, but also a positive duty to engage in discussions of public affairs, for without an informed public opinion to which officials must adjust their actions, the citizenry soon loses its capacity to govern the governors. Improper official conduct can be curbed, unwise or unfair legislation can be repealed, only if the political processes that presuppose public participation are allowed to operate without oppressive restrictions.

Moreover, experience has taught that expression of ideas—even "radical" or seemingly silly ideas—serves as a desirable stimulant to overcome social lethargy. Useless notions are usually exposed fairly quickly or, more probably, are simply ignored; they do small harm. Occasionally, on the other hand, an idea that at first evoked scorn and hostility manages to achieve acceptance, to become in its turn one of the "eternal verities" that may some day be upset by changed conditions and a yet better idea. The ebb and flow of freely expressed opinions may produce no immediately discernible effect, but in the aggregate, just as surely as tides affect a coast line, they do subtly and sometimes dramatically alter a country's shape without, however, shattering it to bits. When ideas can compete, a nation escapes the unyielding rigidities that sooner or later lead to violent change because they cannot be broken down except by an explosion. The stifling of criticism and protest precludes evolutionary gradualism. Criticism, on the contrary, creates awareness of defects; and when awareness has been created, elimination, or at least diminution, of the defects may follow. The expression of dissatisfaction, far from being a disservice to society, is a preservative of it. The "troublemaker's" complaints draw attention to problems that, if long unnoticed, might become dangerously intensified. Often the troublemaker exaggerates the size of the problem, or misconceives the remedy for it. But he does provoke reexamination of the settled way of doing things, and he does bring into the light of public consciousness issues that might otherwise remain hidden in some dark corner.

The other great social justification for encouragement rather than restriction of discussion is, of course, our mounting awareness that we human beings are woefully ignorant and that we may perhaps learn if only we are willing to listen.

Judge Learned Hand, one of the greatest of American jurists, once characterized the spirit of liberty as "the spirit which is not too sure that it is right." The history of civilization provides many clear and saddening proofs that men rarely know as much as they believe they do. The Western world, to mention one instance, was for a long time less tolerant of different religious faiths than oriental countries have traditionally been. Not many centuries ago men were burned at the stake for being heretics—that is, for expressing beliefs that would now not cause a moment's concern to anyone at all, and that have in some respects become part of the accepted faith of those whose predecessors built the fires. In one country that professed to be deeply Christian in its convictions, men killed one another because they could not agree whether the sign of the cross should be made with two fingers or with three—and both sides *knew* they were right. In America only two hundred and sixty years ago some righteous, well meaning people arranged to hang a number of poor old women who were thought to be witches; and when a few skeptics had the courage to express doubt that the women were in fact witches, the doubters themselves were promptly accused of being witches—because their accusers *knew* a witch when they saw one.

The theme need not be elaborated. There are few countries that can look backward into their past without an ashamed awareness of the part played in their culture by credulity, intolerance, and wickedly closed minds. Yet we would err greatly if we were to conclude that the oppressors of bygone days were invariably insincere—or, indeed, that they were less intelligent than are we ourselves. They imposed their wills on others not to perpetuate errors but to preserve what they regarded as truths. After great suffering their mistakes were demonstrated. We, who are the intellectual beneficiaries of painful, long forgotten struggles toward enlightenment, have at last come to believe that the ultimate good is not likely to be attained by enforced dogmas, but "is better reached by free trade in ideas—that the best test of truth is the power of the thought to get itself accepted in the competition of the market. . . ." [1]

Nowhere has this been more apparent, century after century, than in science. Nevertheless, Galileo was forced to confess error when his astronomical observations came in conflict with what the theologians thought they knew. Three hundred years later, German scientists fell into disrepute during the Hitler régime if their findings did not sustain the racist theories decreed by the dictatorship to be true. In order to learn about physical and nervous reactions to acute fear, one physiologist conducted harrowing researches upon living victims drawn from concentration camps and prisoner of war barracks. First, he tormented and destroyed a number of Poles and other people whom the Nazis regarded as "inferior." He reported that they did not live comfortably with fear; and he was warmly applauded for the scholarly thoroughness with which he had proved this point. Then he was given a batch of Norwegian prisoners, upon whom to continue his devilish researches. When he reported that they, the Nordics who in the German myth were a separate and superior breed of men, reacted exactly as had the inferior Slavs, he himself was promptly cast into a concentration camp. That fate was no doubt a deserved end for this particular scientist, but he arrived at the end for a wrong reason; he deserved to be imprisoned for lending himself to so barbarous a research program, but not for truthfully stating its results. Just so, within the recent past, scientists in Stalin's Russia were exiled or liquidated because they clung to the verifiable results of laboratory tests instead of acknowledging a "truth" that was never accepted outside the Soviet Union and has already, within the space of but a few years, lost its force even in Russia. The Lysenko theory concerning genetic change may conceivably not be the nonsense that most biologists believe it to be; but surely its virtues could not be established, as Stalin sought to do, by suppressing all objections to it. Advance in science has come not by proclaiming the truth but by acknowledging the doubt; more and more clearly, as learning progresses, we perceive that unresolved questions far outnumber the few answers we think we know. So long as questions remain, society must cherish minds that are eager to engage in unhampered questings.

But these generalities, sound though they may be, are not decisive of every case. Other social considerations may at times compete with them for primary recognition. Let us examine several problem areas in which the competing considerations can be readily identified.

LICENSING OF SPEECH

Since the freedom of speech is constitutionally guaranteed against being abridged, the state has no power to require that a speaker obtain a license to say whatever he wishes to say. No public body can insist that its approval of a speech is needed before the speech can be made. If prior approval were necessary, the speaker's freedom would be an illusion—for, by hypothesis, approval could then be withheld if some public functionary were dissatisfied with the speaker's purposes or with the content of his remarks. The United States Supreme Court some years ago struck down a Texas statute that barred labor union officials from making public speeches to enlist support for their unions, unless the speakers had first registered with a state agency and had paid a license fee. The statute, while superficially a measure merely to regulate the occupation of "labor union organizer," was in reality a direct restraint upon a sort of speaking with which the Texas legislature had little sympathy. As such it was unconstitutional. Justice Jackson, in a concurring opinion, declared: ". . . it cannot be the duty, because it is not the right, of the state to protect the public against false doctrine. The very purpose of the First Amendment is to foreclose public authority from assuming a guardianship of the public mind through regulating the press, speech, and religion. In this field every person must be his own watchman for truth, because the forefathers did not trust any government to separate the true from the false for us." [2]

That sounds like good sense. It is up to us to exercise our own judgment about the soundness of the views other people express; we have not delegated to any public authority the responsibility of guarding our minds from error. We must be our "own watchmen for truth."

What, however, shall we say about governmental licensing that deals not with the contents of a speech, but with the time and place at which it can be made? This problem arises most urgently when speakers wish to use a public facility—a park or a street corner or a schoolhouse, for example. The man who rents a private building to which he seeks to draw an audience is different from the man who wants to address his remarks to anyone who happens to be strolling along the footpath. The Constitution cannot be "treated as a promise that everyone with opinions or beliefs to express may gather around him at any public place and at any time a group for discussion or instruction." [3] A demonstration on Main Street at the rush hour could no doubt be restrained, because the demonstration, regardless of its purpose, would be an undue menace to the safety of others who wanted to use the street for more normal purposes. A clamorous meeting in front of the public library might be an objectionable interference with the use of the library, while the same meeting might be entirely proper at some other spot in the same vicinity. A heated debate within the precincts of a cathedral might be deemed a desecration, though if it were held elsewhere, it might be a contribution to public information. Variables in the circumstances of time and place do, therefore, justify some degree of official control. Difficulties occur, nevertheless, when an ostensibly reasonable regulation of public property is susceptible of being used in actuality as a means of regulating speech.

An episode involving the religious sect of Jehovah's Witnesses serves as useful illustration. This sect, as is generally known, has not emphasized the possession and maintenance of massive meeting places, nor does it have an extensive organization of priests, clergymen, or religious supervisors. Instead, it seeks to propagate its faith by distribution of printed material and by sermons preached in the highways and byways. Its ministers are, as I understand the matter, self-appointed and uncompensated; they are individuals sufficiently dedicated to the dogmas of the faith to be willing to devote their time to spreading them. Jehovah's Witnesses base their teachings on their own understanding of the Bible. They have a strong aversion to more highly organized religious groups, especially to the Roman Catholic Church. Since they sometimes express their aversion in a rudely positive way, the Witnesses are not always the most popular members of the community. Moreover, Witnesses refuse to salute the American flag and they resist military service; this brings them into conflict with some of the "superpatriotic" groups.

In a small city in the state of Maryland, the Witnesses sought permission to deliver a series of Bible talks in the public park. When permission was denied by the local governing body, the Witnesses nevertheless proceeded with their plans. Two speakers were arrested though there was no evidence whatsoever of disorder, threats of violence, or any other unseemly conduct. When a fine of twenty-five dollars was imposed, the Witnesses carried an appeal through the courts until finally their case came to the United States Supreme Court. There the convictions were set aside. The Court noted that the original denial of the requested permit had not been based on some defensible ground of public safety or convenience. "The conclusion is inescapable," said Chief Justice Vinson, "that the use of the park was denied because of the City Council's dislike for or disagreement with the Witnesses or their views. The right to equal protection of the laws, in the exercise of those freedoms of speech and religion protected by the First and Fourteenth Amendments, has a firmer foundation than the whims or personal opinions of a local governing body." [4]

Does this case mean that in the United States men may roam at large through the public parks, pausing to make a speech whenever and wherever they please? Does it mean that no authority can control the way in which public places are to be used, so that parks can be preserved for quiet enjoyment by persons who go there to look at the flowers, to rest, and to contemplate rather than to hear speeches? Does it mean that public speaking cannot be regulated, through licensing, in a way that will minimize the risk of disorderly assemblages, interference with traffic, and so on? Of course the case means none of these things. It means only this: If a license is required as a prerequisite to a speaker's use of a public area, the licensing official must be given some definite, reasonable standards to apply when he exercises his discretion; those standards must be clearly designed to protect a public interest rather than to control the content of the speaker's utterance; and the licensing official must actually rather than merely apparently base his decision on the standards that have been prescribed.[5]

A series of decisions well illustrates the application of these generalized propositions. The mayor of a large industrial city was empowered by local ordinance to withhold permits to deliver speeches in a park if there were a likelihood of a riot or other serious disorder—which certainly sounds reasonable. But this particular mayor seemed consistently fearful that a riot would develop whenever any of his political opponents wanted to use the park. Finally they went to court to restrain him from interfering with their proposed meetings; and they succeeded because the Court found that the licensing power was not in fact being used to preserve the peace, but as an "instrument of arbitrary suppression of free expression of views on national affairs." [6] In another case, a police chief was authorized to license the use of "sound trucks"—vehicles equipped with sound amplifiers; but since no guidance was given to him to decide how his judgment should be exercised, and since he was therefore free to impose restraints upon speakers he did not like, the ordinance was declared invalid.[7] In yet another case an ordinance that required a permit to distribute pamphlets was held invalid because the licensing power was "not limited to ways which might be regarded as inconsistent with the maintenance of public order or as involving disorderly conduct, the molestation of the inhabitants, or the misuse or littering of the streets." [8]

A strong reaffirmation of the Supreme Court's suspicion of a broadly-stated licensing power susceptible of being abused to restrain free speech, occurred in 1951.[9] A fanatical street preacher named Kunz sought a license to conduct meetings or hold religious services on the streets and in the parks of densely populated New York. The applicable New York ordinance was not confined to traffic control, but allowed the Police Commissioner to revoke or refuse a license for street preaching if he found that the speaker was likely to "ridicule" or "denounce" any form of religious beliefs, or to preach or expound atheism or agnosticism. Kunz had several years previously run into difficulties when, in a crowded place, he had made some extremely scurrilous attacks on Catholics and Jews; he liked to talk about brotherly love, but he was rather narrow in defining who his brothers were. It was because of his past offensiveness that the Police Commissioner denied him a license when he applied for one in 1948. Kunz proceeded to speak without a license, was arrested, and was fined ten dollars.

The American Civil Liberties Union came to Kunz's help and, despite the only nominal fine involved, carried his case to the Supreme Court. Nobody in his right mind could place much value on the vituperative harangues that Kunz was in the habit of delivering. Why, then, were fair-minded believers in civil liberties willing to lend their aid to this disreputable and distasteful person? The answer is that constitutional issues have to be fought out on their own merits, rather than on the merits of the individual in connection with whom the issue may have arisen. Slight invasions of the Constitution can provide the breach in the wall through which more serious assaults may later pour. The particular instance under consideration may, as the Supreme Court remarked many years ago, perhaps be "the obnoxious thing in its mildest and least repulsive form; but illegitimate and unconstitutional practices get their first footing in that way, namely, by silent approaches and slight deviations from legal modes of procedure." [10] The stealthy encroachment is in the end more dangerous than the frontal attack on constitutional liberty, because the defenders of freedom may be unaware that their position is being undermined. In Kunz's case, the applicable ordinance did not simply permit appropriate steps to be taken to protect the community's peace and order, if the speaker's actions were to place them in jeopardy. In addition, the ordinance allowed the Police Commissioner to suppress a particular sort of speech entirely—and this, the Supreme Court said, could not be constitutionally done to Kunz's speaking any more than to yours or mine.

This is not to say that the American Constitution protects every verbal utterance. Words can in themselves be a form of action. A man could not, for example, verbally offer a bribe to an official and then resist prosecution on the ground that he was merely exercising his freedom of speech. Similarly, attacks upon reputation through the spreading of false or malicious words, whether written or spoken, can be proceeded against civilly and in some instances criminally. The words themselves are in the nature of an aggression, and the Constitution does not protect aggressors.

What, then, about some of the utterances of a man like Kunz, embodying outrageous attacks upon another man's religion or ancestry? How far can a speaker go in the direction of infuriating his listener under the guise of enlightening him? Connecticut some years ago recognized a distinction between conveying information and conveying insults in public. It enacted that "No person shall address any offensive, derisive or annoying word to any other person who is lawfully in any street or other public place, nor call him by an offensive or derisive name. . . ." A prosecution under this statute was quickly sustained by the Supreme Court. The Court said, in an opinion by Justice Murphy (who was extremely sensitive, perhaps almost unduly sensitive, to any limitations upon speech), that the Constitution gives no protection to libelous or "fighting" words—that is, to words "which by their very utterance inflict injury or tend to incite an immediate breach of the peace. . . ." Utterances of that sort, Justice Murphy continued, "are no essential part of any exposition of ideas, and are of such slight social value as a step to truth that any benefit that may be derived from them is clearly outweighed by the social interest in order and morality." [11]

Now, to come back to Kunz, note that he was not being prosecuted for having spoken "fighting" words or, indeed, for any other sort of improper utterance. He was prosecuted for insisting on speaking at all after a public official had attempted to muzzle him because the official thought he would not like Kunz's speech. That sort of suppressive action is very different indeed from a proceeding in which a man may be held accountable for whatever misdeeds he has actually committed.

Let me add a further comment about the sort of speaking that may come from the lips of men like Kunz or Jehovah's Witnesses or other deeply convinced but not necessarily wise people. The community must avoid too readily identifying their utterances as insulting or otherwise punishable; the community must cultivate a high degree of toleration—or, to put it differently, a high boiling point. In a Jehovah's Witnesses case some years ago, the United States Supreme Court stated the matter well and forcefully in these terms: "In the realm of religious faith, and in that of political belief, sharp differences arise. In both fields the tenets of one man may seem the rankest error to his neighbor. To persuade others to his own point of view, the pleader, as we know, at times, resorts to exaggeration, to vilification of men who have been, or are, prominent in church or state, and even to false statement. But the people of this nation have ordained in the light of history, that, in spite of the probability of excesses and abuses, these liberties are, in the long view, essential to enlightened opinion and right conduct on the part of the citizens of a democracy." [12]

There is one additional point to be made about licensing or similar regulatory moves that have an impact upon freedom of expression. As has been said, no restraint can be justified unless it is clearly and closely related to the protection of some identifiable public interest. But bear in mind, please, that the public interest in free speech is itself so very great that it cannot easily be outweighed by some competing interest. This may be illustrated very briefly. "Handbills" or "circulars" or "leaflets"—flimsy sheets of printed matter that are handed out on the streets or stuffed into the doors of residences—are a common way of conveying information or opinion, and are especially useful for organizations that do not have ready access to the newspapers or radio. One trouble with them, however, is that persons to whom they have been handed often throw them aside after a brief glance at their contents. Soon the street is a mess, with discarded papers fluttering about and adding to the street cleaner's headaches. May a city constitutionally prohibit or limit handbill distribution in order to keep the streets clean of litter? Keeping the streets clean is surely a permissible public aim. But, says the Supreme Court, the dissemination of information is much too important an interest to be sacrificed for such a relatively minor gain.[13]

Similarly, the Supreme Court has taken a somewhat dim view of statutes that forbid knocking on doors or ringing doorbells in order to deliver unsolicited handbills or other messages. The statutes have been justified by their sponsors as necessary to protect against crime and as assuring quiet for householders who work at night and must sleep during the day. But the Court has felt that "Freedom to distribute information to every citizen wherever he desires to receive it" is "clearly vital to the preservation of a free society." [14]

The dangers of distribution, it was concluded, can be and should be controlled by methods short of restricting the dissemination of ideas. The soundness of that conclusion can well be debated. The late Professor Zechariah Chafee, a keen analyst of civil liberties problems, did not calculate the relative values precisely as did the Supreme Court. Of all the methods of spreading unpopular ideas, he asserted, house-to-house visitations were "the least entitled to extensive protection. The possibilities of persuasion are slight compared with the certainties of annoyance. Great as is the value of exposing citizens to novel views, home is one place where a man ought to be able to shut himself up in his own ideas if he desires. . . . Freedom of the home is as important as freedom of speech." [15] Whether you agree with Professor Chafee or with the Supreme Court, you will realize that you are weighing competing values and are not resting your decision on an undebatable absolute.

How can we decide whether speech has been unconstitutionally restrained or whether, instead, the public has imposed a permissible regulation to safeguard some other social interest? In seeking to answer that question we may perhaps be able to summarize this branch of the discussion.

No single inquiry will yield the desired answer. Five lines of thought must be followed in order to arrive at a conclusion.

First, since we have just seen that the relative weight of competing public interests must be appraised, we must know with precision just what other public interest has been thought to necessitate the regulation of speech. We have observed that it must be a very considerable interest—something more, for example, than keeping the streets clean. Justice Brandeis, one of the outstanding judges in American history and one whose views command mounting respect as time passes, said some thirty years ago that even immediate danger cannot justify a suppression of speech "unless the evil apprehended is *relatively serious*. Prohibition of free speech and assembly is a measure so stringent that it would be inappropriate as the means of averting a relatively trivial harm to society." [16] If regulation of speech is to be valid, it must reflect a good faith effort to maintain some one of what Justice Frankfurter has called the "indispensable ends of modern community life."

Second, since the effort to maintain one of these "indispensable ends" must have been undertaken in good faith, we must know whether the regulation is consistently and fairly applied. Keeping the traffic flowing through a city's streets may be a permissible objective; and, to achieve that objective, a city could control parades and street meetings even though the control had an impact on the freedom to speak. But if the licensing official were to allow the parades of his political friends and forbid the parades of his political foes, we might conclude that the real basis of decision was the official's sympathy (or lack of sympathy) with the parading group. This would be constitutionally objectionable, for there would then be an official interference with the dissemination of ideas. In addition, it would no doubt run afoul of the constitutional command that no person shall be denied the equal protection of law, a provision that serves as a further safeguard against discriminatory treatment.[17]

Third, since precensorship, through licensing or otherwise, has much more sweeping consequences than the application of a judgment after the event, we must take an interest in the particular method used to limit speech. It is one thing to punish a man for abusing his opportunity to speak; that is done when all the circumstances are known. It is another thing to keep him from speaking altogether, lest he say or do something objectionable. That type of prior control may cut off large amounts of speech that would never in fact have been improper.[18] Hence, prior controls over speakers are likely (as in the *Kunz* case, discussed earlier) to arouse a great deal of justified concern.

Fourth, since some words are, as we have noted, a form of action rather than a communication of beliefs or information, we must analyze what sort of speech has been subjected to public regulation. "Fighting words," if they can be cautiously identified, do not give rise to constitutional concern. Apart from such an extreme illustration, we recognize that the public can properly be more troubled about some kinds of speaking than about others. For example, the blaring noise of loud-speakers carried through the city's streets may acutely disturb the public peace, and the fact that the noise consists of spoken words makes it no less disturbing. Or, for another example, a door-to-door seller of brushes or vacuum cleaners might not be entitled to claim for his memorized "sales talk" delivered to unwilling householders precisely the same constitutional protections as should surround a speech advocating, let us say, drastic constitutional revision. Commercial words, though spoken, are distinguishable from the speaking with which the Constitution is mainly concerned.

Fifth, since the time and place of the public speaking bear on the question of whether it conflicts with other public interests, we must know as much as possible about the surrounding circumstances. Regulation of speaking in a private auditorium would obviously raise different questions from regulation of speaking in a public place. While regulation of the use of public premises may be permissible, the regulation must still be no more stringent than necessary. Hence, it is pertinent to inquire into the availability of suitable sites for speaking that will not interfere with other public uses of parks, streets, school buildings, and so on. To deny a permit to hold a meeting in the village schoolhouse during classroom hours is clearly unobjectionable; to deny a permit for evening use might be indefensible. Generalization is not helpful. Particulars must be sought in order to judge, case by case, whether freedom of speech has been unconstitutionally restrained by reason of having been unnecessarily restrained.

THE HOSTILE AUDIENCE

The preceding section of this discussion considered when and how steps can be taken to limit speechmaking that may possibly disrupt the community's tranquillity. Now let us turn to the extremely difficult problem that arises when a speaker's words have actually aroused the hostility of his audience, and thus have created an existing rather than merely a speculative danger of public disorder. Perhaps the problem can be put into focus by the case of a university student named Feiner, who was arrested in the city of Syracuse, New York, in the following circumstances.[19]

Feiner was an enthusiastic member of a somewhat radical youth group, sponsoring a meeting to discuss racial discrimination and civil liberties. Permission to hold the meeting in a public schoolhouse had been obtained, but was later withdrawn. The sponsors then arranged to have their meeting in one of the local hotels. Feiner went to a street corner, stood on a box, and began making a speech to denounce the authorities for having withdrawn the schoolhouse permit and to urge his listeners to attend the hotel meeting. His doing so was perfectly legal; in that particular city no rule placed any limits on street meetings.

Feiner attracted about seventy-five to eighty listeners. He made strongly derogatory remarks about the Mayor of Syracuse, the President of the United States, and the American Legion, an organization whose local units often mistakenly believe they protect the American tradition by seeking to suppress whatever views the Legion dislikes. Feiner blamed the American Legion for having pushed the local authorities into cancelling the schoolhouse meeting. He also loudly advised Negroes that their rights were being disregarded and urged them to band together; one witness, who seems to have been believed by the judges, testified that Feiner had told Negroes they should rise up in arms, though other witnesses said Feiner had merely urged them to go together with him, arm in arm, to the hotel meeting. In any event, whatever it was that Feiner said, the crowd grew restless. The sidewalk was packed with listeners, and pedestrians had to move out into the street in order to proceed on their way. Some of the audience were favorable to Feiner, but others were markedly hostile. A disgusted and angry listener said to one of the two policemen who were present that if the officer did not make Feiner stop, then he would do so himself. Finally the policemen feared that fights might break out. They asked Feiner to end his meeting. He refused. After a few minutes they asked him a second time to stop his speaking, in order to maintain the peace. Again he refused. Then they arrested him on the charge of disorderly conduct. He was tried, convicted, and sentenced to thirty days in jail.

Feiner was in a place in which he had a right to be; his was a lawful meeting at the outset. He did nothing but speak. Disorder was not threatened by him, but by those in his audience who disliked what he said. The charge against him was, in essence, that he had used language that was likely to cause a breach of the peace. You can see at once how easy it might be to use that sort of charge against any unpopular speaker.

The majority of the United States Supreme Court, in any event, concluded that the police had in this case exercised a reasonable discretion to prevent a public disturbance. The arrest of Feiner, the Court thought, was not a masked attack on the views he expressed, but reflected an honest fear that disorder was likely as a reaction to them. Hence, said the majority opinion, the community was simply maintaining peace and order on its streets, and this invaded none of Feiner's constitutional rights.

The dissenting judges saw the case differently. They feared—and, I must confess, I agree with them—that the Court had approved a readily available technique by which cities and states could subject public speeches to local police supervision. The facts, according to the dissenters, did not show "any imminent threat of risk or uncontrollable disorder. It is neither unusual nor unexpected that some people at public street meetings mutter, mill about, push, shove, or disagree, even violently, with the speaker. Indeed, it is rare where controversial topics are discussed that an outdoor crowd does not do some or all of these things." But even if a critical situation had been present, the dissenters asked, why were the police not obligated to protect Feiner's constitutional right to talk? Perhaps, they conceded, the police can at some point interfere with a lawful public speech in order to preserve order;

but that point is not reached until all reasonable efforts have been made to support rather than restrain the speaker. In Feiner's case, the police had made no effort to quiet the restless crowd, or to clear a path on the sidewalk for those who wished to pass through, or to discourage the man who threatened to attack the speaker. "Instead, they shirked that duty and acted only to suppress the right to speak."

The single effective answer to this dissent, in my estimation, is to appraise the facts differently. Probably we would all agree that one or two policemen could not be expected to protect a speaker against a howling mob of a thousand opponents armed with clubs; the speaker's interest in continuing his speech must in some circumstances yield to the pressing necessity of restoring quiet. As one of the judges in Feiner's case stated the matter, "It is not a constitutional principle that, in acting to preserve order, the police must proceed against the crowd, whatever its size and temper, and not against the speaker." The dangerous aspect of Feiner's case is, at bottom, the Court's readiness to believe that the police had no practical choice other than the one they made.

Still, the *Feiner* decision has not obliterated the important proposition that the police must be vigilant peace officers for the speaker as well as for his hearers. The Jehovah's Witnesses, who may not prove to be the world's most important religious movement but who have certainly made some great contributions to American constitutional law, have often furnished a reminder that speakers are entitled to be safeguarded. About a decade ago, for example, a group of the Witnesses had been physically assaulted during a meeting in a small city park, and were driven from the town. They sought to return soon thereafter, to continue their zealous preaching. The police turned them away, and refused to give them a permit for which they had properly applied. Then the Witnesses asked judicial help in persuading the police to do their duty. The court directed the police to let the Witnesses enjoy their constitutional rights, saying that "no effort whatever was made to protect those who were attempting lawfully to exercise those rights" and that there was no evidence that such an effort, if it had been made, could not have preserved law and order.[20]

Another case deserves to be stated at length because it presents so sharply the clash of social values, the value of unhampered discussion as against the value of public order. Ten years ago a discredited Catholic priest named Terminiello was an active participant in movements that capitalized on religious and cultural differences within America. One night in Chicago he made a violently anti-Semitic speech to a largely favorable audience in a private meeting hall. Outside the hall were massed about a thousand hostile demonstrators. A number of clashes occurred before, during, and after the meeting. Terminiello's address inflamed tempers on both sides. He was arrested for having caused a breach of the peace, though in fact the violent episodes—such as throwing rocks through the windows of the meetinghouse—were initiated by Terminiello's opponents and not by his supporters. The lower court thought, however, that a speaker could be convicted for disturbing the peace if his speech "stirs the public to anger, invites dispute, brings about a condition of unrest, or creates a disturbance. . . ." The Supreme Court by a divided vote decided that this was too broadly stated a rule, especially when the objectionable speech had been made in a private hall and nobody was compelled to expose himself to it. Justice Douglas, who wrote the majority opinion, declared that one of the foremost functions of free speech is not to soothe but to stimulate dispute. In democracies, he said, speech "may indeed best serve its high purpose when it induces a condition of unrest, creates dissatisfaction with conditions as they are, or even stirs people to anger." [21]

Justice Jackson, the most vigorous of the dissenting judges, had strong distaste for rabble rousers like Terminiello. He had closely studied the conditions that surrounded Hitler's rise to power in Germany. Partly as a result of that study he tended rather consistently to place a very high value on public order as against free speech, and he had little patience with the notion, expressed years ago by Justice Brandeis, that the way to deal with falsehoods and fallacies is through "more speech, not enforced silence." * In Terminiello's case, he rather sharply remarked: "There is danger that, if the Court does not temper its doctrinaire logic with a little practical wisdom, it will convert the constitutional Bill of Rights into a suicide pact."

There is much to be said on both sides of the debate about the relative merits of order and freedom. This is the sort of problem that the philosopher Bertrand Russell described as "one of balance; too little liberty brings stagnation, and too much brings chaos." [22]

Arresting a man like Terminiello may make him seem to be a martyr; and his beliefs, compounded of folly and malice that might be recognized for what they are if they were freely exhibited, may acquire a little of "the glamour of the forbidden" if they are subjected to official restraints. President Woodrow Wilson, who was an astute politician as well as a political philosopher, thought that if a man is a fool or a scoundrel, "the best thing to do is to encourage him to advertise the fact by speaking. It cannot be so easily discovered if you allow him to remain silent and look wise, but if you let him speak, the secret is out and the world knows that he is a fool. . . ." [23]

On the other hand, the German experience that had so impressed Justice Jackson does have relevance for us. During the republican régime before Hitler, freedom of speech was officially supported no matter what might be the attendant disorders. The recurrence of

* The quoted words occur in the famous concurring opinion in *Whitney* v. *California*, 274 U.S. 357, 377 (1927), in the following context: "Those who won our independence by revolution were not cowards. They did not fear political change. They did not exalt order at the cost of liberty. To courageous, self-reliant men, with confidence in the power of free and fearless reasoning applied through the processes of popular government, no danger flowing from speech can be deemed clear and present, unless the incidence of the evil apprehended is so imminent that it may befall before there is opportunity for full discussion. If there be time to expose through discussion the falsehood and fallacies, to avert the evil by the process of education, *the remedy to be applied is more speech, not enforced silence.* Only an emergency can justify repression. Such must be the rule if authority is to be reconciled with freedom. Such, in my opinion, is the command of the Constitution."

disorder had a tendency to encourage among many Germans a sentiment that democracy could never successfully maintain the peace. Thus was created a sort of longing for the "discipline" that the totalitarians promised to achieve. Once totalitarian controls were in fact imposed, of course there was an end of liberty altogether. This experience has led some thoroughly sincere (though, in my own opinion, poorly informed) believers in democracy to feel that a free society can best be maintained if the individual's freedom of expression is curtailed. To the argument that such a course involves adopting a sort of totalitarianism in order, ostensibly, to avoid the rise of totalitarianism, they answer that the other course—protecting the individual's complete freedom of expression—involves an ultimate destruction of freedom by the very attempts made to preserve it.[24]

Without attempting to settle this debate, I think that a few conclusions can be safely suggested concerning the problem of the hostile audience.

First. A speaker who seeks out an actively hostile audience for the very purpose of creating a disorder can claim no invasion of constitutional freedom if his speech is halted. Such a case resembles the "fighting words" situation discussed earlier. On the other hand, if the speaker is engaged in a genuine effort to communicate, but is faced by an audience so hostile that it may create a disturbance in order to halt the speech, the speaker ought to be protected to the fullest possible extent.

Second. Even if the audience is already behaving in a disorderly or threatening manner, the authorities should conscientiously attempt to preserve the freedom of speech and assemblage *unless*, as indicated above, the speaker has himself for some reason utilized the crowd's preexisting hostility *or* there is a clear likelihood that continued speech will lead to riotous activities that cannot effectively be controlled.

In general, governmental units, from local to national, can as a practical matter prevent violent interferences with speech if they wish. Suitable preventive and protective steps are most likely to be taken if the police are firmly told that a speaker cannot be charged with the crime of inciting a disturbance of the peace unless the police themselves have first done everything possible to protect the speechmaking.[25]

LABOR UNION PICKETING

A chief mechanism of local labor union expression in the United States continues to be the picket line, consisting of unionists or their sympathizers who walk up and down near the place of business involved in a dispute, carrying signs that urge support for their cause.

Bear in mind that concentration of ownership of newspapers may make it very difficult for unions to put their case before the public. In the United States the number of daily newspapers is constantly declining. In 1909 there were 2600 dailies. By 1947 the number had decreased to 1750. At that time only one-twelfth of the cities in which daily papers were published had any competing dailies; rival newspapers existed only in the larger cities, and in ten states not a single city had a competing daily.[26] Today the concentration of newspaper ownership is certainly no less marked. This means that if one newspaper is hostile to the union, or if a single editor decides that the union's contentions are not newsworthy (as, indeed, they rarely are, in any broad way), no word of the controversy is likely to appear in the daily press. If information is to be given at all, it must be given directly and at the scene of action.

A sharp distinction must be drawn between informing and intimidating. Picket lines are not allowed to form physical blockades, or to turn themselves into mobs calculated to scare away potential customers or job seekers. When that occurs, as sometimes it does, the law treats the pickets like any other disorderly assemblage of persons. The question remains, however, whether workers who wish simply to walk up and down carrying signs are to be regarded as exercising their freedom to speak. If so, the workers are within the range of constitutional protection.

Some twenty years ago one of the states in which unions have been numerically and politically weak enacted a general prohibition of picketing near business premises with the intent of influencing persons not to have dealings with the picketed enterprise. The Supreme Court in a ringing decision held that this statute was constitutionally defective.[27] "In the circumstances of our time," the Court declared, "the dissemination of information concerning the facts of a labor dispute must be regarded as within that area of free discussion that is guaranteed by the Constitution. . . . Free discussion concerning the conditions in industry and the causes of labor disputes appears to us indispensable to the effective and intelligent use of the processes of popular government to shape the destiny of modern industrial society. . . . The range of activities proscribed [by the statute under discussion], whether characterized as picketing or loitering or otherwise, embraces nearly every practicable, effective means whereby those interested—including the employees directly affected—may enlighten the public on the nature and causes of a labor dispute. The safeguarding of these means is essential to the securing of an informed and educated public opinion with respect to a matter which is of public concern. . . . '[The] streets are natural and proper places for the dissemination of information and opinion; and one is not to have the exercise of his liberty of expression abridged on the plea that it may be exercised in some other place.' "

Note two things about this excerpt from the Court's opinion. First, the judges recognized the interest of the public in receiving information, as well as the interest of the unionists in distributing information; this, I think, is a matter that needs constant reemphasis. Second, the judges spoke in such sweeping terms that American labor organizations fell easily into the optimistic belief that their picketing activities would henceforth be entirely beyond control, so long as they were conducted peacefully.

The later development of this subject has sharply illustrated, however, that general pronouncements are unlikely to settle constitutional controversies that arise out of ever-changing facts rather than out of philosophical abstractions.[28] Within the very next year after the decision just discussed, the Supreme Court began to qualify the unqualified language it had used. There came before the Court a case involving some truck drivers who picketed perfectly peacefully, but who engaged in violent misdeeds elsewhere whenever they had a chance to terrorize their opponents. The Court was unimpressed by the fact that the picketing itself had been unobjectionable. It was so "enmeshed" with violence that, in the Court's eyes, it was no longer to be regarded as "the workingman's means of communication," but as an instrument of force. So long as the union pickets did no more than ask the public to bring economic pressure on the employer, the picketing deserved protection. But when it became a coercive device, it lost its value. The violence that was linked with the picketing had generated a "momentum of fear" that would, the Court believed, continue even though the future picketing might be conducted in the most delicate and gentlemanly way. So the Court sustained an injunction against the picketing that the unions had hopefully regarded as untouchable.[29]

The next significant development in this field occurred when a state attempted to localize the area of industrial dispute. A union was seeking to represent the employees of a building construction company. The company ignored the union. A restaurant owner made a contract with the construction firm to erect a new building for him. Then the union began to picket the restaurant. The purpose of the picketing was to discourage patronage of the restaurant, perhaps as a lesson and a warning to other businessmen who might be thinking of entering into construction contracts. The picketing was peaceful; the signs the pickets carried were truthful about the controversy. Could the state interfere with this information-dissemination by the union? Yes, said the Supreme Court, it was constitutional to forbid the "conscription of neutrals" who had "no relation to either the dispute or the industry in which it arose." The union's fight was with the building contractor and not with the restaurant owner, and the fight ought not to be allowed to spread beyond its natural boundaries.[30]

Then, a few years later, arose a case that put a really deep dent in the original doctrine about peaceful picketing. A group of ice peddlers organized themselves into a union in order to better their incomes and working conditions. One of the wholesale ice distributors, the Empire Company, refused requests to stop selling to non-union peddlers, and the union began to picket that distributor. Soon Empire had lost 85 per cent of its business. It then asked a court to restrain any further picketing, even though peaceful, on the ground that if Empire were to yield to the union's pressure, it would violate a state statute requiring it to sell to all comers on a non-discriminatory basis. The Supreme Court agreed with Empire.[31] It brushed aside the union's argument that the picket line was merely publicizing facts, in accordance with its constitutional rights. The primary end of the picketing, the Court asserted, was to force Empire to violate the law; exercising the union's freedom of speech would be fair enough, but here the union and its friends were really exercising their economic power to compel observance of union policies rather than state policies. The state, through its statutes, had decided that the selling practices the union was trying to thrust on Empire were "against the interests of the whole public." And the state had power, under the constitution, to restrain union conduct that jeopardized observance of the state's laws. "It had never been deemed an abridgment of freedom of speech or press," the Court added, "to make a course of conduct illegal merely because the conduct was in part initiated, evidenced, or carried out by means of language, either spoken or printed."

In recent years a succession of cases has demonstrated still further that free speech through peaceful picketing is far from an unqualified right in the United States. Injunctions have been sustained when picketing has been used to achieve a specific "unlawful objective" as in the *Empire* case just discussed. Restraints have also been sustained when the picketing has not come in conflict with any statute at all, but has merely been used to attain an end that runs strongly counter to the courts' notions of public policy and community interest.* Recently the Supreme Court reaffirmed the implications to be drawn from this series of cases, and recognized that they had "established a broad field in which a State, in enforcing some public policy, whether of its criminal or its civil law, and whether announced by its legislature or its courts, could constitutionally enjoin peaceful picketing aimed at preventing effectuation of that policy." [32]

The dissenting justices in this case—Chief Justice Warren and Justices Black and Douglas—think that the Court has now gone much too far. They fear that "State courts and state legislatures are free to decide whether to permit or suppress any particular picket line for any reason other than a blanket policy against all picketing" —which everyone would still regard as an unconstitutional interference with unions' right to communicate. The dissenters would like the Court to say that picketing "can be regulated or prohibited only to the extent that it forms *an essential part of a course of conduct* which the State can regulate or prohibit."

Whatever one may think of the development of doctrine in this field, one must recognize that it has moved a long way from its starting point, if, indeed, it has not almost completed a full circle. Picketing, far from being immune against governmental inter-

---

* Leading cases are *Hughes* v. *Superior Court*, 339 U.S. 460 (1950), and *International Brotherhood of Teamsters* v. *Hanke*, 339 U.S. 470 (1950). The Hughes case involved picketing to compel a California grocery store to hire Negro employees in proportion to Negro customers. California's courts have long been hostile to discrimination based on race or color. The picketing was subjected to judicial restraint because, if continued, it would compel the store owner to select his employees according to their color rather than according to their capabilities, and this would be against public policy. In the *Hanke* case the union picketed the establishments of self-employed dealers in used automobiles; the purpose was to make them observe the same closing hours and other conditions as were maintained by employers who had entered into contracts with the picketing union. The picketing was forbidden by the courts because, if successful, it was thought likely to upset the best interests of the larger group in the community. This decision has been regarded as establishing the "community interest rule" and as opening the way for state injunctions thought necessary to protect the amorphous "public interest" against "undesirable" picketing.

ference in the United States, can be restrained whenever the courts are willing to recognize a reasonable basis for the restraint. The most that can be said about peaceful picketing is that it is *presumably* a form of speech that deserves constitutional protection; those who wish to limit it must still bear the burden of showing a justification for the restraint they seek to impose. But the Supreme Court's decisions have made that burden an extremely light one. States are limited in some areas of labor relations—including the control of picketing—by federal statutes that have a status superior to state laws; but the constitutional protection of free speech is no longer a major barrier to be surmounted before picketing can be halted.

Enactment of the Labor-Management Reporting and Disclosure Act of 1959 [33] brought to a sharp point these observations concerning the evolving law of picketing. Two years of legislative hearings had drawn public attention to abuses of some labor unions' power. Picketing, the evidence indicated, had often been perversely used. Unscrupulous persons, it was shown, had in the past threatened to throw picket lines around business premises unless extortionate demands were met. Sometimes the extortioners created wholly spurious labor organizations for no apparent purpose other than to intimidate those from whom they sought to extract "payoffs." On other occasions, members of bona fide unions had been used by reckless leaders to picket honestly resistant businessmen. At times the businessman was caught between a cross-fire of demands by two unions; if he yielded to one, he might be picketed by the other with placards that denounced him as "unfair to organized labor." Even when no genuine controversy existed, picketing could cause severe economic hardship not only by discouraging patronage (especially in the case of small establishments such as restaurants and retail stores), but also by inducing other unionists to cease providing services to the picketed premises; tradition influences union members not to cross a picket line, and they rarely study the merits of the particular case before acting in accord with the general tradition. These unlovely realities aroused Congressional determination to place previously unheard of restraints upon picketing.

In sum, the 1959 statute gave the National Labor Relations Board jurisdiction over a new type of unfair labor practice, abusive picketing. Picketing may be limited if its declared purpose is to cause an employer to deal with a union as representative of the employees— unless the union has first been certified, after the appropriate governmental proceedings, as the true representative of those employees. This prohibition of so-called "organizational picketing" is operative where the employer has already recognized some other labor organization in circumstances not open to legal challenge; or where an official election of a collective bargaining representative has been conducted within the past twelve months; or where the picketing group, which purports to be engaged in a campaign to organize the previously unorganized (and hypothetically oppressed) employees of a non-union employer, has not shown its good faith by promptly petitioning the National Labor Relations Board to poll the affected employees. These limitations, Congress believed, were needed to prevent spurious picketing.

At the same time, the 1959 enactment recognized that picketing still does have legitimacy as a means of communication. After spelling out the restrictions summarized above, the statute adds that limits on attempts to recruit new adherents to the union are not intended "to prohibit any picketing or other publicity for the purpose of truthfully advising the public (including consumers) that an employer does not employ members of, or have a contract with, a labor organization . . ." This preservation of the right to publicize facts is, however, immediately qualified by one further proviso: the right to picket in order to advise the public still exists, the statute says, "unless an effect of such picketing is to induce any individual employed by any other person in the course of his employment, not to pick up, deliver or transport any goods or not to perform any services."

These recent developments reflect well-justified antagonism toward men with hard fists and soft morals in the labor movement. Some union officers, as well as some racketeers simply masquerading as unionists, have irresponsibly or venally distorted practices that were legitimate in origin, and are still essential to bona fide unions. Congress faced the problem of striking down the distortions without fatally weakening the unions' opportunity to publicize controversies. The approach taken in the 1959 statute is moderate. It does not prohibit picketing in all circumstances, and does not, at least on the surface, limit it at all in connection with genuine work stoppages. It says no more, basically, than that the appearance of controversy shall not be counterfeited when no controversy truly exists. Twenty years of Supreme Court decisions clearly establish that picketing is not untouchable merely because it is not violent. The power of Congress to limit this form of expression as now it has done seems beyond question. If, despite the moderation of the new law, the statutory restraints are applied in an overly harsh manner, judicial relief will no doubt be forthcoming. It will come, however, in the form of judgments that picketing has been unduly restrained in particular cases, and not in the form of embracive decisions that picketing (because it is a species of speech) must remain forever beyond Congressional control.

This discussion of three areas in which free speech questions arise, may be closed by a no doubt superfluous observation. You will have noted that emphasis throughout has been on judicial action, on what the judges did and thought. This is a natural way for a lawyer to talk when he is discussing constitutional law problems. Let us, however, not be deluded by this kind of analysis into thinking that freedom is to be won or lost only, or even chiefly, in courtrooms and lawyers' offices. Judge Hand, ripe in wisdom and rich in honor, has spoken words that serve as a fitting end to this chapter: "I often wonder whether we do not rest our hopes too much upon constitutions, upon laws, and upon courts. These are false hopes; believe me, these are false hopes. Liberty lies in the hearts of men and women; when it dies there, no constitution, no law, no court can save it; no constitution, no law, no court can even do much to help it. While it lies there it needs no constitution, no law, no court to save it." [34]

Chapter 4

FREE SPEECH AND
THE COMMUNIST CONSPIRACY

The American system of government rests on a theory that, to some people, has always seemed the height of foolishness. The nation has bet its life upon the proposition that "right conclusions are more likely to be gathered out of a multitude of tongues, than through any kind of authoritative selection." [1]

The American Constitution in unconditional language says that the freedom of speech and of the press should not be abridged. The soundness of the principle underlying that brave declaration is now once more undergoing an agonizing reappraisal. The world, contorted by a clash of ideologies, lives in fear that the war of words and ideas may become in fact a ruinous war between nations. The tensions aroused by that fear stir impatience with the traditional counsels of toleration. Free trade in ideas, many people feel, is a supportable policy when the times are quiet and when there is ample opportunity for a ruminative exchange of views. But when desperate perils may be near at hand, a diversity of ideas comes to be regarded as divisive, and dissent comes to be equated with disaffection. Then arises a demand for modification of the faith reflected in constitutional provisions like those now under discussion.

This demand at present draws not only its inspiration but its chief justification from the ambiguous character of the Communist Party. The "class war" is more than a figure of speech to Communists. They deem themselves to be engaged here and now in a war against the existing social order, for which they wish to substitute their own dictatorship. To that end they—or, at least, some of them—are able to justify in their own minds the use of tactics that bear no relationship to the ordinary contests for power within a democratic framework. Identifying their cause with that of the Soviet Union, they have faithfully followed the convolutions of policies designed by that great power for its own national interests alone. Politically-inspired espionage on behalf of the Soviet Union has been proved beyond doubt in a number of dramatic instances. Infiltration of labor unions and other organizations has occurred so that they might be maneuvered not for the interests of their members or in furtherance of their declared purposes, but in order to advance a cause to which the membership has not knowingly given its allegiance. Guile and stealth have been used to intensify rather than to lessen the frictions that inevitably arise in a complex society, so that dissension may be aroused and faith in governmental processes may be diminished.

But along with the clandestine, conspiratorial, criminal, and corrupt activities which the Communists justify as unpleasant necessities in the class struggle, can be found another aspect of the Communist Party. It seeks to function as an open and public organization, devoted to political agitation unrelated to violence. It propagandizes as do other political parties. It appeals for votes. It attempts to gain adherents by persuasion. It appeals to the discontented and the disillusioned, promising (as do other political parties) that its program will end their difficulties.

Many supporters of democratic principles are unable to distinguish between the two aspects of the Communist Party. Political activity by Communist zealots, they maintain, is a deceptive device. The Communists, these persons say, do not really intend to debate ideas and to abide by majority conclusions; their advocacy is intended not to enlighten judgment but to create internal disaffection; their aim is not persuasion of the present majority, but the development of an atmosphere in which a militant minority can seize power; hence, even their seemingly innocent words and deeds must be regarded as steps in a totalitarian conspiracy aimed at destroying the freedom the Constitution is dedicated to preserving. It matters not that their number is small—according to official estimates that some observers believe to be four times too high, only 25,000 in the United States, a nation of over 170,000,000. These few, it is argued, are so single-minded, so totally committed to their cause that they constitute a grave and continuing threat to constitutional liberties.

This chapter will explore the extent to which sentiments of the sort just described may validly be reflected in statutes that limit Communist propaganda and Communist political agitation.

Before turning to the issues that touch directly upon freedom of expression, we may usefully note that undesirable conduct—as distinct from words—is already interdicted by many laws.[2] Thus, for example, penal statutes deal firmly with crimes of action (such as sabotage) and with crimes of stealth (such as espionage and disclosure of official information). Violence, whether or not aimed at overthrow of the government, is not tolerated. The ingress of aliens who might endanger the nation is regulated, and contact is maintained with the aliens who have been allowed to enter. The domestic agents of any "foreign principal" are required to register with the Department of Justice, and to disclose their activities in behalf of their principal.

The pages of statute books alone are not relied upon to serve as impregnable shields against malefactors. Active and seemingly effective counterespionage work is undertaken as a normal ingredient of police administration.

But measures like these have not completely quieted concern. In America, perhaps more acutely than in most other countries, the feeling has been manifested that since Communist beliefs may give rise to dangers that might not be detected until too late, the nation's defense requires suppressing the teaching and advocacy of Communism itself. If Soviet espionage agents are likely to be recruited from those who are now or who in future might become Communists, then those who are pro-Communist must be exposed and recruitment of converts must be blocked. Views like these underlie the measures that seek to restrict belief and utterance, and that attempt to stigmatize individuals not for their positive deeds but for their supposed allegiances.

As often happens when emotions are at flood tide, a critically detached view of these measures is not easily acquired. A succession of "loyalty programs" and "personnel security programs" has been aimed at eliminating Communists and their sympathizers from posts in government and industry. After a dozen years of exertions that affected perhaps as many as twenty million Americans, a strikingly small number of individuals were ousted from employment—not because they were Communists, but because they were deemed to be somehow connected in a sympathetic way with Communists or Communist organizations. Though not found guilty of affirmative wrongdoing, they were condemned to wear through life a "badge of infamy" [3] because there was found to be reasonable doubt as to their "loyalty." Those who were directly destroyed in this manner were few, but undoubtedly the sorry fate of these few induced in many others a determination to avoid all peril by sterilizing their minds and associations.

Gradually a few strong voices began to point out the dangers to democracy that flourish in a climate of fear; pressures toward pallid conformity suppress not merely antisocial deviations but also constructive criticisms and enriching innovations and thus lead to a stagnant society.*

The pursuit of disloyalty, often misguided and sometimes dema-

---

* See, e.g., Judge Learned Hand's "Address before Convocation of the University of the State of New York," October 25, 1952, reprinted in *The Spirit of Liberty, Papers and Addresses of Learned Hand* (Irving Dilliard ed., 1953), p. 284: "Risk for risk, for myself, I had rather take my chance that some traitors will escape detection than spread abroad a spirit of general suspicion and distrust, which accepts rumor and gossip in place of undismayed and unintimidated inquiry. I believe that that community is already in process of dissolution where each man begins to eye his neighbor as a possible enemy, where non-conformity with the accepted creed, political as well as religious, is a mark of disaffection; where denunciation, without specification or backing, takes the place of evidence; where orthodoxy chokes freedom of dissent; where faith in the eventual supremacy of reason has become so timid that we dare not enter our convictions in the open lists, to win or lose. Such fears as these are a solvent which can eat out the cement that binds the stones together; they may in the end subject us to a despotism as evil as any that we dread. . . ."

gogically spurred by extremists, became alarmingly intensified before, at last, it came under judicial scrutiny. Then, largely as a result of judicial decisions which in one respect or another criticized the immoderate and uncritical procedures that the loyalty probers had used,[4] a measure of calm was restored. Meanwhile, evidence mounted that the scattershot methods of these programs caused many casualties without uncovering the active plotters they were meant to hit. Not a single spy has been brought to light by all the federal government's loyalty and security proceedings over a span of a dozen years; as a matter of fact, so far as is now known, not a single criminal prosecution of any character whatsoever has been initiated as a result of information gained through these programs. This does not mean, of course, that there have been no Communist plotters, no spies, no criminals. The contrary is known to be the case, for a number of them have been convicted after open trials. As one of the more prominent espionage agents has pointed out, however, the Soviet Union's spies in the United States are instructed to shun all contact with Communist organizations and to avoid reading any Communist publications, lest suspicions be stimulated. In all probability the dangerous spies do not go about in bright red—or even pink—plumage.

THE SMITH ACT: ILLEGAL ADVOCACY

Discussion of recent American legislation aimed at subversive sentiment rather than subversive action must commence with a statute of 1940, commonly referred to as the Smith Act.[5] This Act subjects to severe penalties all persons who, individually or as a group, "advocate . . . or teach the duty, necessity, desirability, or propriety of overthrowing or destroying any government in the United States by force or violence. . . ."

Not until 1948 was this law turned against the Communists, who were undoubtedly its chief targets when it was adopted. In 1941 it had first been used as the basis of prosecuting a small group of Marxists who were strongly anti-Stalin and anti-Soviet; believers in civil liberties protested its use on that occasion, though the Communists were apparently untroubled so long as their enemies were being harassed. In 1943 the law was used in a sedition trial against twenty-eight alleged Nazi sympathizers; again civil libertarians protested, while the Communists were silent. Neither of these cases reached the Supreme Court.[6] In 1948, however, an indictment based upon the statute was lodged against eleven top leaders of the Communist Party in the United States. After a long and dramatic trial had resulted in their conviction, they appealed to the higher courts. Ultimately, in *Dennis* v. *United States*,[7] the Supreme Court upheld the constitutionality of the law and sustained the convictions.

This highly significant decision can be evaluated only in the light of the precise accusation against the defendants.

The defendants in the *Dennis* case were not charged with having conspired to overthrow the government. Nor were they accused of having taken steps in that direction. Rather, they were charged with having conspired to *advocate* and *teach* the necessity or desirability of overthrowing the government. They were not accused of having taught the technology of violence; that is to say, they were not charged with having given vocational training in how to make bombs at home, or how to steal guns from military warehouses, or how to plan a quiet assassination. They were, instead, accused purely and simply of having banded together to advocate a doctrine.

Undoubtedly their purpose in doing so was to influence conduct, not immediately but at some moment in the indefinite future. The Communist leaders were not "closet philosophers," interested in ideas entirely divorced from action. They meant that their ideas should ultimately be transformed into deeds. Nevertheless, neither they nor the Government of the United States had any expectation that this transformation from argument into performance would occur instantly, or even soon.

During previous years the Supreme Court had with a fair degree of consistency applied in free speech cases a formula that became known as the "clear and present danger" test. It had first been stated by Justice Holmes in a 1919 case involving prosecution for

attempted discouragement of military recruiting during the First
World War:

> The question in every case is whether the words used are used in such
> circumstances and are of such a nature as to create a clear and present
> danger that they will bring about the substantive evils that Congress has
> a right to prevent. . . .[8]

A few years later, in one of his great dissenting opinions that
afterward came to be regarded as a much more authoritative pro-
nouncement than the utterance of the then majority, Justice Brandeis
elaborated the thought by asserting that "no danger flowing from
speech can be deemed clear and present, unless the incidence of the
evil apprehended is so imminent that it may befall before there is opportunity for full discussion. If there be time to expose through discussion the falsehoods and fallacies, to avert the evil by the processes
of education, the remedy to be applied is more speech, not enforced
silence." [9]

Expressions like these became a part of the American credo, and
were reflected in numerous judicial decisions between 1930 and
1950.[10] Then came the *Dennis* case. There was in that case no proof
of imminent danger; there was no proof that steps had been taken
that led directly from talk to action; there was no proof that the
eleven defendants' advocacy would be likely to have discernible
results before it could be offset by sounder counsels or by suitable
protective measures. Nevertheless, the Court held that the Smith
Act presented no unconstitutional interference with freedom of expression. The Government, said the Court, need not delay its defense against subversion until revolution is actually at hand; it need
not "wait until the *putsch* is about to be executed, the plans have
been laid and the signal is awaited." To decide whether reasonable
restraints have been imposed the courts must in each case "ask
whether the gravity of the 'evil,' discounted by its improbability,
justifies such invasion of free speech as is necessary to avoid the
danger."

What the Court was saying, in other words, was that speech may be restricted if there is a probability of its producing at some time—not necessarily immediately—a relatively serious danger. If the evil is a minor one, it must be plain and close at hand to justify restraints upon expression—upon "advocacy" or "teaching." [11] But as to serious dangers, the element of imminence that was embodied in the "clear and present danger test" was discarded. Dennis and his colleagues, it had been found, had intended that the government should be overthrown by violence "as speedily as circumstances permit." Their words were calculated to bring about this result—and that sufficed to justify their suppression.

Formulated in this way, the chief opinion in the *Dennis* case [12] gave rise to considerable concern about the possible expansion of governmental authority to punish undesired talk. The "clear and present danger test" had emphasized the need for a close causal connection between speech and antisocial action if speech were to be limited. Thus it had effectively destroyed the notion that words could be punished if only they were thought to have a "reasonable tendency" toward evil. To sustain restraints upon free communication, two elements were required: nearness in time and probability of outcome. *Dennis* seemed to minimize those elements. In doing so it might perhaps open the door to restrictions that were the products of excessive nervousness rather than urgent necessity. The long-range effect of words is always difficult to gauge; for that very reason, in fact, the Supreme Court had on an earlier occasion held to be unenforcible a penal statute that forced a defendant to guess whether the speech he uttered today might have consequences at some time in the indefinitely prolonged future.[13] But it is always easy to fear that the words of an evilly disposed person may have some untoward results sooner or later—disregarding the fact that later happenings are likely to divert the impact of the words, whatever may be the speaker's hope when he spoke them. True, Dennis and his codefendants had been found not to be casual political philosophers; they were engaged, rather, in a systematic course of indoctrination and instruction with the intent that governmental power should be illegally seized as soon as might be feasible. Still, there is a vast difference between bad intent and bad behavior. A man may talk often and wistfully about the desirability of robbing banks; he may even organize a seminar to discuss the inequity of keeping all that beautiful money locked up, instead of in the pockets of deserving robbers; but until he takes some step in the direction of the substantive crime—until, in short, he does something more than express the opinion that bank robbery is a highly desirable way of making a living—he has not yet committed a punishable offense.[14] If people like Dennis were to be imprisoned on the charges that had been brought against them, it would not be because they had begun to effectuate a coup. As Justice Douglas pointed out in his dissenting opinion, they were not shown to have engaged in "the teaching of methods of terror and other seditious conduct," such as espionage, street warfare, or assassination; behavior of that sort could no doubt have been prosecuted, just as could the hypothetical bank robber if he had initiated a course in which to train his confederates in the arts of safecracking and pistol shooting. Nor were they being proceeded against because society was otherwise helpless; "the invisible army" of which they were the chieftains, Justice Douglas sarcastically said, was "the best known, the most beset, and the least thriving of any fifth column in history. Only those held by fear and panic could think otherwise." There was in his view no escape from the conclusion that these defendants were prosecuted because they organized the teaching of noxious doctrine, and not because that doctrine had in fact produced a peril to the good order of society.

Among those who felt that Congress could reasonably shut off talking lest it conduce to gravely dangerous action, were many who perceived the possible undesirable consequences. Justice Frankfurter, who joined in sustaining the Smith Act, observed that even the advocates of revolution serve usefully as social critics. By capitalizing on existing defects they may prod other people toward making reforms that protect society rather than weaken it, and to that extent destroy the ammunition of the revolutionary forces. Moreover, he added, "suppressing advocates of overthrow inevitably will also silence critics who do not advocate overthrow but fear that their criticism may be so construed. No matter how clear we may be that the defendants now before us are preparing to overthrow our Government at the propitious moment, it is self-delusion to think that we can punish them for their advocacy without adding to the risks run by loyal citizens who honestly believe in some of the reforms these defendants advance. It is a sobering fact that in sustaining the convictions before us we can hardly escape restriction on the interchange of ideas."

At that time there was little public concern about the possibly diminished freedom to exchange thoughts. The ideas of the Communists, tinged as they were with violence, were held in such general distaste that the *Dennis* decision was readily and on the whole uncritically embraced as a vindication of American ideals.* Six years later, however, the Supreme Court again had occasion to consider the constitutionality of the Smith Act when it was sought to be applied to fourteen second-level Communist leaders who had been convicted of conspiring to advocate overthrow. In *Yates* v. *United States* [15] the Court "clarified" the *Dennis* case—or, to state the matter more candidly, drastically curtailed it.

The Court flatly declared in *Yates* that the advocacy and teaching of forcible overthrow, no matter how evil may be the intent of the advocate or teacher, is not prohibited by law so long as it is not accompanied by "any effort to instigate action." Justice Harlan, for the majority, reaffirmed "the distinction between advocacy of abstract doctrine and advocacy directed at promoting unlawful action"; and the Smith Act was interpreted as being intended to preserve that distinction. True, the *Dennis* case had somewhat obscured the dividing line. But the Court now asserted that "the essence of the Dennis holding" was much narrower than had been

* Justice Black, dissenting in *Dennis*, had closed his opinion with the following sad (but prophetic) words: "Public opinion being what it now is, few will protest the conviction of these Communist petitioners. There is hope, however, that in calmer times, when present pressures, passions and fears subside, this or some later Court will restore the First Amendment liberties to the high preferred place where they belong in a free society."

supposed. The case should be regarded as holding that "indoctrination of a group in preparation for future violent action, as well as exhortation to immediate action, by advocacy found to be directed to 'action for the accomplishment' of forcible overthrow, to violence as 'a rule or principle of action,' and employing 'language of incitement' . . . is not constitutionally protected when the group is of sufficient size and cohesiveness, is sufficiently oriented towards action, and other circumstances are such as reasonably to justify apprehension that action will occur."

Justice Clark, who dissented in the *Yates* case, remarked that he had "read this statement over and over" without quite being able to grasp its meaning, because he could "see no resemblance" between what the Court now said and what it said had been said in the *Dennis* case. Others may well have the same difficulty as Justice Clark. Nonetheless, the implications of Justice Harlan's explanation of the *Dennis* holding are clear and important. He is saying that mere doctrinal justification of forcible overthrow is not punishable, even if the speaker hopes that those who hear his ideas will some day act upon them by becoming revolutionaries. That sort of advocacy is too remote from specific action. What made Dennis' advocacy objectionable was (according to the present opinion) that it constituted "indoctrination preparatory to action." It was not the statement of an idea which at some point might lead others to engage in unlawful action; it was advocacy that the unlawful action be taken. "The essential distinction," Justice Harlan added, "is that those to whom the advocacy is addressed must be urged to *do* something, now or in the future, rather than merely to *believe* in something."

Of course this contraction of the *Dennis* holding does not dispose of all the difficulties. As the Court itself recognized, "distinctions between advocacy or teaching of abstract doctrines, with evil intent, and that which is directed to stirring people to action, are often subtle and difficult to grasp." Justice Holmes remarked in a memorable aphorism, "Every idea is an incitement." [16] Yet, one can recognize a qualitative distinction between a speaker who expresses the opinion before a student audience that all law professors are scoundrels whose students should band together to beat them within an inch of their lives, and a second speaker who, taking up that theme, urges the audience to obtain baseball bats, meet behind the law faculty building at three o'clock next Thursday afternoon, and join him in attacking any professor who can then be found. The first speaker, in Justice Harlan's view, should not be prosecuted; the second has stepped over the line between advocating a belief and advocating an illegal action.

The upshot of all this was that the Court set aside the convictions of the fourteen men and women involved in the *Yates* case, because the trial court had not clearly observed the distinction just stated. As to five of the defendants, the Court ordered outright dismissal of the charges because there was no evidence at all tending to show that they had engaged in incitement to action. As to the other nine, the Court ordered retrials because it felt that a jury could possibly find knowing participation by them in a conspiracy to urge others to do unlawful things.

Even this "clarification" of *Dennis* did not satisfy Justices Black and Douglas. All of the defendants, in their view, should have been acquitted. Most of the evidence against Yates and the others had consisted of books, pamphlets, newspapers, and manifestoes which, as Justice Black put it, "are turgid, diffuse, abstruse, and just plain dull"—or as many others have observed, are more likely to induce profound slumber than to arouse violence. It seemed to these two Justices going too far to convict present-day defendants because they endorsed what Marx or Engels or some other Communist deity had written a hundred or more years ago. The Court's suggested differentiation between advocacy of *belief* and advocacy of *doing* was unsatisfactory to the dissenters. The Constitution, they said, forbids any interference with people who are simply "talking about public affairs, whether or not such discussion incites to action, legal or illegal." * They marked the contrast between dictatorship, which must ruthlessly stamp out causes and beliefs opposed to their

* The dissenters found support for their view in one of Thomas Jefferson's statements (quoted in 12 Hening's Stat., Virginia 1823, c. 34, p. 85): ". . . it is time enough for the rightful purposes of civil government, for its officers to interfere when principles break out into overt acts against peace and good order. . . ."

régimes, and, on the other hand, democracies which are committed to the view that free expression of all ideas, unpopular as well as popular, is the best way to assure continuance of democratic government. And they concluded that "The First Amendment provides the only kind of security system that can preserve a free government—one that leaves the way open for people to favor, discuss, advocate, or incite causes and doctrines however obnoxious and antagonistic such views may be to the rest of us."

The aftermath of the *Yates* case is interesting. By the end of 1956 convictions of Communist leaders under the Smith Act had numbered 114. Many of these cases were still pending in the appellate courts when the *Yates* decision was announced in June of 1957. On one ground or another, convictions were set aside and new trials were granted to many of these defendants. The Department of Justice itself dropped the prosecution of a considerable number, on the ground that they could not properly be convicted on the basis of the evidence now available. Most significantly of all, the cases against the nine remaining defendants in *Yates,* as to whom the Supreme Court had refused to dismiss the charges, were abandoned by the prosecution because there was insufficient evidence that they had advocated action as distinct from opinion.[17] After all the clamor, after all the expressed alarm about the peril into which the United States was being plunged by this handful of misguided fanatics, the prosecution felt itself unable to show persuasively that the Communist spokesmen had engaged in the forbidden incitements to illegality.

This should stimulate a sober second look at the surface attractions of programs of suppression and coercion. Occasionally the supporters of these programs are scoundrels who falsely parade themselves as upholders of democracy; but more often they are good and sincere men. Men genuinely devoted to worthy ends sometimes endorse efforts to force unanimity of sentiment, not because they consciously espouse authoritarianism, but because they hope thus to assure maximum support for the nation and its people. No matter how well intentioned they may be, however, those efforts themselves create a graver danger than they overcome. The perils sought to be suppressed are regularly overestimated. History shows in one example after another how excessive have been the fears of earlier generations, who shuddered at menaces that, with the benefit of hindsight, we now know were mere shadows. This in itself should induce the modern generation to view with prudent skepticism the recurrent alarms about the fatal potentialities of dissent. In any event, in a world torn between the merits of freedom and the blandishments of totalitarian power, the lovers of freedom cannot afford to sacrifice their moral superiority by adopting totalitarian methods in order to create a self-deluding sense of security. Suppression, once accepted as a way of life, is likely to spread. It reinforces the herd urge toward orthodoxies of all kinds—religious, economic, and moral as well as political.*

The sounder course, dictated by decisions that preceded *Dennis,* is to disregard advocacy and teaching, even though its ultimate goal may be acts, unless there is imminent danger that unlawful conduct will be induced.[18] At a particular time and in particular circumstances a speaker may properly be deemed an actionist. Realistically considered, there can in fact be such an offense as inciting a riot; there can in fact be such an offense as organizing violent steps that are calculated to disturb public order or to lead to overthrow. The use of one's vocal cords or of one's typewriter may, therefore, properly be regarded as punishable action in some situations. Those situations, however, do not arise when there is still ample opportu-

---

* Years ago, in the midst of a great war, the United States Supreme Court saw and stated the issue in terms that have the continuing ring of truth:

"As first and moderate methods to attain unity have failed, those bent on its accomplishment must resort to an ever-increasing severity. As governmental pressure toward unity becomes greater, so strife becomes more bitter as to whose unity it shall be. . . . Ultimate futility of such attempts to compel coherence is the lesson of every such effort from the Roman drive to stamp out Christianity as a disturber of its pagan unity, the Inquisition, as a means to religious and dynastic unity, the Siberian exiles as a means to Russian unity, down to the fast failing efforts of our present totalitarian enemies. Those who begin coercive elimination of dissent soon find themselves exterminating dissenters. Compulsory unification of opinion achieves only the unanimity of the graveyard." *West Virginia State Board of Education* v. *Barnette,* 319 U.S. 624 (1943).

nity for the force of words to be dissipated by other and better words, or by feasible defensive measures, or (most significantly) by the course of events that the speaker does not control. The man who urges an angry mob to follow him into action, then and there, is creating an immediate threat to public safety. But a man who urges an audience to follow him into action when the time is ripe, at some uncertain date in the future, is not a present menace, though he may be a profound irritation. Two things argue against dealing with him or his kind at that stage. First, society should conserve its energies, using them only for real rather than supposititious problems. Second, when immediacy of danger is not the test, the boundaries between permissible and impermissible talk become too hard to draw. When that happens, the people at large are discouraged from talking at all about things that matter deeply, lest they be adjudged to have overstepped the lines. A free society can better stand the risks of talk than the risks of silence.

THE INTERNAL SECURITY ACT OF 1950
(McCARRAN ACT)

When war broke out in Korea in 1950, the already large public resentment of Communists found expression in new federal legislation. Arguing that legally admissible evidence to sustain convictions of Communists was difficult to obtain, and contending that further laws were needed to expose conspirators against the nation, Congress enacted the Internal Security Act of 1950.[19] It commences by reciting the legislative conclusion that the world Communist movement has as one of its purposes the establishment in the United States of a totalitarian dictatorship, to be brought about by treachery, deceit, infiltration, sabotage, and terrorism. The statute also states that American Communists have transferred their allegiance to a foreign power, and that they constitute a present danger to America's security. These legislatively declared findings are said to make necessary the following steps proposed in the statute:

1. Creating a new crime, consisting of joining with others "to perform any act which would substantially contribute to the establishment within the United States of a totalitarian dictatorship . . . the direction and control of which is to be vested in . . . any foreign government . . .";

2. Providing administrative machinery (the Subversive Activities Control Board) to determine what organizations are "Communist-action" or "Communist-front" groups. Such groups are required to register, and they and those connected with them then suffer certain disabilities;

3. Setting up a system of preventive detention of potential spies and saboteurs in the event of war or other presidentially declared national emergency;

4. Stiffening existing laws aimed at espionage; and

5. Erecting still further barriers against entry into or residence within the United States by Communist-tainted aliens.

For present purposes discussion will be confined to the first two of these five phases of the so-called McCarran Act.

The new sedition provision. Since the statute seeks to penalize only joining with others to perform *acts* that contribute toward creating a foreign-controlled dictatorship, it seems at first glance to be free from the objections previously voiced against penalties upon mere advocacy. But a second glance shows the present provision to be so broad, so vague, so threatening as to be constitutionally objectionable. It does not clearly indicate the behavior it is intended to forbid, and thus fails to afford a person an adequate guide as to whether or not his conduct is criminal.

Of course antisocial acts may validly be prohibited; such things as sabotage and violence, whether or not aimed at establishing a foreign dictatorship, can be—and long since have been—declared to be criminal. What else was the new statute intended to reach? Does it mean to penalize acts which, while wholly innocent in themselves, are objectionable because they might somehow facilitate the undesired end result? It is a basic proposition in a constitutional

society that crimes should be defined in advance, and not after action has been taken. "The standards of certainty in statutes punish-
ing for offenses," the Supreme Court has declared, "are higher than
in those depending primarily upon civil sanction for enforcement.
. . . There must be ascertainable standards of guilt. Men of common intelligence cannot be required to guess at the meaning of the
enactment. . . ." [20] And in another case, involving a statute which
forbade committing "any act injurious to . . . the public morals,"
the Court said that reasonable standards of guilt must be provided
if a statute were to achieve a valid purpose. "Legislation may run
afoul of the Due Process Clause because it fails to give adequate
guidance to those who would be law-abiding, to advise defendants
of the nature of the offense with which they are charged, or to guide
courts in trying those who are accused." [21]

The first branch of the statute now under discussion seems clearly
deficient by these tests. No effort has been made to enforce it,
and its patent invalidity will in all likelihood discourage any reliance upon it. Nevertheless, like other extreme and careless laws,
this one may have a subtly restricting effect upon freedom, for
men may fear to do innocent things that could conceivably be made
the basis of an accusation under such sweeping language. Printers,
for example, might refuse to print a Communist paper. According
to report, Madison Square Garden, a large meeting hall in New
York which even during World War II continued to rent its auditorium to groups that were antiwar and assertedly pro-Nazi, has
now refused to rent the same facilities to "subversive" organizations; the refusal is seemingly induced at least in part by doubt
whether furnishing a hall for such groups would be deemed a violation of this statute. Following Madison Square Garden's lead,
other auditoriums have adopted the same policy. And thus freedom
of assembly and freedom of speech are wounded though the government itself has not fired a single shot in a campaign to apply this
restrictive statute.

Registration. The McCarran Act divides Communist organizations into two classes: "Communist-action" organizations, which

are controlled from abroad in order to achieve the purposes of the world Communist movement, and "Communist-front" organizations, which are those that are controlled and manipulated by Communist-action groups though their immediate purposes seem quite proper and their members may be unwitting dupes. Both types are required to register. If the Attorney General believes that an unregistered organization should register, he may begin proceedings before the Subversive Activities Control Board to obtain an order from that body. Elaborate procedures are prescribed to be followed by the Board, but once it has finally ordered that there be registration, heavy penalties are incurred by noncompliers. Moreover, registration itself involves substantial burdens intended to restrict the organization's functioning. Members and sources of funds must be recorded by Communist-action groups; activities and expenditures must be described; members are barred from certain private as well as public employments and from obtaining passports; registered groups must label their printed matter or radio broadcasts as Communist propaganda.

Needless to say, no organization has voluntarily registered under the provisions of this law, for to have done so would have been an acknowledgment, to all intents and purposes, that the organization was reprehensible. So the Attorney General on November 22, 1950, began proceedings to compel the Communist Party to register. Hearings commenced on April 23, 1951, and lasted until July 1, 1952. The Board's decision, 251 pages long and reaching the expected conclusion, was announced on April 20, 1953, two years after the hearings started. But that was far from the end. The Communist Party went to the courts, to attack the statute and the order made under its authority. While the case was still pending, the Communist Party moved that the hearing be reopened because evidence had come to light that several of the witnesses against it were perjurers, who had become thoroughly discredited even in the eyes of those who had previously regarded them as reliable informants. In 1956 the Supreme Court held that the proceedings should be returned to the Board, "to make certain that the Board

bases its findings upon untainted evidence." [22] The Board then reopened the case, reconsidered the matter, and reached the same
conclusion, namely, that the Communist Party is a "Communist-
action organization" and must register. But the matter remained
unsettled, for in 1959 the case was once again in the courts. On
July 30th of that year the United States Court of Appeals in the
District of Columbia upheld the Board's decision, by a divided
vote.[23] Further judicial proceedings seemed probable. Nine years
had then passed since the statute had been enacted, but as yet nobody had registered—though, in addition to the Communist Party,
a few other groups had by then been ordered to do so and proceedings had been begun against twenty more. It may be noted,
however, that the very act of commencing a proceeding to force
an organization's registration does in itself subject that group to
considerable public opprobrium and thus does have immediately
damaging consequences.

The ultimate effects of the McCarran Act are difficult to gauge.
Of course its sponsors meant that it should cripple the Communist
movement in America. Perhaps it will have that result, though no
one can yet say whether it will ever do more than lead to changes
in name and appearance. President Truman, acting on the advice of
the Departments of State, Defense, and Justice (of which the F.B.I.
is a part), as well as the Central Intelligence Agency, sought unsuccessfully to prevent passage of the act; the government agencies
asserted that their operations would be seriously damaged if, as they
feared might happen, the Communists were to be "driven under-
ground" and were forced to become an even more secret movement.[24] Moreover, the act contains provisions of extremely doubtful
practical wisdom—such as one directing the Secretary of Defense
to publish a list of industrial establishments engaged in important
military production, and forbidding any Communist to seek work
in those establishments. The publication of such a list would very
probably be warmly welcomed by hostile espionage agents, who
would thus be spared the trouble of locating the nation's industrial
nerve centers. But it is not the purpose here to debate the political

consequences of the statute. We are now concerned solely with its bearing on political liberty.

Laws of this type must inevitably restrict the freedoms of speech and assembly. The McCarran Act, for example, sets forth, as one of the important criteria for judging the character of an organization brought before the Subversive Activities Control Board, the extent of its adherence to the expressed policies of the Soviet Union. Thus, if an organization were to devote itself to, say, supporting the admission of Red China into the United Nations, or to control of nuclear weapons according to the Russian instead of the American prescription, or agitating for the withdrawal of American air bases from the periphery of the Soviet Union, it might at least conceivably have to face demands that it register as a Communist organization— for all of these are among the declared objectives of the Soviet Union, though all of them are also conscientiously supported by persons who have independently arrived at the same conclusions. If people cannot meet when they wish and espouse whatever views they choose, without risking the pains and penalties of forced registration, they are to that extent less free than they were before.*

THE COMMUNIST CONTROL ACT OF 1954

In 1954, the Congress of the United States grew impatient. The McCarran Act of 1950 had failed to bring about the demise of the supposed Communist Menace. The registration procedures required by that statute had proved to be just as cumbersome as President Truman had predicted they would be, when he had unsuccessfully tried to block enactment. So now a new effort was made, motivated partly by genuine exasperation and partly, it is believed, by the desire of certain "liberal" legislators to demonstrate that they

* Reference may here be made to the discussion in earlier pages of the problem of license requirements in connection with exercise of the right to speak. See pages 45–55, above; and note especially *Thomas* v. *Collins*, 323 U.S. 516 (1945), in which Justice Rutledge declared that "As a matter of principle a requirement of registration in order to make a public speech would seem generally incompatible with the exercise of the rights of free speech and free assembly."

were at least as vigorously anti-Communist as were their political opponents.

The Communist Control Act of 1954 [25] has the announced purpose of "outlawing" the Communist Party in the United States; but thus far its consequences remain highly doubtful. The act begins by stating the Congressional conclusion that the Communist Party is not in fact a political organization, but is instead a conspiratorial and revolutionary movement that serves as agent of a hostile foreign government. As such, the Communist Party is declared to be a present and continuing danger to national security. This legislative finding, the statute continues, justifies withholding from that party any of the rights or privileges enjoyed by "legal bodies created under the laws." The statutory language is vague, but its sponsors declared at the time that it was intended, among other things, to prevent the Communist Party from making leases or contracts, from suing in the courts, or from appearing on the ballot.

Article I of the American Constitution provides, in Section 9, that "No Bill of Attainder or ex post facto Law shall be passed." An "ex post facto Law" is one which declares to be a crime conduct which was not illegal when it occurred.[26] A bill of attainder, according to an important decision of the Supreme Court, is a legislative act, no matter what its form, that applies "either to named individuals or to easily ascertainable members of a group in such a way as to inflict punishment on them without a judicial trial." [27] Measured by this test, the Communist Control Act of 1954 may readily be deemed unconstitutional as an attempt to punish an allegedly conspiratorial group without affording the group the protections of a trial. At least debatably, however, no "punishment" is involved in withdrawing recognition of an organization's legal status. Hence it may be well to consider the merits of the approach here taken by Congress, without predispositions based on constitutional provisions of uncertain applicability.

The chief issue, in my opinion, is the desirability of seeking to bar Communists (or any other unpopular group) from participating in the democratic process of elections. As of 1951, eight of the states had excluded from a place on the ballot for state and local elections any party which used "Communist" in its name, or which was connected with the Communist Party of the United States; other states withheld electoral rights from groups that advocated forcible overthrow of the government.[28] The validity of these laws was doubtful,[29] and they did not appear to have any great impact upon political events. The 1954 federal statute now sought to do on a nation-wide basis what some of the states had been attempting in a piecemeal manner.

There is a superficial plausibility about denying to the enemies of democracy the opportunity to use its machinery. But, when the matter is considered more closely, the unreasonableness of this step becomes plain. The foundation stone upon which democratic institutions are built is the voters' opportunity to choose freely among competing candidates and programs. They may choose well or poorly, but they must be able to choose freely if democracy is to preserve its meaning. Moreover, if vote-seekers are flatly forbidden to make electoral appeals to vote-givers, strong support is lent to the argument that basic changes can never be achieved by democratic means, but must be produced by revolution.

Charles Evans Hughes made this point tellingly as long ago as 1920. A former Governor of New York, former Justice of the Supreme Court, and former Republican candidate for the presidency of the United States, Hughes—who subsequently became Secretary of State and, later, Chief Justice of the United States—did not hesitate to oppose the action of the New York legislature in refusing to allow five elected Socialists to take their seats, because in those days the Socialist Party was deemed "subversive." When the ousted men appealed to the courts, Hughes appeared as counsel in behalf of the most prominent association of lawyers in New York, to support the Socialists' rights. He deemed it "a most serious mistake to proceed, not against individuals charged with violation of law, but against masses of our citizens combined for political action, by denying them the only recourse of peaceful government; that is, action by the ballot box and through duly elected representatives in legislative bodies." The question to be weighed, as this distinguished jurist so well saw, is not whether the aims of a political group are deeply obnoxious to the present majority; the question, rather, is whether the channels of peaceful persuasion shall be kept open so that there can never be justification for resort to force.

Another debatable provision of the 1954 statute adds "Communist-infiltrated organizations" to the categories of "Communist-action" and "Communist-front" groups that had been recognized by the McCarran Act of 1950. Like the other two types, "Communist-infiltrated" organizations are subjected to various burdens, requirements, and penalties. While general in form, this part of the new statute seems particularly directed at labor organizations, which, if found to be "Communist-infiltrated," are to lose the protections of the laws that compel employers to bargain collectively with their employees' chosen representatives. That is to say, even if workers freely chose to be represented by a condemned union, the employer could refuse to deal with it.

The term "Communist-infiltrated," added to the other adjectives that have been used to characterize groups in which Communists are thought to play a part, is obviously difficult to define. The statute says that it connotes an organization which has been substantially directed or controlled by individuals who within the past three years have been knowing Communists or foreign agents, and which has served within that period as a means of aiding or supporting the Communists or a foreign Communist government, or impairing America's military strength or industrial capacity. The Attorney General may file charges against such an organization, which is then entitled to a hearing before the Subversive Activities Control Board created by the McCarran Act of 1950.

The first proceeding initiated by the Attorney General under this branch of the statute illustrates both the possible uses and the possible perils of the law. The case still remained under consideration in 1960, and no opinion is ventured here concerning the merits. It involves the International Union of Mine, Mill and Smelter Workers, long regarded as a "left-wing" union. Some years ago it had been expelled from the Congress of Industrial Organizations along with several other labor organizations that were deemed to be too heavily influenced by Communist leaders. Nevertheless, the union continued to represent a number of metals miners and related workers. The officers of the union had sworn that they were not Communists, and the union was legally recognized as bargaining representative for the employees of some important companies. Within the labor movement and among knowing persons, nevertheless, the union was still widely thought to be very "left-wing." Now, by proceeding under the Communist Control Act of 1954, the Attorney General was officially seeking to brand it. It was not necessary for him to show that the nominal leaders of the union were Communists; it would suffice if he could show that there was "effective management" of its affairs by one or more individuals who could be closely tied to the Communist Party. To some observers this seemed a desirable means of revealing not only to the public but to the union members themselves the political links of their organization's managers.

On the other hand, in order to stigmatize the defendant union the statute required more than showing the presence of an effective Communist in the Union's councils. The statute required that the union be "actively engaged in" giving support to the Communist Movement. To establish that branch of his accusation against the Mine, Mill and Smelter Workers, the Attorney General cited a number of actions taken and views espoused by the union. Among them was the union's opposition to the Labor-Management Relations Act of 1947 (the Taft-Hartley Act), the Communist Control Act of 1954, and certain other legislative proposals of an avowedly anti-Communist nature. Now, it is true that these were actively opposed by the Communist Party, which obviously preferred to be free from the harassments and restraints the new laws were likely to bring. But the statutes were energetically fought against as well by a great many non-Communist and, indeed, strongly anti-Communist organizations, including virtually the whole labor movement of the United States, which felt that these measures embodied objectionable and perhaps dangerous policies. To include such things in the proofs of Communist activities is, in effect, to warn all other organizations that opposition to anti-Communist measures may lead to official scrutinizing and, conceivably, to the charge of "Communist infiltration." Repression of free discussion is almost certainly not the direct objective of the Communist Control Act. But it might well prove to be its achievement, if proceedings under its terms were ever to become frequent.

George Santayana once described fanatics as those who redouble their effort when they have forgotten their goal. Measured by that test, the sponsors of the Communist Control Act came perilously close to the line of fanaticism. Constant concern about the Communist Menace had dulled analysis of its precise nature. As a result, true aim was not always taken when countermeasures against the Menace were being launched. The only legitimate goal of these countermeasures was the preservation of a free society against the threat of totalitarianism. Too often, however, moves have been defended on the ground that they have been directed against Communism, without sufficient attention to the question of whether they have been directed toward Democracy.

The Communist Menace is not in America primarily a matter of ideology. Communist ideas have made little headway in countries that have retained a measure of social mobility, that have developed an equitable economy, and that have been willing to cope with problems rather than simply deny their existence. The need, then, is not to stamp out the expression of communist philosophy. The need is to deal with the actualities of danger. Externally, these are military in character. They must be dealt with by the instruments of diplomacy, by the thrust and counterthrust of power, and eventually by genuine international accord; peaceful coexistence is the only practical alternative to glorious no-existence. Internally, the menace lies in the possibility of espionage, sabotage, or similar activity purposefully related to the supposed interests of a present or potential adversary in the military realm. Clandestine crimes of these types will not be effectively controlled by the mechanisms of registrations, purges, and political purity tests that play a large part in current legislation.

The late Justice Jackson, though concurring in the *Dennis* decision that upheld the constitutionality of the Smith Act, expressed doubt about the long-range effectiveness of efforts to halt Communism by jailing Communists.[30] His words on that occasion have broad significance. "No decision by this Court," he said, "can forestall revolution whenever the existing government fails to command the respect and loyalty of the people, and sufficient distress and discontent is allowed to grow up among the masses. Many failures by fallen governments attest that no government can long prevent revolution by outlawry. Corruption, ineptitude, inflation, oppressive taxation, militarization, injustice, and loss of leadership capable of intellectual initiative in domestic or foreign affairs are allies on which the Communists count to bring opportunity knocking to their door." As these remarks suggest, the true hope of safeguarding democratic institutions against subversion lies in perfecting those institutions, rather than in toying with totalitarian-style weapons.*

* Compare the statement of Sir Hartley Shawcross, former Attorney General of the United Kingdom and Chairman of the Council of the Bar of England:

". . . in the course of the centuries we had built up both a body of law and a tradition of respect for the great number of individual liberties which in their sum have made our people perhaps peculiarly tolerant of others— and themselves free. At all events that is our aim: freedom and toleration. But we believe that it is only realizable as an aim if it is also practiced as a means. Indeed I would think our experience has suggested that while it is possible to buy a little temporary safety by giving up some liberty, the transaction is often one which in the end leaves neither safety nor liberty." Shawcross, "The Experience of Nation States," 54 *Columbia Law Rev.* 734, 735–736 (1954).

And note also the appeal addressed by one of the most famed professors of Japan, Sakae Wagatsuma, to the youth of that country, demoralized by national defeat: "A false patriotism will destroy our country. But a people without patriotism, too, cannot escape destruction. Therefore, our duty now is to make our country such that it can be loved by all of us. There lies the secret of our change to democracy." These remarks, first published in 1949 in Professor Wagatsuma's paper on "Economic Reconstruction and Control Legislation," are quoted in his "The Japanese Legal System 1945–1955," 12 *Monumenta Nipponica* 105, at 119 (1956).

Chapter 5

THE FREEDOM NOT TO SPEAK

The preceding chapters have considered various aspects of the freedom to speak. Now let us turn to the question of whether there is any freedom to remain silent.

Free speech, as we know, finds its chief impersonal justification in the fact that unrestricted discussion is in the long run (and often in the short run) likely to advance the welfare of a democratic society. Obviously, this same justification does not support a right to keep one's mouth closed. If there is any freedom not to speak, its existence must be explained in somewhat different terms.

Freedom not to speak connotes the right to remain silent in the face of governmental effort to compel speech. Analysis will be aided if three different kinds of silence are separately recognized. They have been well described as follows: "first, the right not to say what one does not believe; second, the right not to say what one does believe; and third, the right not to say what one knows." [1]

THE RIGHT NOT TO SAY WHAT
ONE DOES NOT BELIEVE

During many centuries of human experience attempts have been made to coerce the expression of beliefs that were not honestly held. It is one of the ironies of history that these efforts have most often been undertaken in the name of God; in many times and in many places infidels have been compelled by fear to profess religious convictions they did not in fact hold—all to the greater glory of a Supreme Being who could presumably have gotten along without these grudging acknowledgments. In retrospect we can see how silly a procedure this was. At any given moment, however, mankind seems to be entirely capable of repeating the blunders of its past. The world has by no means seen the last of organized campaigns to suppress dissent by enforcing a superficial unanimity.

The American Constitution does seek to guard against this possibility in the field of religion. The First Amendment provides in part that "Congress shall make no law respecting an establishment of religion, or prohibiting the free exercise thereof." Similarly, through interpretation of the Fourteenth Amendment, the several states have been deemed to be barred from coercing the acceptance of theological doctrine or suppressing unorthodox religious views.

There remains room, however, for compulsion in respect of philosophical or political expression. This possibility was sharply revealed as a reality some fifteen years ago in a United States case widely known as the "flag salute case."

Recent years have seen the introduction into many American schoolrooms, though by no means in all, of a little ceremony that includes the group recitation of the following pledge: "I pledge allegiance to the flag of the United States of America and to the Republic for which it stands, one Nation under God, indivisible, with liberty and justice for all." While the children dutifully begin their school day by mouthing these words (which probably mean very little to most of them), they stand stiffly at attention, executing a salute in the direction of the flag that is displayed in a corner of the room.

Few youngsters would hesitate to join in this recital, though in form it pledges their allegiance to a symbol of secular government, and embodies an expressed belief in a deity. Suppose, however, that children were instructed by their parents not to voice the indicated sentiments. This actually happened when members of the Jehovah's Witnesses sect forbade their children to participate in the ceremony.* One of the states, moved by the excessively fervid spirit of the war years, decreed that any child who refused to salute the flag should be expelled from school. The validity of the decree was challenged on behalf of one of the expelled children, and thus was presented to the Supreme Court the issue of whether the Government can constitutionally compel an individual to affirm a particular belief. The Court concluded that society has a very slight interest, if any interest at all, in making people profess a belief they do not in fact hold. Freedom to remain silent in the face of any such attempt was regarded as being almost unlimited.[2]

Out of this petty case involving the little child of fanatical parents came some stirring affirmations of democratic sentiment. The majority opinion written by Justice Jackson recalled, first of all, that the motives behind efforts to compel unanimity of belief are often perfectly proper, though the results of the efforts are almost always bad. "Struggles to coerce uniformity of sentiment in support of some end thought essential to their time and country," Justice Jackson said, "have been waged by many good as well as by evil men." But good motives have not sufficed to prevent the loss of liberty. Even good men may resort to more and more severe measures when their initial efforts to attain a common faith do not succeed. Then, as the pressure to achieve unity becomes ever more intense, "strife becomes more bitter as to whose unity it shall be." Attempts to compel acceptance of officially endorsed doctrine were sure to fail in the end, Justice Jackson asserted; this, he said, was the lesson of every such effort from the early Roman campaign to make Christians express belief in the Roman emperor's divinity to the then current efforts of totalitarian régimes, with which the United States was at war, to stamp out all dissent. "Those who begin coercive elimination of dissent," he remarked, "soon find themselves exterminating dissenters. Compulsory unification of opinion achieves only the unanimity of the graveyard."

* At the time in question, it should be noted, the words "under God" did not appear in the pledge to the flag. They were added pursuant to a Congressional resolution in the postwar years, when a surge of official piety was experienced in the United States.

The constitutional provisions that protect freedom of expression and belief were of course designed to prevent just that sort of development. The framers of these provisions were not frightened by the prospect of dissidence or, even, eccentricity and abnormality. They are a price that society can well afford to pay in return for what Justice Jackson characterized as "intellectual individualism and the rich cultural diversities that we owe to exceptional minds." In the flag salute case the particular device that was sought to be used was not very imposing, and the refusal of a handful of children to accept the state's command seemed harmless to others. Still, the goal toward which the state was striving could be stated in fairly impressive terms. After all, the state was attempting nothing less than to foster national unity and to stimulate patriotic sentiment in the midst of a grueling war. But this did not impress the Supreme Court deeply. As Justice Jackson put it, "freedom to differ is not limited to things that do not matter much. That would be a mere shadow of freedom. The test of its substance is the right to differ as to things that touch the heart of the existing order.

"If there is any fixed star in our constitutional constellation, it is that no official, high or petty, can prescribe what shall be orthodox in politics, nationalism, religion, or other matters of opinion or force citizens to confess by word or act their faith therein. . . ."

This story would be incomplete if there were no mention of the fact that, only three years earlier, the Supreme Court had been unable to perceive the truth of these very same propositions. In 1940 a "flag salute" case had come to the Court from another state. On that occasion eight of the nine justices had shrugged off any concern about the petty imposition that then seemed to be involved.[3] Only Justice Stone, who later became Chief Justice, worried enough to write a dissenting opinion. He protested against coercing belief merely because the legislative body thought the public interest would thus be served. "History teaches us," he wrote, "that there have been but few infringements of personal liberty by the state which have not been justified, as they are here, in the name of righteousness and the public good, and few which have not been directed, as they are now, at politically helpless minorities. The framers [of the Constitution] were not unaware that under the system which they created most governmental curtailments of personal liberty would have the support of a legislative judgment that the public interest would be better served by its curtailment than by its constitutional protection. I cannot conceive that in prescribing as limitations upon the powers of government, the freedom of the mind and spirit secured by the explicit guarantees of freedom of speech and religion, they intended or rightly could have left any latitude for a legislative judgment that the compulsory expression of belief which violates religious convictions would better serve the public interest than their protection."

The reversal of judicial sentiment in the space of three short years, so that Justice Stone's solitary dissent became in effect the majority view of the Supreme Court, is one of the great personal triumphs in the annals of American jurisprudence. The present position of the Court seems sound on legal, philosophical, and psychological grounds. Devotion to the principles of the Constitution, sharing in the aspirations it embodies, and loyalty to the nation that seeks to translate those aspirations into realities are indeed desirable. But they cannot successfully be compelled. National unity becomes an empty sham if it is built on words extorted from unwilling lips.

THE RIGHT NOT TO SAY WHAT ONE DOES BELIEVE

While society may not have a legitimate interest in making a person declare a belief that he does not in fact hold, there may perhaps be a more readily identifiable interest in making him disclose his real beliefs. Consider the most obvious example, that of a foreigner who seeks to become a naturalized citizen. There would be an incongruity if citizenship were voluntarily assumed by a man who detested the form of government that prevailed in his adopted country. Nothing is forced on him if he is asked whether he truly believes in—will support and defend—the constitutional foundations of the nation to which he intends to link himself.

All cases, however, are not so clear as the one just stated. In some situations, the compulsion to declare one's beliefs may have at least an indirectly coercive effect upon freedom of thought or conscience. "A requirement that adherents of particular religious faiths or political parties wear identifying arm-bands, for example, is obviously of this nature." * If exposure to ridicule, hostility, or oppression is the cost of holding a belief, liberty becomes an illusion.

Nevertheless, the pertinence of an individual's belief to some acknowledged public interest is sometimes at least debatably present. A decade ago, for instance, concern was felt in the United States about the influence of Communists in some of the labor unions. At that time, as is still true today, the Government maintained a special tribunal (the National Labor Relations Board) to protect unions and their members against unfair practices by employers. The tribunal's purpose was to safeguard collective bargaining between the employees' representatives and their employer. Many people, however, were reluctant to further the interests of Communist-led unions, because those unions were accused of engaging in political (rather than economic) strikes and were suspected of readiness to disregard the nation's best interests in times of crisis. Why, it was asked, should the Government use any of its facilities to strengthen that sort of union? The upshot of the discussion was that every union leader was by law required to file a "non-Communist oath" before his union could gain access to the National Labor Relations Board.

This oath requirement was soon attacked as an interference with freedom of thought, speech, and association. The Supreme Court rejected this view, and upheld the new law. The statute, according

* *American Communications Association* v. *Douds*, 339 U.S. 382 (1950). This, in essence, is what the Supreme Court feared was behind a move by the State of Alabama in 1956 to compel the National Association for the Advancement of Colored People to submit its membership lists to public inspection. In *N.A.A.C.P.* v. *Alabama*, 357 U.S. 449 (1958), the Court held that this requirement was a substantial and unconstitutional restraint upon the members' exercise of their right to freedom of association. The Court noted "the vital relationship between freedom to associate and privacy in one's associations," and remarked that "Inviolability of privacy in group association may in many circumstances be indispensable to preservation of freedom of association, particularly where a group espouses dissident beliefs."

to the majority of the Court, did not prohibit any beliefs at all; the union leaders could go on believing whatever they wished without being penalized, nor was any punitive action taken against the unions. All that had been done, said the Court, was to fix the conditions upon which a union could use a public tribunal.[4]

Some critics regarded this decision as not realistic or candid. Barring a union from the public facilities open to other unions, the critics said, had the same effect as a more conventional punishment. It would impose a real disadvantage on Communist-led unions, and therefore would place pressure on the membership to change the leadership. This in turn, it was argued, meant that union officials who were Communist adherents would suffer loss of jobs and influence, thus being "punished" for the beliefs they had been forced to disclose.

The answer to this line of argument is especially interesting because it is so broadly applicable throughout this field of law. It runs like this: The government was not obligated to provide a labor tribunal in the first place; use of such a facility is not something that can be claimed as a constitutional right, but is a mere "privilege" that can be withdrawn at will; therefore Congress did not overstep permissible boundaries when it decided that the "privilege" of resorting to the National Labor Relations Board should be extended only to bona fide labor unions, which were regarded as serving the public interest; Congress could reasonably conclude that a Communist-led union was not of that sort; the oath requirement was a practical and unobjectionable means of determining whether a union was of the one type or the other.

Soon another case reached the Supreme Court, raising the same kind of question in a different way. The city of Los Angeles, California, required every municipal employee to declare formally that he did not advocate overthrow of the government by force or other unlawful means, and had no connection with any organization that advised such a revolutionary course. A number of civil servants in Los Angeles resisted the requirement, partly on the ground that they did not know exactly what it meant and partly on the ground that they should not be compelled to disclose their beliefs in any event. When they persisted in their refusal to execute the demanded declarations, the city discharged them. A majority of the Supreme Court held that the requirement was valid.[5]

The Court thought, in Justice Clark's words, that "a municipal employer is not disabled because it is an agency of the State from inquiring of its employees as to matters that may prove relevant to their fitness and suitability for the public service. Past conduct may well relate to present fitness; past loyalty may have a reasonable relationship to present and future trust. Both are commonly inquired into in determining fitness for both high and low positions in private industry and are not less relevant in public employment." The oath requirement in this instance was thought to be a sensible way of establishing an employee's qualifications; and, to whatever extent it might serve to limit the political beliefs or activities of the municipal staff, the requirement was regarded as "reasonably designed to protect the integrity and competency of the service."

The dissenting judges gave great weight, on the contrary, to a factor concerning which the majority had been silent. The oath about associations and beliefs (or, rather, nonbeliefs) made an irrational demand, they thought, because to some extent it searched into a man's past without clear relationship to his present attitudes. But it had an even more sweeping effect. It restrained individuals in forming mental attitudes, by creating a repressive atmosphere "uncongenial to the spiritual vitality of a democratic society." "It is bound to operate," Justice Frankfurter asserted, "as a real deterrent to people contemplating even innocent associations. How can anyone be sure that an organization with which he affiliates will not at some time in the future be found by a State or National official to advocate overthrow of the government by 'unlawful means'? All but the hardiest may well hesitate to join organizations if they know that by such a proscription they will be permanently disqualified from public employment. These are considerations that cut deep into the traditions of our people. Gregariousness and friendliness are among the most characteristic of American attitudes.

Throughout our history they have been manifested in 'joining.' " *

At any rate, during recent years there have been mounting discouragements of the former tendency to join organizations because of agreement—or partial agreement—with their objectives. Oath requirements have increased by leaps and bounds. Not all of the new requirements are valid. In fact, just one year after the Los Angeles case discussed above, the Supreme Court declared unconstitutional a state statute that required every public employee to swear that he had not at any time during the preceding five years been a member of an organization listed by the Attorney General as a "Communist front" or "subversive" organization. The fault in that particular statute was that an employee could be discharged because of membership in such an organization even though he might have known nothing at all of its purposes and activities. It was unreasonable, the Court said, not to differentiate between knowing and innocent association.[6]

In the case just mentioned, Justice Black wrote a concurring opinion that well summarizes the feeling of many who deplore the spreading growth of laws to force disclosures of belief. "Governments," he said, "need and have ample power to punish treasonable acts. But it does not follow that they must have a further power to punish thought and speech as distinct from acts. Our own free society should never forget that laws which stigmatize and penalize thought and speech of the unorthodox have a way of reaching, ensnaring and silencing many more people than at first intended. We must have freedom of speech for all or we will in the long run have it for none but the cringing and the craven."

---

* Most social historians would, I think, agree with Justice Frankfurter that the United States has been a nation of "joiners" and that the resultant spread of organized community activity of every type and description has greatly aided the nation's development. Compare, however, J. Edgar Hoover, director of the Federal Bureau of Investigation, who has declared: "One of the great *weaknesses* of all Americans, whether adult or youth, is to join something." Hearings before House Committee on Un-American Activities, on H.R. 1884, H.R. 2122, 80th Cong., 1st Sess., 46; quoted by Justice Clark in *Wieman* v. *Updegraff*, 344 U.S. 183, 190 (1952).

We in America have recently gone through a period of excessive nervousness during which neighbor too often eyed neighbor with suspicion, and during which a number of truly silly things were done in the name of national security. As of January 1, 1951, for example, nine American states as well as Hawaii and Alaska required all public employees to execute elaborate oaths concerning their belief (or lack of belief) in unlawful change of the governmental structure, and twenty-seven jurisdictions imposed similar requirements especially on schoolteachers.[7] Laws of this type, it will be noted, are not concerned with forbidden activities, but are aimed at those who advocate or teach the propriety of forbidden activities in any circumstances at all, even though there is no present likelihood of actual misconduct. These "oath laws" have had their vogue in America not because they have been shown to be helpful in reaching a desired result, but, rather, because their sponsors confused their emotional satisfactions with positive accomplishments. In one state, to cite a most extreme example, a needy person who applies for public assistance must swear that he is non-Communist in his orientation (unless he happens to be blind, in which case, through legislative carelessness, he may apply for benefits without making a public proclamation about his beliefs); in another state, an unemployed person who seeks payment of unemployment insurance benefits must take an oath that he is politically pure and sweet.[8] Laws like these cannot be justified as needed protections of society; they have been enacted, rather, as a means of expressing the legislators' strong hatred of Communism.

"Oath laws" typically fail to create confidence in the public service they were intended to purify, because they fail to uncover the dangerous plotters whose existence was assumed when the laws were passed. For the most part, the people who lose their jobs because of this type of statute are not Communists at all, but are persons whose conscience prevents their satisfying the new requirements. In the large industrial city of Detroit, for example, a loyalty oath was demanded of all municipal employees; only one refused, in the end, to declare his beliefs—and that one was a member of the sect of Jehovah's Witnesses rather than of the Communist Party.*

Despite their unproductivity, laws of the same type spill over into other parts of the community. Thus, for example, a Texas statute enacted in 1952 requires each applicant for a pharmacist's license to swear that "he is not a member of the Communist party or affiliated with such party, and that he does not believe in and is neither a member of nor supports any group or organization that believes in, furthers or teaches the overthrow of the United States Government by force or any illegal or unconstitutional methods." There seems to be no reasonable connection between this oath requirement on the one hand and, on the other, the public health which is supposedly the object to be protected when a pharmacist seeks a license. An even more extreme example could at one time be found in the state of Washington, where would-be veterinarians were compelled to sign a non-Communist oath before they were allowed to care for sick animals.[9]

Beyond much doubt, requirements like these would be declared unconstitutional if they were ever suitably challenged. The Supreme Court has never said that individuals must reveal their beliefs whenever directed to do so. The right of silence cannot be destroyed at will. Before a man may be forced to state what is in his own mind, there must be a demonstrably strong public interest in what may be disclosed.[10] As yet, we have no reason to think that a widely expanded official concern with what private persons think and

---

* When the oath requirement seemed not to have exposed hordes of subversives, the city of Detroit launched in 1949 a "loyalty program" that would weed out the Communists and their sympathizers. After two years of operation, this program had produced serious doubts about the "loyalty" of only one employee, the driver of a garbage collection wagon, whose position seemed not to be of very large strategic importance. In 1952 I wrote, with reference to this farce: "But will the voters now be persuaded that the city government is not after all overrun by the Communists? More likely they will be convinced that the 'Reds' have yet again demonstrated their extraordinary wiliness. The stage will then be set for some new, more stringent approach to ridding the municipality of its hypothetical underminers." *The States and Subversion*, at pp. 370–371.

whom they know is the right way—or, even, a permissible way—to go about saving society from being subverted.*

THE RIGHT NOT TO SAY WHAT ONE KNOWS

More than two hundred years ago a famous English judge declared that "the public has a right to every man's evidence." [11] Four years ago the Supreme Court of the United States restated his thought, but with a necessary qualification: ". . . it is every man's duty to give testimony before a duly constituted tribunal *unless he invokes some valid legal exemption in withholding it.*" [12] Thus, for example, in most jurisdictions doctors, lawyers, and clergymen need not disclose information given them in their professional capacity. Those and similar "testimonial privileges" reflect policy choices. It is more important, for example, to encourage a confident relationship between husbands and wives than to have their testimony in court proceedings; it is more important that patients

* In 1958 the Supreme Court in two test cases strongly intimated its doubts on this score. California gave certain property-tax exemptions to veterans and to religious organizations. It provided at the same time, however, that any applicant for exemption must take an oath that he did not advocate the overthrow of the government, or advocate the support of a foreign government in event of hostilities against the United States. In order to test the validity of this law, certain veterans and a church applied for the tax exemption but declined to execute the oath. California then of course denied the exemption, saying that it was in any event a mere gratuity which could be granted or withheld as the state saw fit. When the state action was challenged in cases that came before the Supreme Court, the Court bluntly disposed of this contention, saying: "To deny an exemption to claimants who engage in certain forms of speech is in effect to penalize them for such speech. Its deterrent effect is the same as if the State were to fine them for this speech. The appellees [the California tax officials] are plainly mistaken in their argument that, because a tax exemption is a 'privilege' or 'bounty,' its denial may not infringe speech. . . . [T]he denial of a tax exemption for engaging in certain speech necessarily will have the effect of coercing the claimants from the proscribed speech." The cases were finally decided, however, on the narrow ground that the procedural provisions of the state law were defective. "When the State undertakes to restrain unlawful advocacy it must provide procedures which are adequate to safeguard against infringement of constitutionally protected rights—rights which we value most highly and which are essential to the workings of a free society." *Speiser* v. *Randall,* 357 U.S. 513 (1958), and *First Unitarian Church* v. *Los Angeles,* 357 U.S. 545 (1958).

consult their doctors freely than to have the testimony of the doctors.

In addition to these exemptions, and much more importantly, the United States Constitution and most of the state constitutions as well protect an individual against compulsion to testify against himself. The Fifth Amendment provides in part that no person "shall be compelled in any criminal case to be a witness against himself"—a provision that has long been construed as meaning that a person cannot be compelled in any sort of proceeding at all to furnish evidence that might tend to be incriminating if there were later to be a "criminal case." *

The privilege against self-incrimination, thus so firmly imbedded in the legal system, does undoubtedly serve on occasion to save some thoroughly guilty rascal from the necessity of cooperating in efforts to convict him. Nevertheless, a prominent scholar not long ago described the privilege as "one of the great landmarks in man's struggle to make himself civilized." [13] If the effect of our constitutional provisions were merely to save criminals from their just fate, nobody could speak of the privilege in such glowing terms. The fact is, of course, that the present-day privilege is a reaction against past abuses, and a safeguard against their recurrence.

In America the early settlers were mindful that organs of English government had often seized persons on suspicion of crime, had put them on oath, and had then asked questions intended to force a self-

---

* See E. M. Morgan, "The Privilege Against Self-Incrimination," 34 *Minnesota Law Rev.* 1, at 31 (1949).

The Fifth Amendment, it should be noted, is a limitation upon the federal government rather than upon the separate states. All but four of the states do have constitutional provisions of their own that are couched in somewhat the same terms as the Fifth Amendment. The Supreme Court has held, however, that a state, not being bound by the Fifth Amendment, has power to limit "the privilege against self-incrimination" in some respects. See *Twining* v. *New Jersey*, 211 U.S. 78 (1908); *Adamson* v. *California*, 332 U.S. 46 (1947). In the latter case, however, the Court noted that "The due process clause forbids compulsion to testify by fear of hurt, torture or exhaustion. It forbids any other types of coercion that fall within the scope of due process." These matters are discussed in an earlier chapter, at pages 24–28, above.

disclosure of wrongdoing. The penalties for refusing to answer were severe; and in those days people who had sworn to tell the truth genuinely feared God's wrath if they were to tell lies instead. Moreover, the interrogation frequently bore on political or religious orthodoxy, rather than on activities now regarded as criminal in nature; this served to intensify the citizenry's repugnance toward the practice of compelling self-incrimination.

In modern times, not only in America but in many other countries with far different traditions, sorry experience proved that irresponsible methods were encouraged when public authorities were in a position to demand testimony upon the basis of which the witness could later be prosecuted. The Supreme Court summed up the matter recently by acknowledging that increased difficulty in proceeding against a possibly guilty man is an evil, to be sure, but that this must be weighed against an even more far-reaching evil, namely, the possible recurrence of harsh inquisitorial methods. "Prevention of the greater evil was deemed of more importance than occurrence of the lesser evil," said the Court. "Having had much experience with a tendency in human nature to abuse power, the Founders sought to close the doors against like future abuses by law-enforcing agencies." [14] Moreover, as was observed by Dean Wigmore, the great authority on the law of evidence, unrestrained questioning of suspects has led in many countries to official reliance on torture: "If there is a right to an answer, there soon seems to be a right to the expected answer—that is, to a confession of guilt. Thus the legitimate use grows into the unjust abuse; ultimately, the innocent are jeopardized by the encroachments of a bad system." [15]

In any consideration of constitutional developments in this area, initial stress must be laid on the proposition that the privilege against self-incrimination is limited to *communication*. The sorts of abuses that gave rise to the privilege had to do with verbalization rather than with what has been called "nonassertive conduct." Hence a defendant or a suspect in a criminal matter cannot refuse, for example, to provide his fingerprints, or to exhibit a scar by which he might be recognized, or to try on an article of clothing that was left at the scene of a crime, or to stand up so that witnesses can identify him.

On the other hand, when words rather than physical externals are involved, the privilege is very broad indeed. A witness need not be guilty of anything in order to be able to refuse to speak. The privilege, as has been said, can shield the innocent against providing circumstantial evidence suggestive of a nonexistent guilt.[16] In one well known recent case the Court held that a school board could not properly dismiss a professor solely because he had refused to answer questions on the ground that his answers might incriminate him. "The privilege," said the Court, "serves to protect the innocent who otherwise might be ensnared by ambiguous circumstances." Because this is so, the Court strongly condemned "the practice of imputing a sinister meaning to the exercise of a person's constitutional right under the Fifth Amendment. . . . The privilege against self-incrimination would be reduced to a hollow mockery if its exercise could be taken as equivalent either to a confession of guilt or a conclusive presumption of perjury." [17] Being mindful that "ambiguous circumstances" may make an innocent witness reluctant to produce evidence that would draw the circumstantial net even tighter, the Court has not insisted that testimony must be given unless it would affirmatively indicate the commission of a crime by the witness; the privilege can be claimed whenever an answer would furnish (or, in fact, lead to) "a link in the chain of evidence." [18] Of course it is not for the witness, on his own unsupported assertion, to determine whether his answer would be incriminating. The court continues to have a responsibility in that regard. Plainly, however, a witness cannot be required to prove in any very complete way that he will actually be exposed to danger if he does answer; if he were required to make that sort of proof, he would have to disclose the very things he is reluctant to reveal. Hence, as the Supreme Court has said, "To sustain the privilege, it need only be evident from the implications of the question, in the setting in which it is asked, that a responsive answer to the question or an explanation of why it cannot be answered *might* be dangerous because injurious disclosure could result." [19]

The proposition must be stressed, however, that the privilege is against self-*incrimination*, that is, involvement in possible criminal proceedings. Hence, mere fear of embarrassment or even disgrace does not afford a foundation for claiming the privilege. Moreover, the privilege is entirely personal to the one who claims it. An individual, therefore, cannot refuse to give testimony because it might tend to incriminate someone else. The most important consequence of this view of the privilege is that a corporation executive, or an official of a large unincorporated association such as a labor union, cannot withhold testimony or documentary evidence that might tend to incriminate his organization.[20] And this is true even though the evidence in question might incriminate him as well.[21] The American courts take the view that the privilege against self-incrimination had the historic purpose of "protecting only the natural individual from compulsory incrimination through his own testimony or personal records," which means that "the papers and effects which the privilege protects must be the private property of the person claiming the privilege, or at least in his possession in a purely personal capacity"; if he possesses evidence simply as the custodian or representative acting on behalf of a corporation or other organization, the witness cannot withhold it.[22]

Another extremely important point is that the privilege against self-incrimination can be lost by waiver. That is to say, it must be specifically invoked, though not by any set form of words.[23] Even when it has been claimed, however, it can be deemed to have been waived if the witness has answered other questions to which the present inquiry is related. In a widely criticized decision in 1951, the Supreme Court held that a defendant who had already in general terms revealed some elements of his past conduct, could not rely on the privilege against self-incrimination when he was then asked to disclose further details.[24] The dissenting judges remarked that this holding created a real dilemma for witnesses: "On the one hand, they risk imprisonment . . . by asserting the privilege prematurely; on the other, they might lose the privilege if they answer a single question. The Court's view makes the protection depend on timing so refined that lawyers, let alone laymen, will have difficulty in knowing when to claim it."

Most professional commentators shared the dissenters' belief that the decision was poorly reasoned and would lead to unfortunate results. Their concern has been borne out by events. As Dean Griswold observed several years later, "As a consequence of this case, witnesses who have legitimate fears of prosecution, but who might be willing to cooperate as far as they could, are induced (if not actually compelled) to refuse to answer any questions at all." [25] In recent times, many witnesses have simply identified themselves and have then declined to speak further; their theory, sustained by the courts, has been that even if they merely denied some atrocious allegation, they would open themselves to a thorough search into related matters that might have a possibly self-incriminating tendency.

This sort of difficulty has intensified a fairly general impatience with the whole idea of the privilege. One can safely say that this is not one of the more popular constitutional protections, for the public usually perceives it not as a bulwark against abuse, but as a screen behind which wrongdoers and recalcitrant witnesses hide. There is nothing new about this. More than a hundred years ago law enforcement officials complained that they were prevented from obtaining necessary evidence in important proceedings. The suggestion was then made, and accepted by Congress, that witnesses should be immunized against prosecution if they were forced to give incriminating testimony. That is to say, an individual who might know about evidence that would incriminate not only himself but some other wrongdoers as well, was to be given an "immunity bath" in return for his surrendering his constitutional privilege of silence.

The first so-called "compulsory testimony act" was adopted in 1857. It had some unexpected consequences. Wily criminals sometimes managed to have themselves called as witnesses and then, in response to too loosely phrased questions, would disgorge admissions of their own past misdeeds—for which they could not thereafter be prosecuted. In one case, a pair of rascals who, unbeknownst to anybody, had cheated the government out of two million dollars, succeeded in testifying against themselves before anyone had discovered their misdeeds; then, freed from the fear of prosecution, they were able to enjoy their ill-gotten millions in peace and quiet. Naturally, episodes like this one led quickly to a tightening up of the statutes.[26]

The most important contemporary "immunity bath" statute was enacted in 1954. It provides, in substance, that whenever the Attorney General decides that testimony is needed in a national security case (such as one involving espionage or sabotage), he may ask a court to instruct a witness to testify or produce evidence; if a court does so order, the witness may not refuse to answer because of possible self-incrimination, but he cannot thereafter be prosecuted in any court if he claims his constitutional privilege before complying with the court's order. The validity of this statute was attacked by a witness whose testimony was sought in connection with investigation of an espionage group of which he had allegedly been a member. The witness argued that while the statute did immunize him against prosecution, it did not give him protection against other undesirable things (such as dismissal from his job, expulsion from his labor union, and "general public opprobrium"—or loss of face) that might arise because of his testimony. The Supreme Court emphasized, however, that the Constitution protects only against possible *incrimination*—that is, from governmental actions of a punitive character. "Immunity displaces the danger. Once the reason for the privilege ceases, the privilege ceases." On this reasoning, the statute was upheld.[27]

Chapter 6

LEGISLATIVE INVESTIGATIONS

As the preceding chapter showed, the government's need for information sometimes comes into direct conflict with the individual's right to remain silent. The discussion in that chapter related particularly to judicial proceedings and to the investigations that may prepare the way for later trials. Now attention will be centered on investigations that are conducted not as an element of judicial proceedings, but as an element of legislative activity.

If a society is to be wisely and effectively governed, those who make its laws must be well informed. In the United States as in other countries information comes to legislators from many sources —from official reports, from constituents, from so-called "pressure groups" (that is, from organizations representing those who may have some special interest), and from personal experience or study. Moreover, action is rarely taken on any important proposal unless it has first been referred to a committee of the legislature, which ordinarily conducts a hearing so that supporters and opponents of the measure may bring facts and arguments to the legislators' attention. The United States does not resemble countries in which the legislative program comes almost exclusively from the Cabinet. In such countries the pertinent factual background and policy considerations are normally explored in the relevant ministries, rather than by the members of the legislative body itself. In America, by contrast, the legislature (at least hypothetically) makes an independent study of the matters that relate to suggested statutes. Of course it sometimes happens in the United States, as in other countries, that important matters are referred to specially created commissions, to study and ultimately to report their findings and recommendations.

In the main, information flows freely to the legislature. Persons who have an interest in the subject matter clamor to be heard. Documentary and oral statements are provided in abundance. Occasionally, however, the needed insights can perhaps not be acquired unless compulsion is used to get at the facts. A suspicion may exist, let us say, that practices connected with the Stock Exchange may be jeopardizing the interests of investors. But the extent and the precise mechanics of those practices may be only partially understood. Before a suitably protective statute may be framed, more information must be obtained. Those who possess the information may be reluctant to divulge it. Can governmental force then be used to overcome their reluctance?

That question has been answered affirmatively almost since the nation's beginnings, although the American Constitution contains no specific reference to the problem. Congress has freely investigated (as have also state legislatures to a much lesser degree) whatever may bear upon the lawmaking or money-appropriating functions. The earliest Congressional inquiry occurred as long ago as 1792, when an effort was made to find out who was to blame for a disastrous defeat inflicted upon American troops by an Indian chieftain with the unimpressive name of Little Turtle. The trouble on that occasion seems to have been a failure to provide necessary supplies for the troops. About a hundred and sixty years later Congress investigated almost precisely the same sort of problem, when an American commander in Korea charged that his army's operations had been hampered by ammunition shortages.[1]

This kind of inquiry into the way that governmental powers have been exercised by the executive branch seems a bit bizarre to persons in countries in which the Cabinet is composed of members of the Parliament. In such countries, if the Government does something of a shockingly inept character, it may be turned out of office by a vote of no confidence. In the United States, by contrast, the chief executive—the President—will remain in office for a fixed term of years no matter how much or how little Congress may sympathize with his conduct of public affairs. Congressional investigations serve as one way of focussing attention upon the functioning of government. As a result of these investigations, improvements are often quickly achieved and policies are often altered, even without the enactment of any new statutes and without any major personnel changes. To some extent legislative investigation of this nature serves the same purpose as a special tribunal of inquiry, appointed to examine into some alleged misbehavior in government. The tribunal method, which has been highly refined in Britain and no doubt elsewhere, is in many respects preferable to the American system. When conduct of an assertedly illegal or unethical nature is to be investigated, a legislative committee is perhaps not the best equipped body to search for the facts; the temptation becomes too great to approach the case with an eye to partisan political advantage, newspaper headlines, and personal aggrandizement.

Inquiries into the way existing laws are being administered do not as a rule raise many problems of Congressional power. Witnesses who hold public office are usually cooperative (or at least try to give the impression that they are), even when they face the possibility of severe embarrassment because of the matters under investigation. Of course a legislative committee cannot always pry into the confidential communications that may pass between the President and his aides, any more than it can interfere with the day-to-day functioning of a court. After all, there are three separate branches of government, and each one has its own responsibilities that cannot be interfered with by another branch. For the most part, however, Congress has only minor irritations in obtaining information from persons in the executive branch.[2] The more difficult questions of power arise when the legislature seeks to compel persons outside the government to testify about matters they would prefer to leave shrouded in silence.

The Supreme Court has long since concluded that Congress (usually acting through one of its committees) may inquire into conditions pertinent to proposals for legislative action; and it may also inquire into matters that might possibly show the need for statutes that have not yet even been proposed. To assure the effectiveness of its inquiries, the legislative body is thought to need the authority to compel testimony. The need is probably much exaggerated. If an important investigation is to be made in Great Britain, for example, it is turned over to a specially created body, called a Royal Commission of Inquiry, composed of particularly qualified members rather than jacks-of-all-trades politicians and not at all dependent on the power to subpoena testimony or documents. Be that as it may, American legislators believe that they must have the subpoena power. And the Supreme Court has upheld punishment of obstructive witnesses, either imposed by the legislature itself [3] or, pursuant to a general statute, by a criminal court.[4] The use of compulsion has by no means been rare, and it has become much more frequent in recent years. Ever since 1857 it has been a penal offense to refuse to respond to questions asked lawfully by Congress. During the ninety-two years between 1857 and 1949, 113 witnesses were cited for contempt of Congress, as the offense is called. From 1950 to 1952—a mere two years—117 witnesses were cited for contempt.[5]

These figures do not indicate a sudden growth in contemptuous refusal to answer questions. Rather, they suggest that many more questions are being asked, and that the areas of inquiry have been undergoing change. From 1789, the first year of the United States' existence under the Constitution, until 1925 Congress had authorized a grand total of 285 investigations, usually by special committees with fairly specific purposes and only a limited life. During the two years 1950–1952, Congress authorized 225 separate investigations—though most of the controversial matters arose in only a few of this large number.[6] The tendency to concentrate on investigation rather than on legislation continues to be marked. In addition to the specially authorized inquiries, one must also take account of the work of certain permanent committees which proceed to make investigations under very broadly stated grants of power. For example, the late Senator McCarthy, a demagogue who at one period provided the newspapers with much sensational material, functioned as chairman of a committee instructed simply to study "the operation of Government activities at all levels with a view to determining its economy and efficiency."

The present frequency of investigations means, of course, that Congressional committees are more likely to touch more people in more compelling ways than in former times. This inevitably occasions debate as to whether questions asked by this or that committee are of a lawful character and must therefore be answered.

The Supreme Court has said in sweeping terms that the legislative power to investigate may not be used to delve into "private affairs unrelated to a valid legislative purpose," [7] and does not extend to an area in which Congress could not enact any constitutional legislation.[8] Moreover, the power to investigate does not override the specific guarantees of the Constitution, particularly the privilege not to give evidence of a self-incriminating tendency.[9] Finally, "a witness may rightfully refuse to answer where the bounds of the power [conferred on a committee to make an investigation] are exceeded or where the questions asked are not pertinent to the matter under inquiry." [10]

Notwithstanding these limitations on the investigating power, the United States Congress during the past twenty years has tolerated an extraordinary series of actions conducted in its name and with the support of its authority. Real or supposed threats to the United States Government and to "the American way of life" have occasioned almost continuous inquiries into so-called "un-American activities" and subversive movements. The investigations have sometimes ranged far and wide, so that no very clear concept of what was truly un-American seemed to emerge. Occasionally it seemed that anything a particular investigator happened to dislike might be branded as un-American and disloyal. When the investigating power fell into the hands of political extremists and charlatans, as unfortunately it did, it was used sensationally rather than constructively. The investigations at times became ends in themselves. They were not always conducted as serious efforts to obtain information needed in the discharge of legislative responsibilities, but were intended to "expose" organizations or individuals of whom the investigators disapproved.

While Communism and Communists were often the declared objects of these exposures, the Congressional investigators were occasionally careless in formulating their charges or in developing their proofs; and, in any case, those who were denounced by the investigators had small chance to defend themselves against their accusers. Some investigations seemingly had as their chief object the infliction of punishment on individuals for holding the wrong opinions or for having engaged in conduct that was not punishable by legal means, even though it may have been highly unpopular. A man could not, for example, be punished by law for having been a Communist years ago, or for having urged friendship with the Soviet Union, or for having criticized the government of Generalissimo Chiang Kai-shek. But when such a man was "exposed" by a legislative investigating committee with the innuendo that he might be a concealed Communist, he might lose his job or his good name.

On some occasions committee investigators summoned private citizens before them and proceeded to ask searching questions about what had previously been regarded as their personal lives and affairs —their beliefs, their associations, and their political orientations. These unwilling witnesses were then faced with difficult choices. If they answered, they surrendered their privacy. If they refused to respond at all, they risked being proceeded against for "contempt of Congress" in blocking its inquiries. And if they refused to respond to questions on the ground that their answers might possibly incriminate them, then of course they aroused the disapproval of their employers and acquaintances, who were prone to conclude that the claim of the privilege against self-incrimination was the virtual equivalent of a confession of guilt. Suppose, for example, that a man had been a Communist during his years as a university student, 1938–1942. He had dutifully read Marx and Lenin and had talked about the sovietization of America, but had never become deeply involved in party affairs. Then he had terminated his membership completely, though he still occasionally saw some of his former Communist friends. Now, having meanwhile become a successful journalist or movie actor or radio technician, he is suddenly called before a Congressional committee that is investigating un-American activities. "Are you now or have you ever been a member of the Communist Party?" he is asked. He cannot truthfully answer that he has not been. If he answers that he has been, the door will then be open to a flood of other questions; he will be asked to name all others whom he knew as Communists, and so on. If instead of answering, he claims the privilege against self-incrimination, the next question may be, "Did you ever commit espionage or sabotage?" He never did, but once he has begun to use the privilege against self-incrimination, he will probably have to continue to do so; he cannot pick and choose among the questions that are put to him, and as a result he may find himself virtually destroyed by the scandalous implications of the questions he must decline to answer, despite his being wholly innocent.

A decision of the Supreme Court in 1957, *Watkins* v. *United States*,[11] shed much new light on this sort of problem.

John Watkins was a labor union official who had long been suspected of Communist leanings. In 1954 he was commanded to appear before a Congressional committee that had already received evidence about his alleged Communist connections. Watkins made a complete and candid statement about himself. He said that he had never been "a card-carrying member of the Communist Party," though he had "cooperated with the Communist Party and participated in Communist activities to such a degree that some persons may honestly believe that I was a member of the party." But he declined to say, in response to a question, whether certain other persons were known by him to be Communists; as to that, he declared: "I do not believe that any law in this country requires me to testify about persons who may in the past have been Communist Party members or otherwise engaged in Communist Party activities but who to my best knowledge and belief have long since removed themselves from the Communist movement. I do not believe that such questions are relevant to the work of this committee nor do I believe that this committee has the right to undertake the public exposure of persons because of their past activities. I may be wrong, and the committee may have this power, but until and unless a court of law so holds and directs me to answer, I most firmly refuse to discuss the political activities of my past associates." This refusal to answer led to Watkins' being prosecuted for contempt of Congress. He was convicted, and was sentenced to pay a fine of one hundred dollars and to be imprisoned for a year. He appealed this judgment, and thus the stage was set for a final review by the Supreme Court.

The Supreme Court reversed Watkins' conviction and ordered that the proceedings against him be terminated. The narrow ground of decision was, simply, that a witness can be compelled to answer only those questions that are really pertinent to a matter under proper investigation; and that the purpose of the inquiry must be stated with sufficient clarity so that a witness can intelligently judge whether he is being asked a relevant or an irrelevant question.[12]

The opinion by Chief Justice Warren, however, went much further than needed to dispose of this case. It contained some strong general statements that, while not a part of the Court's actual decision, did disclose the direction of some judges' thinking about legislative investigations. Thus, for example, the Chief Justice declared that "There is no general authority to expose the private affairs of individuals without justification in terms of the functions of the Congress. . . . Nor is the Congress a law enforcement or trial agency. These are functions of the executive and judicial departments of government. No inquiry is an end in itself; it must be related to and in furtherance of a legitimate task of the Congress. Investigations conducted solely for the personal aggrandizement of the investigators or to 'punish' those investigated are indefensible. . . . We have no doubt that there is no congressional power to expose for the sake of exposure. The public is, of course, entitled to be informed concerning the workings of his government. That cannot be inflated into a general power to expose where the predominant result can only be an invasion of the private rights of individuals." *

Elsewhere in his opinion, Chief Justice Warren reflected the sentiment, shared by many believers in civil liberties, that legislative investigations are capable of being misused to impose an undesirable degree of conformity upon the public at large. "Abuses of the investigative process," the Chief Justice said, "may imperceptibly lead to abridgement of protected freedoms. The mere summoning of a witness and compelling him to testify, against his will, about his beliefs, expressions or associations is a measure of governmental interference. And when those forced revelations concern matters that are unorthodox, unpopular, or even hateful to the general public, the reaction in the life of the witness may be disastrous. . . . Nor does the witness alone suffer the consequences. Those who are identified by witnesses and thereby placed in the same glare of publicity are equally subject to public stigma, scorn and obloquy. Beyond that, there is the more subtle and immeasurable effect upon those who tend to adhere to the most orthodox and uncontroversial views and associations in order to avoid a similar fate at some future time. That this impact is partly the result of non-governmental activity by private persons cannot relieve the investigators of their responsibility for initiating the reaction." †

* Woodrow Wilson, a professor of political science before he was president of the United States, once declared that "The informing function of Congress should be preferred even to its legislative function." This statement, appearing in his *Congressional Government* (1901) 303, has often been seized upon by Congressional "exposers" as a justification for their activities. Chief Justice Warren, in the opinion quoted above, points out, however, that Wilson was talking about Congressional power "to inquire into and publicize corruption, maladministration or efficiency *in agencies of Government*." See also James M. Landis, "Constitutional Limitations on the Congressional Power of Investigation," 40 *Harvard Law Rev.* 153, 168–194 (1926); Telford Taylor, *Grand Inquest* (1955), ch. VI; Alan Barth, *Government by Investigation* (1955), ch. III.

† In *Sweezy* v. *New Hampshire*, 354 U.S. 234 (1957), the Supreme Court held that an investigating agency in the State of New Hampshire had no power to force a lecturer to tell it what he had said in a lecture to some university students, because the inquiry into that matter had not clearly been authorized by the state legislature. In the course of his opinion in this case Chief Justice Warren spoke very feelingly about the dangers of governmental invasion of

These strong words adequately suggest the dangers of unbridled legislative inquiries and reflect a judicial willingness to support resistance to the most blatant abuses. Just two years later, however, the Chief Justice's ringing declarations lost some of their ring when the Supreme Court announced a five-to-four decision in *Barenblatt* v. *United States*.[13]

Barenblatt, a former college instructor, had been summoned before a subcommittee of the House Committee on Un-American Activities during the course of an inquiry concerning alleged Communist infiltration into the field of education. Another witness had told the committee that Barenblatt had been a member of a Communist group while he had been a graduate student. Now the committee asked Barenblatt five questions: Was he at this time a Communist? Had he ever been one? Did he know the earlier witness as a Communist? Had he been a member of a certain club during his student days? Had he been a member of another named student organization at that time? Barenblatt refused to answer these questions, but he expressly disclaimed any reliance on the Fifth Amendment protection against self-incrimination. Instead, he denied that the committee had power to inquire into his "political" and "religious" beliefs or any "other personal and private affairs" or "associational activities." His refusal led to his indictment for contempt of Congress. He was ultimately convicted, being sentenced to six months' imprisonment and a fine of $250. The Supreme Court upheld this judgment.

In doing so, the Court passed on three major issues raised by Barenblatt: the power of the House Committee on Un-American

---

"liberties in the areas of academic freedom and political expression." "Scholarship," he asserted, "cannot flourish in an atmosphere of suspicion and distrust. Teachers and students must always remain free to inquire, to study and to evaluate, to gain new maturity and understanding; otherwise civilization will stagnate and die. . . . All political ideas cannot and should not be channeled into the programs of our two major parties. History has amply proved the virtue of political activity by minority, dissident groups, who innumerable times have been in the vanguard of democratic thought and whose programs were ultimately accepted. Mere unorthodoxy or dissent from the prevailing mores is not to be condemned. The absence of such voices would be a symptom of grave illness in our society."

Activities, the unclarity of the relation between the questions asked and any proper subject matter of inquiry, and the impact on First Amendment freedoms (that is, freedom of speech and association) if inquiries such as these were to be allowed.

The Committee on Un-American Activities is authorized by its parent, the House of Representatives, to investigate "(1) the extent, character, and objects of un-American propaganda activities in the United States, (2) the diffusion within the United States of subversive and un-American propaganda that is instigated from foreign countries or of a domestic origin and attacks the principle of the form of government as guaranteed by our Constitution, and (3) all other questions in relation thereto that would aid Congress in any necessary remedial legislation." All the Justices regarded this as indeed a vague charter; but the majority felt, nevertheless, that the original grant of power should now be read in the light of the "persuasive gloss of legislative history" that had been added in the years since the Committee's creation. As is well known, the Committee has over the course of more than twenty years conducted one investigation after another into alleged Communist activities; well aware of this, each new Congress renewed the Committee's authority and gave it increased financial support. The majority of the Court concluded, therefore, that investigations like the one in which Barenblatt had become entangled were well within the Committee's intended scope, as it had come to be understood through contemporary political usage.

Justice Black, in dissent, was dissatisfied with this approach. Like the majority, he believed the authorizing resolution placed only very shadowy boundaries upon the Committee's powers; but, unlike the majority, he was unwilling to look elsewhere for light that might chase away the shadows. "Perhaps," he said sarcastically, "if Barenblatt had had time to read all the reports of the Committee to the House, and in addition had examined the appropriations made to the Committee he, like the Court, could have discerned an intent by Congress to allow an investigation of communism in education. . . . [W]e are dealing here with governmental procedures which the

Court itself admits reach to the very fringes of Congressional power. In such cases more is required of legislatures than a vague delegation to be filled in later by mute acquiescence. If Congress wants ideas investigated, if it even wants them investigated in the field of education, it must be prepared to say so expressly and unequivocally. And it is not enough that a court through exhaustive research can establish, even conclusively, that Congress wished to allow the investigation."

If the Committee did have the power to inquire into "Communist infiltration" among educators, then the issue of pertinency that had been decisive in the Watkins case, discussed above, was not very troublesome. Only a month earlier the Court had unanimously reaffirmed its view that a recalcitrant witness cannot be punished when he has not had opportunity to understand why questions have been put to him, because the information given him is "too wavering, confused and cloudy." [14] The Barenblatt decision marks no withdrawal from that position. In this instance, however, the Committee had informed the witness about the intended aim of its questioning; Barenblatt, unlike Watkins, well knew the Committee's purpose. At least some of the questions he refused to answer were plainly relevant to that purpose.

Having decided that the House of Representatives had empowered the Committee to ask the questions it did ask, the Court now was compelled to consider Barenblatt's final objection that the whole undertaking was beyond the pale of constitutionality. Justice Harlan emphasized, for the majority, that the Court's function in passing on that grave issue was "purely one of constitutional adjudication in the particular case and upon the particular record before us, not to pass judgment upon the general wisdom or efficacy of the activities of this committee in a vexing and complicated field."

The heart of the majority conclusion is not that Congressional investigations are wholly unrestrained by the First Amendment protections against invasions of free speech and association. It is, rather, that when First Amendment rights are claimed as a shield against governmental interrogation, "resolution of the issue always involves a balancing by the courts of the competing private and public interests at stake in the particular circumstances shown."

The "balancing" in this case, as the majority saw it, was between Barenblatt's desire as an individual to be free from inquiry into his political relationships and other personal affairs and, on the other hand, the nation's "right of self-preservation" as manifested by numerous enactments aimed at the Communist Party because of its ultimate revolutionary purpose. The Committee's investigation, the majority stressed, was not concerned with what Barenblatt or any-one else taught in the classroom, or with the field of education as an end in itself; this might have invalidated the Committee's program, for at least arguably these are matters beyond Congressional control through legislation, and perhaps for that reason beyond its in-vestigatory power. Here, said Justice Harlan, the Committee was investigating potential overthrow of the government; and "an in-vestigation of advocacy of or preparation for overthrow certainly embraces the right to identify a witness as a member of the Com-munist Party"—which, the opinion noted, has been found not to be "an ordinary political party" at all.

The dissenting opinion of Justice Black attacked this branch of the Court's opinion most vigorously. First, the Court's "balancing test" was rejected when ideas and not conduct were at stake. The First Amendment says that "Congress shall make no law . . . abridg-ing the freedom of speech . . . or the right of the people peaceably to assemble. . . ." Justice Black (and Chief Justice Warren and Justice Douglas, who joined in his opinion) felt that the other judges had now amended this to say "Congress shall pass no law abridging freedom of speech, press, assembly and petition unless Congress and the Supreme Court reach the joint conclusion that on balance the interests of the Government in stifling these freedoms is greater than the interest of the people in having them exercised." Even if that were the correct view of the Constitution, the dissent continued, the majority had applied its own test carelessly. The Court had weighed Barenblatt's right to refrain from revealing Communist affiliations against the Government's right to preserve itself. That, Justice Black contended, mistook the factors that should be weighed. First, he said, "it completely leaves out the real interest in Barenblatt's silence, the interest of the people as a whole in being able to join organizations, advocate causes and make political 'mistakes' without later being subjected to governmental penalties for having dared to think for themselves. It is this right, the right to err politically, which keeps us strong as a Nation. For no number of laws against communism can have as much effect as the personal conviction which comes from having heard its arguments and rejected them, or from having once accepted its tenets and later recognized their worthlessness. Instead, the obloquy which results from investigations such as this not only stifles 'mistakes' but prevents all but the most courageous from hazarding any views which might at some later time become disfavored. This result, whose importance cannot be overestimated, is doubly crucial when it affects the universities, on which we must largely rely for the experimentation and development of new ideas essential to our country's welfare. It is these interests of society, rather than Barenblatt's own right to silence, which I think the Court should put on the balance against the demands of the Government, if any balancing process is to be tolerated. Instead they are not mentioned, while on the other side the demands of the Government are vastly overstated and called 'self-preservation.' It is admitted that this Committee can only seek information for the purpose of suggesting laws, and that Congress' power to make laws in the realm of speech and association is quite limited, even on the Court's test. Its interest in making such laws in the field of education, primarily a state function, is clearly narrower still. Yet the Court styles this attenuated interest self-preservation and allows it to overcome the need our country has to let us all think, speak, and associate politically as we like and without fear of reprisal. . . .

"Moreover," he continued, "I cannot agree with the Court's notion that First Amendment freedoms must be abridged in order to 'preserve' our country. That notion rests on the unarticulated premise that this Nation's security hangs upon its power to punish people because of what they think, speak or write about, or because of those with whom they associate for political purposes. . . . I challenge this premise, and deny that ideas can be proscribed under our Constitution. I agree that despotic governments cannot exist without stifling the voice of opposition to their oppressive practices. The First Amendment means to me, however, that the only constitutional way our Government can preserve itself is to leave its people the fullest possible freedom to praise, criticize or discuss, as they see fit, all governmental policies and to suggest, if they desire, that even its most fundamental postulates are bad and should be changed. . . . On that premise this land was created, and on that premise it has grown to greatness. Our Constitution assumes that the common sense of the people and their attachment to our country will enable them, after free discussion, to withstand ideas that are wrong. To say that our patriotism must be protected against false ideas by means other than these is, I think, to make a baseless charge. Unless we can rely on these qualities—if, in short, we begin to punish speech—we cannot honestly proclaim ourselves to be a free Nation and we have lost what the Founders of this land risked their lives and their sacred honors to defend."

It may well be, as the majority implied, that the Communist Party has illegal as well as legal aims. But, said Justice Black, there are dangers in denying to members of any group the protections the Constitution affords uncompromisingly to all. Members of the Party who either singly or collectively commit violations of law should be prosecuted. But so long as their conduct is permissible, the Justice went on, Congress should be deemed to be wholly without power, either by statute or by inquisition, to delimit "the freedom of individuals to think what they please, advocate whatever policy they choose, and join with others to bring about the social, religious, political and governmental changes which seem best to them"—even though, to the rest of us, those changes may seem disastrous.

This opposition of ideas between the majority and the minority of the Court was a prelude to their final sharp clash. In the Watkins case, it may be recalled, Chief Justice Warren had declared flatly that "there is no congressional power to expose for the sake of exposure." Barenblatt now asserted that this was the whole reason for his having been called as a witness. Another witness, Crowley, had already admitted having once been a Communist, and he had identified Barenblatt as having been a fellow member. So, said Barenblatt, nothing was to be gained, in the way of new information, by asking him whether he knew Crowley or whether he had been a Communist; whatever his answers might be, they could contribute nothing to a valid legislative purpose. Not so, said the majority. The investigation was valid in its inception because it purported to be primarily into matters that might bear upon legislative proposals. "So long as Congress acts in pursuance of its constitutional power," Justice Harlan wrote, "the judiciary lacks authority to intervene on the basis of the motives which spurred the exercise of that power." Here, the record did not firmly establish that the Committee was seeking to pillory witnesses or that it had summoned Barenblatt or other witnesses indiscriminately and without belief that pertinent information might be forthcoming.

At this point Justice Brennan, who had not thought it necessary to pass upon the other issues that had been debated in the opinions, joined the other three dissenters in concluding that the investigation had had no purpose except "exposure purely for the sake of exposure," and that this was a purpose to which a witness' First Amendment rights cannot validly be subordinated. Justice Black, in this branch of his opinion, expressed no doubt about the patriotism and sincerity of the Un-American Activities Committee's members. But he concluded that the Committee's own utterances showed that its "chief aim, purpose and practice . . . is to try witnesses and punish them because they are or have been Communists or because they refuse to admit or deny Communist affiliations." Punishment by humiliation, he observed, is no novelty; branding, the pillory, and ostracism are well known examples. The House Committee has declared its dedication to a program of "pitiless publicity and exposure." Indeed, the very investigation that had in the end led to Barenblatt's conviction had, in the Committee's own words, been initiated "in order to demonstrate to the people of Michigan the fields of concentration of the Communist Party in the Michigan area, and the identity of those individuals responsible for its success." [15] That, Justice Black believed, showed a clear intent to bring about exposure as an end in itself or as a type of punishment for past wickedness; the investigation was launched not to obtain material for Congressional consideration but to "name names" in Michigan. Punishment by the Government, the four dissenting Justices asserted, could be imposed only after trial by duly constituted courts. The Committee's activities in this instance should have been evaluated, the minority thought, in the light of its own claims and reports; these showed that the Committee's purposes were not legislative, but were in fact an encroachment on the judicial function.

This lengthy description of the Barenblatt case perhaps points up the grave difficulties that lie before the courts when confronted by challenges to legislative power. Overturning the work of a co-ordinate branch of government is no lightly undertaken task in any circumstances. It becomes even more onerous when cloudily perceived motives are assigned as reasons for invalidating an outwardly legitimate exercise of legislative authority. No matter how offensive may be the motives of individual legislators, legislative investigation has great values. Too hasty interference by the courts might well impair the capacity of the legislatures to make wise choices in discharging their great responsibilities.

The future of this subject is far from plain. One thing does stand out very sharply, despite the divisions of opinion within the Supreme Court. Every one of the present Justices does seemingly assume responsibility to review closely cases in which witnesses and Congressional investigators have become ensnarled. This is noteworthy because for some years the Court appeared disinclined to examine those cases at all. The Barenblatt case, moreover, has reaffirmed rather than destroyed the view that exposure and punishment are not permissible objectives of legislative inquiries. True, Justice Harlan and his fellow judges of the majority did not find in the record of that particular case the indications that scored so heavily with the minority; the majority was unwilling to impute improper motives that would exclude a proper legislative purpose, but neither the majority nor the minority said that purposes were irrelevant.[16] Finally, nothing in the Barenblatt case diminishes in any way restraints on legislative investigators that have previously been established, such as their obligation to recognize a witness' right to avoid self-incrimination, their duty to remain within the scope of whatever authority may have been conferred by the parent legislative body, and their need to enlighten a witness' judgment concerning the pertinency of the questions to which answers have been demanded.

Potentially, legislative investigation is a strong resource of democracy. Like other valuable resources, however, it can be depleted and dissipated by reckless use. The task here, as elsewhere in public law, is to be vigilant against procedural deficiencies and unworthy motivations, while preserving the power of democratic government to be effective government.

Chapter 7

THE FREEDOM OF MOVEMENT

The United Nations' "Universal Declaration of Human Rights" was promulgated not as a code of laws but as "a common standard of achievement for all peoples and all nations." Article 13 of the Declaration reads as follows:

Paragraph 1. Everyone has the right to freedom of movement and residence within the borders of each state.
Paragraph 2. Everyone has the right to leave any country, including his own, and to return to his country.

The present discussion will consider the extent to which this standard has been attained in the United States, first with reference to movement inside the country and, second, with reference to entrance into and exit from it.

MOVEMENT WITHIN THE UNITED STATES

From the Atlantic on the east to the Pacific on the west, the United States stretches for nearly 3000 miles; from Canada on the north to Mexico on the south, it stretches for 1500 miles. Its total area is more than 3,000,000 square miles, less than half the size of the Soviet Union but still slightly larger than, say, Australia or than Germany, France, Italy, Spain, Greece, Egypt, India, Burma, Thailand, Korea, the Philippines, and Japan combined. That is indeed an extensive area within which one may move without any hindrance whatsoever. Yet this is the actual fact. Without the slightest formality and certainly without the necessity of obtaining anyone's permission, any American may move where he wishes.

This is especially remarkable when one considers the origins of the country. At the time that the British colonies were being established in North America, movement in England was so limited by law and practice that most persons were to all intents and purposes confined within the locality of their birth. It was as though the barriers of modern national frontiers had been erected around the boundaries of each tiny parish throughout the land. Regardless of reasons, regardless of opportunities that a man might have to improve his life if only he could live it elsewhere, most Englishmen of those days had to stay at home.[1] The colonials, naturally enough, tended to react against these constrictions as soon as they had a chance. There was more room in North America than in England— and far fewer people; so nobody worried very much about movement from one place to another.

Nevertheless, even after the revolution of 1776 had severed the ties between the colonies and the British king, there were thirteen quite separate and sovereign states on American soil. Very soon they agreed among themselves to be *united*—to be the United States. Had it not been for that step in the very beginning, the North American continent might today be criss-crossed with the same sort of boundary lines that prevent easy travel from one nation into another.

Nowadays everyone takes it for granted that one can roam at will throughout the whole country. Oddly enough, however, this is one of those freedoms not mentioned in the American Constitution, and nobody is absolutely sure where this ease of movement came from. Nonetheless, on the very few occasions that any state has tried to limit freedom of movement, the attempts have always been declared invalid. About a hundred years ago one of the states put a tax of one dollar on people who wanted to leave the state. The Supreme Court was sure that this was unconstitutional, but the judges were very unclear in explaining their reasoning.[2] A more recent restraint on movement came to light during the great economic depression that beset America during the 1930's. California was the goal of many poverty-stricken people who hoped that they would find either work or a pleasanter climate or a higher standard of relief and welfare services than they had experienced at home. California decided to close its doors to these nonresidents who became burdens on local taxpayers after they arrived. But the Supreme Court held that this could not be done. No state, Justice Byrnes said, could "isolate itself from difficulties common to all of them by the simple expedient of shutting its gates to the outside world." [3] All the Justices of the Supreme Court agreed, but for different reasons; some thought that California was seeking to regulate interstate commerce (a subject solely within the control of the Congress, rather than of the individual states); others thought that a right of national citizenship was being impaired, and they found various grounds for saying that this was forbidden. Frankly, without being technical about the matter, I am satisfied that the right to roam is thoroughly imbedded in the American tradition, and that no interference with that right will ever be tolerated—except, of course, as to persons whose freedom is lawfully restrained, such as persons awaiting trial on criminal charges. In 1900 the Supreme Court said: "Undoubtedly the right of locomotion, the right to remove from one place to another according to inclination, is an attribute of personal liberty." [4] Those words were not necessary to the decision—they were what lawyers call *dicta*, just a sort of passing remark rather than a real judgment—but they do express a mood that is not likely to change.[5]

Freedom of movement within the United States is equally possessed by aliens who are resident in this country. The individual states cannot prohibit their residence or their access to employment.[6] Since 1940, aliens do have to register annually with a federal agency; they do so through any local post office. This does not limit their movement in any respect.

Having now spoken contentedly about the individual's freedom of movement, I must in all candor turn to a most painful episode in American history when Americans of Japanese descent as well as Japanese nationals were entirely deprived of their freedom of movement within the territory of the United States. I refer of course to the wartime "relocation," as it was euphemistically called, of over one hundred thousand men, women, and children, some seventy thousand of whom were American citizens, while inquiry was made into their "loyalty."

This drastic action has never had the approval of all Americans. While war was still in progress, the present dean of the Yale Law School (to mention only one example from many) wrote in a leading periodical: "All in all, the internment of the West Coast Japanese is the worst blow our liberties have sustained in many years." [7] There was an outcry of indignation at the time, and it has continued to this very day. A few words about this sad affair may serve to put it into perspective.

When the United States entered World War II in 1941, there were no immediate mass arrests or evacuations of enemy aliens. Less than three thousand enemy aliens were taken into custody in the early weeks of the war, and they—along with all others who were later detained—were given prompt hearings before boards composed of very high-minded and qualified persons who served on a voluntary basis. A great many were either released outright or were paroled. By June 30, 1944, the number in custody was very little more than six thousand—not a staggeringly large number when it is recalled that there were 1,100,000 enemy aliens in the United States at the outbreak of war. In Hawaii, where almost a third of the population is of Japanese descent, fewer than eight hundred Japanese nationals were detained despite the strong emotions that had been aroused by the Pearl Harbor bombing.

But the moderation and reasonably good sense that had been generally apparent seemed to disappear on the Pacific Coast. There only about one per cent of the population consisted of persons of Japanese descent. Some episodes of signaling to ships at sea had occurred in the early days of the war, and there was some perhaps genuine nervousness about what might happen if Japan were to invade America. But in the months following Pearl Harbor there were no known instances of espionage or sabotage by Japanese-American residents in the West Coast states. Nevertheless the military commander in that area became convinced that a real menace existed, and that there was no time to deal with it on a very selective basis. He may not have been one of the wisest men who ever lived. He sought to justify his moves, for example, by such nonsense as this: "The very fact that no sabotage has taken place to date is a disturbing and confirming indication that such action will be taken." At any rate, with the hearty endorsement of many illiberal elements in the community, he determined that military necessity demanded burdensome restraints upon persons of Japanese background, and then their removal to centers where the demonstrably pure could be separated from the potentially dangerous. Once this not very prudent general had acted, his superiors felt that they had to give him their support as a matter of military morale, if for no other reason. And so, for the first time, Americans penned up a large number of their fellow citizens on the basis of vague and general suspicions, without evidence of individual wrongdoing.

Possibly the West Coast Japanese were singled out for this treatment not because they were genuine perils, but because there was no other ready outlet for the angry tensions of those times. Too many Japanese lived in Hawaii to make them an easy target, and the Italians and the Germans and their descendants in the United States were not only very numerous but were also well intrenched politically. The West Coast Japanese were neither too numerous nor too powerful to be handled. They thus became easy targets of the hatreds and frustrations that war arouses.

When the validity of the military detention decrees came before the Supreme Court, as they ultimately did, the main features of the relocation program were upheld as lawful exercises of military judgment concerning imminent threats to safety.[8] The nine black-robed judges, sitting snugly in their quiet courtroom three thousand miles from the Pacific Coast, were obviously reluctant to override the decision of the man on the spot who bore responsibility for carrying on the war. But the Court's reluctance, no matter how understandable it may have been, was unfortunate. The decisions in those cases, quite apart from their support of an unpalatable invasion of human dignity, seem on the surface at least to strengthen military power in its relation to civil authority, which in the United States has always been paramount both in theory and in fact; we have never yet suffered from the military men's being in a position to dictate our policies. As Justice Jackson said in his dissenting opinion, the principle the Supreme Court applied when it gave its approval to the restrictions on the West Coast Japanese "lies about like a loaded weapon, ready for the hand of any authority that can bring forward a plausible claim of an urgent need." [9]

The episode just described was of course but one among the many horrors brought about by war. We can only pray that something has been learned from those dreadful experiences. In the United States I hope and believe we have learned that mass restraints on freedom of movement and residence are unjust, inefficient, and only artificially related to true national needs.

ENTRANCE INTO THE UNITED STATES

The first European immigrants to the Western Hemisphere were Spanish. Spain required that everyone who crossed the ocean must be licensed. Licenses were extremely difficult to obtain, being issued only to persons of the most rigid political and religious orthodoxy. Persons who traveled without a license were subject to very severe penalties. In the seventeenth century, an unlicensed migrant was sentenced to be a galley slave for eight years; and if he survived that hard life of rowing and misery, he was banished to an African penal colony for an additional ten years. In 1607 Spain decreed the death penalty for a sea captain who carried an unlicensed passenger to the New World.[10] One sometimes hears that it is difficult to get into the United States today. Things have at least improved a little since those early times.

The British, in contrast to the Spanish, were extremely liberal in admitting newcomers into their North American colonies—unlike the French, who tended as did the Spaniards to discourage people from settling in the Western Hemisphere. The young United States started off with the British rather than the French or Spanish attitude toward immigration.

Not until 1875 did the United States begin to enact laws to keep people out of the country—and then only to exclude prostitutes and criminals. Between 1820 and 1900 more than twenty million immigrants had entered the United States; between 1900 and 1910, nearly nine million more came; and up until America's entry into the First World War, in 1917, additional immigrants were entering at the rate of a million a year.

Even so, by comparison with other countries the United States is not physically overcrowded despite its population of about 170 million. In 1955, there were 55 persons per square mile in the United States—as compared with, roughly, 540 in Britain, 645 in Japan, and 750 in Belgium. Nevertheless, Americans were beginning to feel crowded and much less hospitable than they had been when the country consisted of wide, open spaces waiting to be filled. Under present immigration laws, only a few more than 150,000 aliens are theoretically eligible to be admitted each year to become permanent residents, in addition to a considerable number of others who are admissible under special provisions. During 1956, for example, 350,000 immigrants were received in the United States. This number, the largest since 1925, included political refugees from Hungary and elsewhere, families of American citizens, and other "exempt" groups. But only 90,000 regular immigrants entered during the year, as against the 150,000 who were theoretically allowed. The trouble with the present laws, patterned on a statute enacted in 1921, is that they provide for admission on a "quota" basis—that is, a fixed percentage of the number of persons of the same national origin who were resident in the United States in 1910. At that time a very large number of settlers in America had come from England, Germany, Ireland, and the Scandinavian countries. Nowadays there are not so many would-be immigrants from those countries;

the British quota, for example, has not been filled for years. On the other hand, people who wish to move permanently to the United States from eastern or southern Europe—for example, from Greece or Hungary—have to wait for a long time because the quotas for their countries are not so large and there are lengthy waiting lists. The same is true as to countries of the Far East, to which very small quotas have been assigned.[11]

Many disagree with this "national-origins quota system," but Congress does undoubtedly have the constitutional power to control immigration as it sees fit. The admission or exclusion of aliens, the Supreme Court has held, is a sovereign act within the unlimited discretion of Congress.[12] It could, if it wished, prohibit immigration altogether. If, instead, it chooses to allow only a limited immigration, it may place the limits at whatever point it wishes. Since foreigners cannot vote in American elections, some of the Congressmen—especially those who come from states to which there has been little movement of families with overseas connections—are not very much interested in liberalizing the present exclusionary system. Some experts say that by 1970 the United States will have a population of 200 million. To many people that seems quite enough, without encouraging any further immigration. At any rate, we have to recognize that the freedom to come to the United States with the thought of remaining there, simply no longer exists. The door used to be open, but nowadays one needs a special key to unlock it.

The considerations that bear on the admission of temporary visitors into a country are very different from those having to do with permanent residence. In my opinion every country ought to welcome visitors from any other, to wander from place to place gaining new impressions and new ideas—and, occasionally, even leaving a few ideas behind them. An American can travel through most of Europe and, indeed, much of the rest of the world, without the necessity of obtaining any visa or advance permission.

Present American policy is much more restrictive. Partly as a response to the international tensions that have been felt in the United States, with all the concern they have aroused about spies and the like, our laws require people who want to visit the United States even for only brief periods to meet all sorts of tests, almost as though they wanted to stay forever. Checking up very closely on those who plan to join the community permanently may be justifiable; going to the same lengths with temporary visitors seems much less wise.

Preoccupation with the supposed interests of national security has delayed or altogether prevented trips to the United States by persons who are prominent in the social, business, or academic circles of their own lands. This has of course been costly in good will. Various international gatherings that might have much enriched American intellectual life have simply been moved to other countries to avoid the embarrassments of denied or unduly delayed visas. Even professors—and everybody knows that nobody pays any attention to them—sometimes have difficulty in obtaining the visas that would allow them to travel to America.

This somewhat silly business serves to emphasize that courts cannot be relied on to deal with every unjust or unwise exertion of governmental power. Some matters are outside effective judicial control, and the regulation of foreign relations—of which international travel has traditionally been deemed a part—is one of those matters. The citizenry, rather than the judiciary, must take responsibility for discouraging any legislative excesses in those fields.

Another aspect of this topic that deserves special consideration is of a procedural rather than substantive nature. The American courts have taken the position, very broadly stated, that since Congress can decide whom it wants to admit, it can attach to their admission whatever conditions it chooses. Thus, for example, Congress may say that no person who may be deemed a security risk shall be admitted into the United States, and may then provide that the determination is to be made by procedures that would be regarded as unfair if they were to be applied to anybody other than applicants for admission into the country. Persons who want to enter have no rights except those that Congress grants them; nothing is owed to them otherwise.

The hardships of this position may be illustrated by two cases.[13]

Mrs. Ellen Knauff, the German-born wife of an American citizen, was barred from entering the United States because the Attorney General (the head of the Department of Justice, which administers the immigration laws) said her admission would be prejudicial to the country's interests. But he declined to reveal the basis of this finding, nor was he willing that Mrs. Knauff should have a hearing; the Attorney General had acted on "information of a confidential nature" which he desired not to expose. The Supreme Court held, by a one-vote margin, that neither the Constitution nor the existing statutes entitled Mrs. Knauff to have a full hearing; Congress had authorized the Attorney General to act as he did, and the alien applicant had to be content with what was given. Justice Jackson, strongly dissenting from the majority opinion, wrote: "Security is like liberty in that many are the crimes committed in its name. The menace to the security of this country, be it great as it may, from this girl's admission is as nothing compared to the menace to free institutions inherent in procedures of this pattern. In the name of security the police state justifies its arbitrary oppressions on evidence that is secret, because security might be prejudiced if it were brought to light in hearings. The plea that evidence of guilt must be secret is abhorrent to free men, because it provides a cloak for the malevolent, the misinformed, the meddlesome and the corrupt to play the role of informer undetected and uncorrected."

The case created a burst of indignation that was reflected in some Congressional criticism of the procedure Congress had itself permitted. About a year later the Attorney General decided that a hearing could be had. His confidential information could then be disclosed, he thought, without disaster. When the information was exposed to the light of day, it shrank to insignificance. Ultimately it was found that Mrs. Knauff was not a danger after all, and she was then allowed to come into the United States.

The second case involved a cabinetmaker named Ignatz Mezei, who had been born in Hungary but had lived in the United States for many years. He returned to Europe to see his sick mother, who then resided in Roumania, but he never managed to see her because the Roumanians would not give him a visa—perhaps because they feared he might be an American spy. When he came back to the United States, he was denied entry and, like Mrs. Knauff, was given no hearing or information as to the cause of his difficulties. He then applied to twenty-five other countries for admission, but was always rejected; the Communist countries did not want him and the rest were afraid of him, supposing that whatever it was in Mezei that menaced the United States would be equally bad for them. Consequently, Mezei seemed destined to spend the rest of his life in detention at the gates to America, because he was not allowed to pass through the gates and he was unable to go anywhere else.

Once again, by a majority of one vote, the Supreme Court held that the would-be entrant had no rights. Once again Justice Jackson protested. "This man, who seems to have led a life of unrelieved insignificance, must have been astonished to find himself suddenly putting the Government of the United States in such fear that it was afraid to tell him why it was afraid of him. . . . Let it not be overlooked that due process of law is not for the sole benefit of an accused. It is the best insurance for the Government itself against those blunders which leave lasting stains on a system of justice. . . ."

Mezei's case like Mrs. Knauff's had a reasonably happy ending. After three years of detention, he was finally accorded a full hearing before a special board composed of distinguished New York attorneys. They found, upon the basis of evidence that seems to have been available without uncovering any "undercover sources," that Mezei was in fact excludible as a sometime Communist. But they then volunteered the unanimous recommendation that he be allowed to remain at liberty in the United States on parole, as a harmless though perhaps not very praiseworthy character. For the past four or five years Mezei has been living in America without, so far as is known, any unfortunate consequences. His freedom, however, is a matter of administrative grace. As far as the law is concerned, he could have been kept out of the country without ever being told why—and, in his case, being kept out of the country might well have meant being kept in detention for the rest of his life.

Procedural crudities like these are unlikely to be tolerated for long. Congress, it may at once be agreed, has the power to limit freedom of movement into the United States; as one author has said, "the right of entry is a liberty only of American citizens." [14] But in deciding whether or not the applicant has met the conditions laid down by Congress, administrative officials should use methods that lessen the risks of mistake or prejudice. The observance of procedural safeguards has been the foundation stone of barriers against arbitrary, absolutist government. Whether or not aliens who wish to enter the United States have an enforcible right to fair procedures, Americans have a duty not to abandon their own traditional quest for liberty through justice toward all.

FREEDOM TO LEAVE

The Constitution is silent concerning the right of American citizens to depart from this country. In 1868, however, Congress enacted a law (never since repealed) that expatriation is a natural and inherent right that anyone may exercise whenever he wishes. Any contrary policy would be paradoxical in a nation populated by descendants of people who had chosen to leave their own native lands in order to become residents and citizens of America.

To exercise the right of expatriation, a citizen obviously has to get out of his country. In recent years this has not been an automatically easy thing to do. Until the First World War, anyone who wanted to leave the United States for any reason at all was free to do so, unless he was under criminal charges. At present, it is a crime for an American citizen to leave the United States without a valid passport during times of war or national emergency proclaimed by the President.[15] President Truman declared that an emergency did require restrictions on freedom of movement, and President Eisenhower renewed the declaration, which remains in force today. The United States and the other countries in North and South America, however, maintain an easygoing neighborliness in this respect. Travel from this country to the countries of the Western Hemisphere continues to be permissible with much less formality than attaches to other journeying.

The United States is by no means peculiar in insisting that its nationals obtain a passport before leaving the country. Most other nations have the same requirement, and almost all of them require an alien to have a passport in order to be admitted. This constitutes a real shift in emphasis from earlier days. Passports used to be defined merely as a government's "request, that the bearer of it may pass safely and freely." [16] Now, it is more accurate to say that they resemble a license to leave the country, an exit permit rather than a letter of introduction.

Not many people want to leave the United States with the intention of permanently severing themselves from it. But a very large number do want to leave it in order to travel abroad for business or pleasure or education or family visits or some other personal purpose. During the fiscal year 1959, the State Department received 702,021 applications for issuance or renewal of passports. Americans are mobile and curious, and they enjoy seeing the world.

Almost all of the requested passports were issued. Some were held up because of difficulty in establishing the applicant's citizenship; * a few others were denied because the applicants were mentally ill, were fugitives from justice, or were for some similar reason not eligible to leave the country. Until mid-1958 the Department also had the practice of denying or substantially delaying passport issuance in some instances on the ground that the applicant's "travel abroad at this time would be contrary to the best interests of the

---

* Will Rogers, the much beloved American humorist of the preceding generation, once had difficulty in obtaining a passport because he could not readily prove where he had been born. "You see," he said, "in the early days of the Indian territory where I was born there was no such things as birth certificates. You being there was certificate enough. We generally took it for granted if you were there you must have at some time been born. . . . So if you foreigners think it is hard to get in here, you ain't seen nothing. You ought to be an American and try to get out once."

United States." This last ground stimulated much discussion and concern, and finally gave rise to important litigation.

In the United States a passport has at times been regarded as having to do with "foreign affairs." An authoritative digest of international law by a former legal adviser to the State Department declares that a passport is more than a document of identity. It also "indicates that it is the right of the bearer to receive the protection and good offices of American diplomatic and consular officers abroad and requests on the part of the Government of the United States that the officials of foreign governments permit the bearer to travel or sojourn in their territories and in case of need to give him all lawful aid and protection." [17] That seems to suggest that the American Government somehow stands behind every passport holder; it gives him a positive letter of recommendation. By contrast, in most European countries passports are said to be obtained, like automobile licenses, from local police authorities, who check the applicant's criminal record and collect a fee and never give a thought to international relations.[18] The legal philosopher Hans Kelsen, when he was an Austrian judge in 1925, held that "the constitutionally guaranteed freedom of movement included the freedom not only to emigrate, but also to leave the country for short periods of time." [19] This view seems to have generally prevailed among western nations; they issue passports and let the countries of destination decide for themselves whether the passport holders are worthy of being admitted.

The American State Department, taking a contrary stand, some years ago began to assert a discretionary power to grant or refuse a passport, and, in doing so, to evaluate the worthiness of the applicant. The Cold War with the Communist bloc provided a chief justification of the Department's summary withholding of passports. If, as supposed, travel by representatives of the world communist conspiracy were an important and even perhaps essential means of communication and planning, passport controls could be viewed as useful preventives of undesired personal contacts.[20] But, as so often happens, a measure debatably justified by one set of circumstances soon found itself being used in quite different circumstances. The

State Department refused to issue passports to a wide range of unorthodox people who could be linked with Communist plotting only by an extreme stretch of the imagination. And it insisted that no reasons had to be given, no facts had to be proved; it was enough for the Department to say that travel abroad would not be in "the best interests of the United States."

Naturally enough, this extremely blunt action did not long remain unchallenged. The older idea of a passport as an amiable message from one sovereign to another had led to its being regarded as a privilege; after all, if someone chooses not to befriend you, you may be disappointed and may even be hurt, but you do not begin an action in the courts to compel friendship to be given you. In those days, however, the withholding of a passport did not actually prevent travel; the United States did not block a man's leaving, and many countries were willing to receive a visitor without a passport. But now the absence of a passport means a definite loss of the freedom to move beyond national boundaries. Could the State Department impair that freedom without any restraint upon its decisions? In police states, to be sure, residents are accustomed to doing only what they are expressly permitted to do; in a constitutional system, by contrast, citizens have a wider latitude of action in the absence of an express and lawful prohibition. Where did the State Department find its authority to prevent the foreign travel of citizens who had done no wrong, and as to whom no affirmative showing of probable future wrongdoing had been made?

A number of lower court decisions have firmly declared that the State Department must not withhold a passport without first affording opportunity for a full hearing at which there must be disclosure of the reasons for denial, substantial evidence in support of the Department's action, and a chance for rebuttal by the applicant. In 1955 the Court of Appeals for the District of Columbia held in an important case that passport issuance is not exclusively a political or foreign affairs matter within the Secretary of State's exclusive discretion, but is, instead, subject to judicial review because it touches on an individual's basic constitutional rights.[21] Travel abroad, the court said, is just as much a right as is travel within the country, and it cannot be taken away without due process of law.

Finally, in 1958, the Supreme Court was called upon to consider this issue when passports were denied to a well known artist, a psychiatrist, and a nuclear physicist who desired to go abroad.[22] In the first two cases, the applicants had refused to submit affidavits (as required by the State Department's regulations) concerning past or present Communist Party membership; they insisted that all inquiry into questions other than citizenship was irrelevant to the matter under consideration. The physicist, by contrast, readily provided the desired information. He swore that he had never been a Communist, that he had no connections with spies or other improper persons, and that he wished simply to go to India to accept appointment to the staff of a research institute in that country. The State Department nevertheless refused to grant him a passport, basing its refusal on confidential information (from unrevealed sources) that the applicant had had close association with Communist agents. His travel abroad, the Department concluded, would not be in the best interests of the United States.

In the argument of these cases before the Supreme Court the Government startlingly conceded that the right to travel is indeed a part of the "liberty" which cannot be taken away except by due process of law. The majority of the Supreme Court obviously agreed. The Court's opinion, by Justice Douglas, says that "Freedom of movement across frontiers in either direction, and inside frontiers as well, was a part of our heritage. Travel abroad, like travel within the country, may be necessary for a livelihood. It may be as close to the heart of the individual as the choice of what he eats, or wears, or reads." And elsewhere the Court speaks directly of "the citizens' right of free movement" as being a "constitutional right."

Even after these strong expressions, however, the Court decided this trio of cases solely on the basis of statutory interpretation, rather than on the basis of the Constitution itself. The Government had argued, in effect, that the constitutional right of free movement was subject to reasonable limitation in the national interest; and it argued, further, that the Secretary of State's actions in the present instances were reasonable. The Court answered that it did not have to decide the extent to which a passport applicant's "liberty" can be curtailed. "We are first concerned with the extent, if any, to which Congress has authorized its curtailment." After reviewing the statutes from which the Secretary of State derived his power over passport issuance, the Court concluded that he had no "authority to withhold passports to citizens because of their beliefs or associations." Under present laws, the Court said, an exit permit (in the form of a passport) can be denied only if the applicant is not a citizen or if he is engaged in criminal or unlawful conduct.

Future developments can not be foretold. Following the Supreme Court's five-to-four decision that Congress had not as yet given the Secretary of State the powers he had long been exercising, President Eisenhower strongly urged the passage of new legislation. Each day during which the Secretary's discretion was limited was, the President declared, a day of peril for the United States. Congress at first seemed in a mood to respond to the President's advice that it should expressly direct the Secretary to continue pretty much as before. In the autumn of 1959, the feared "peril" not yet having materialized, the House of Representatives adopted a much milder proposal than the President had urged. The Senate took no action during the remainder of that year, though new legislation of some sort seemed likely in the near future. No doubt the constitutional issue that was avoided in 1958 will have to be faced by the Supreme Court at some later date.

Meanwhile, in any event, uncertainty will remain concerning another aspect of the freedom to travel. Quite without reference to the identity of the individual passport-seeker, the State Department regularly restricts the geographical validity of American passports. When they are issued, they bear a stamp saying that they are not valid for travel to countries in which the United States has no diplomatic representation—which now include Communist China, the northern portion of Korea, and a few other Communist-controlled territories. The Government takes the position that it will not facilitate overseas travel to places where it is unable to afford any protection to the traveler. Moreover, discouragement of travel to Communist countries has economic and political consequences that are considered important by those who shape foreign relations policies. The geographical limitation upon passport use has come under increasingly heavy attack, especially by journalists who complain that they have been prevented from making direct observations in China and other places of interest to the American public. During 1957 the State Department began to retreat from its formerly unqualified refusal to allow Americans to travel where they wish, if need be without their own government's assurances of protection. A few news reporters and others have received permission to enter previously forbidden zones; and the belief is widely held that a more flexible policy will soon become applicable to all travelers in relatively peaceful times.

Chapter 8

DESEGREGATING THE SCHOOLS

If your mind is flexible enough to embrace a fantasy, suppose for just a moment that somewhere in the United States a law were passed requiring all children of Irish descent to attend schools apart from the rest of their age group. This wild idea might not have seemed so wild a hundred years ago. Immigrants from Ireland in the pre-Civil War period were, in the North, "often regarded as less desirable than the freed Negro; in the South, they were considered more expendable than the slave and were thus assigned to the more dangerous work. . . . They were warned off from many of the better jobs by the notice, 'No Irish need apply.' Mine and mill workers found themselves relegated, on the basis of their religion and national origin, to the lowest class of jobs." [1] If some vestigial remnant of the hostility of those discreditable days were now to produce an attempted differentiation between Irish-American children and all others, the cry of unconstitutionality would be heard throughout the land. Quite properly so, too. The multitude needs no lawyer to tell it that equal treatment is a chief mandate of the Constitution. A lawyer might refine popular understanding by reciting the words of the Fourteenth Amendment: "No State shall . . . deny to any person within its jurisdiction the equal protection of the laws." He might explain that constitutional insistence upon equality "is not a pedagogical requirement of the impracticable," but is merely a command that whatever distinctions may be made in law shall rest upon a justifiable ground. [2] He might point out that a legislature may make classifications, so long as they reflect real differences related to a permissible objective, and so long as everyone within the class is treated alike. But not very many people could be persuaded that a legislature could reasonably classify children in two groups for purposes of public schooling, Irish-American in one group and the rest of the kids in the other.

In a nutshell, that is the whole issue in the great school desegregation controversy that was brought to a head (though certainly not begun) by the Supreme Court's famous decision in 1954 in *Brown* v. *Board of Education*.[3] One group of children had been, by law, set apart from the others. The separated group was Negro, of course, and not Irish-American. The furore over *Brown* v. *Board of Education* suggests that that constitutes a genuine difference. Is it in fact as great a difference as the furore suggests?

Apart from rather technical points having to do more with the Court's manner of expression than with its conclusion, two rational as distinct from emotional or "instinctive" grounds for opposing the Supreme Court's decision may be said to exist. They can be summarized under two main headings. First, without reaching the merits of the decision, some people believe that the Supreme Court ignored settled constitutional principles in order to rewrite the Constitution according to the taste of the present Justices. Second, some people honestly suppose that treating Negro children differently from others is justifiable because the children represent, as it were, two distinct species.

THE COURSE OF PAST DECISIONS

Differentiation on the ground of color or ethnic origin is no novelty in American law. In 1954, at the time of the Supreme Court's decision, segregated schools were publicly maintained in seventeen states and the District of Columbia. They had existed as recently as a century earlier in as enlightened a commonwealth as Massachusetts. In some of the states, notably California, efforts had long been made, though with only varying success, to prevent persons of oriental descent from enjoying opportunities accorded to others as a matter of course.[4] So there is a genuine foundation for contending that differentiation of this sort had become rooted in America and had therefore impliedly gained constitutional acceptance.

In actual fact, the acceptance was far from being complete. In 1896 the Supreme Court had for the first time upheld a state law that commanded the provision of special accommodations for Negroes. The famous case of *Plessy* v. *Ferguson* [5] decided in that year did not, however, involve education. It involved a requirement that white and colored railway passengers be transported in separate cars. The Court refused to declare the law unconstitutional, saying that keeping groups apart was not objectionable so long as the facilities provided for each group were of the same quality.

The "separate but equal" doctrine thus announced did undoubtedly encourage the view, widely acted upon in later years, that virtually all racial differentiations would be regarded as constitutionally permissible. Fifty-eight years after *Plessy* v. *Ferguson* the great advocate John W. Davis, arguing before the Supreme Court in behalf of segregation in the schools, urged that "somewhere, sometime, to every principle comes a moment of repose when the decision has been so often announced, so confidently relied upon, so long continued, that it passes the limits of judicial discretion and disturbance." [6] But, strikingly, the Supreme Court in all the years after *Plessy* v. *Ferguson* had never once squarely held that the "separate but equal" doctrine announced in a railroad case was decisive of cases in the field of education.

What had happened, in essence, was that the applicability of the doctrine had at first simply been assumed by litigants (so that further consideration of the issue by the Court had not been required); [7] and in cases arising in later years, when the doctrine began to be questioned by litigants, the Court had found that the educational facilities for Negroes were unequal in fact, thus obviating the necessity of deciding whether segregation could have been maintained if qualitative uniformity had really existed.[8] *Brown* v.

Board of Education brought before the Court for the very first time in a clear and unmistakable form the question of whether isolation in education on racial grounds was in itself objectionable, because in that case (and the four companion cases decided with it) the Negro complainants acknowledged that the facilities for their children were, in tangible respects, equal with those provided for white children. Their complaint was that separate educational facilities were inherently unequal, no matter how good they might be in physical terms, because they constituted an unwarranted seclusion of a minority group. The Supreme Court could and did sustain this contention without overruling a single precedent.

Nevertheless, it would be uncandid to pretend that the Supreme Court in 1954 did nothing novel. It did reject the presuppositions underlying its 1896 decision in *Plessy* v. *Ferguson,* and it did repudiate the views that had for many years in many quarters been regarded as logical extensions of that decision. By some this has been denounced as a gross departure from judicial propriety and as a usurpation of constitutional authority.[9]

Reliance on precedents is normally a sound judicial course. It makes for consistency and predictability of results. Businessmen can enter into contracts, property can be bought and sold, lawyers can advise their clients with greater confidence when decisions of past controversies provide a sure indicator of future judicial attitudes. Hence, once an issue of law has been squarely decided by an authoritative tribunal, judges tend not to reexamine the matter anew if the same legal point crops up in a later case. Even if they took no part in the first decision and even if they regard it unfavorably, they are slow to overrule a precedent upon which expectations may have been built. That is all that *stare decisis* means—to stand by the decisions. It is a rule of policy, not a "rule of law." As the Court said many years ago, whether *stare decisis* "shall be followed or departed from is a question entirely within the discretion of the court which is again called upon to consider a question once decided." [10] Judges are free to decide each case without reference to what has gone before; but as a matter of wisdom they choose in most instances to follow in the grooves their predecessors have made, leaving to the legislature the task of rewriting the judicially established rules if they produce socially disadvantageous results.

The judicial choice in this regard has always been flexible, even in the realm of so-called "private law." When constitutional interpretation or application has been involved, the policy of *stare decisis* has had diminished force. In such cases, where judicial mistake is virtually irremediable because of the cumbersome mechanics of amending the Constitution, earlier decisions have frequently been overruled, modified, or simply ignored. "The Court," wrote Justice Brandeis, "bows to the lessons of experience and the force of better reasoning, recognizing that the process of trial and error, so fruitful in the physical sciences, is appropriate also in the judicial function." [11] Another Justice, believing it a healthy practice for a court to reexamine its own doctrine, has expressed the view that responsible government entails the undoing of wrongs it itself has committed. "Respect for any tribunal is increased," he asserted, "if it stands ready (save where injustice to intervening rights would occur) not only to correct the errors of others but also to confess its own." [12] In this light the Court was clearly not indulging in a novel exercise when it reexamined the ideas underlying its earlier acquiescence in racial discriminations.[13] Indeed, the Constitution could never have survived the attrition of the years since its adoption in 1789 if the Supreme Court had in that long interval doggedly refused to adapt the antique text to the changing circumstances of modern times.

In 1868 when the Fourteenth Amendment was adopted, and even in 1896 when the railroad car issue was decided in *Plessy* v. *Ferguson*, public schooling was not centrally significant. In some parts of the country school terms were short and attendance was sporadic; in many communities neither teaching nor equipment was maintained at a level of excellence suggestive of public concern about education. "Today," as the Court's opinion in the 1954 segregation cases remarked, "education is perhaps the most important function of state and local governments. Compulsory school attendance laws and the great expenditures for education both demonstrate our recognition of the importance of education to our democratic society. It is required in the performance of our most basic public responsibilities, even service in the armed forces. It is the very foundation of good citizenship. Today it is a principal instrument in awakening the child to cultural values, and in preparing him for later professional training, and in helping him to adjust normally to his environment. In these days, it is doubtful that any child may reasonably be expected to succeed in life if he is denied the opportunity of an education."

Should the Court have blinded itself to this tremendous alteration in circumstances? Simply because in 1896 the Court had held that segregating Negro railway passengers did not deprive them of equal traveling opportunities, should it in 1954 have refused to consider whether segregating Negro schoolchildren deprived them of equal educational opportunities? These questions answer themselves. The Court did not by willfully indulging its personal preferences undo the settled constitutional judgments of earlier Justices. The Court did discharge its obligation, as constitutional custodian, to decide the case before it in accord with applicable principles— and in the context of mid-twentieth century factual understanding.

ARE NEGROES DIFFERENT?

Among a people professing Christianity and a belief in the brotherhood of God's children, human slavery would have been even less respectable than it was if the slaves had not been regarded as, somehow, subhuman.[14] Early attitudes toward Indians in the Western Hemisphere, especially on the part of the Spanish conquerors, had established a pattern of thought that comforted the "master race" in its exploitation of darker people.

The emotional need for self-justification during the slavery period was reinforced by socioeconomic factors that remained fully operative even after slavery as such no longer existed. In the pre-Civil War period the freed slaves in the South—of whom there were several hundred thousand—were denied most of the rights of truly free men, lest it be supposed that Negroes could genuinely profit by freedom; they were disadvantaged in court proceedings, limited in educational opportunity, restricted in occupational choice, barred from voting, and, in general, doomed to ignorance, impoverishment, and degradation.[15] After the enforced emancipation of the slaves, economic competition for jobs, coupled with the embittering frustrations of the postwar period, led to aggressive efforts to "keep the Negro in his place"—which, inevitably, was lowly. Thus, for example, most of the skilled mechanical work in the ante-bellum South had been performed by Negro slaves, but, a few years after the slaves had been freed, Negroes were held to be wholly incapable of filling the very positions to which they had previously been assigned.[16] The long economic and political decline of the South during the latter decades of the nineteenth century encouraged the search for an approved object of attack; the Negro conveniently served as an outlet for hostilities which could not be safely loosed elsewhere.[17]

Factors like these have left their deep mark on present attitudes toward the Negro.[18] Possibly "the vastly ego-warning and ego-expanding distinction between the white man and the black" [19] might have arisen even if slavery had never existed in the United States, and even if there had been no depressing aftermath of a desperate civil war; caste distinctions have survived in other countries, such as India and Japan, without those same generating causes. But America has never had to put the matter to the test, for slavery instilled in many white men's minds the consoling notion that no matter how wretched they might be, someone else was still lower.[20]

A widespread conviction of Negro inferiority produced, in times past, what sociologists call a self-fulfilling prophecy. The Negro, the argument might run, is mentally incapable of high intellectual achievement. Hence let us not waste our resources in providing him an extensive education. Later, the argument having been acted on, let us now measure the level of intellectual achievement of the Negro. Aha, note how little he has achieved! Didn't I tell you so?

You see, there really was no point in providing him an extensive education, because a dullard like that could never have absorbed it, anyway. The progress from hypothesis to action to preordained conclusion inescapably reminds me of a family friend in Saint Louis. When I was a boy this kindly gentleman owned extensive properties occupied by low-income tenants—or, to put the matter a bit differently, he was a big landlord in the slums. I can remember his saying that he had seriously considered installing bathtubs in his tenements, but had decided against this expensive innovation because he thought his tenants would not take baths even if they had the chance. Afterward, he bemoaned the persistent uncleanliness of the workingmen's families who occupied his houses, and drew comfort from not having wasted money on providing tubs for such smelly people. His prophecy was utterly self-fulfilling.

In the case of the Negro, the belief that he is different—and inferior—has subjected him to numerous discriminations that, in the course of time, have produced some of the very conditions to which they were supposedly a response.* "Jim Crow laws" have effectively reinforced the conclusion that Negroes are unlike other humans, but the conclusion finds little support in objective studies. Environment and opportunity seem to be important determinants of intellectual achievement; northern Negroes consistently outscore southern Negroes on intelligence tests, and approximate the scores of whites in comparable circumstances.[21] Neuroticism and other personality disorders are apparently distributed even-handedly

---

* See, for example, the study of Negro ghettoes in the North, by Morton Grodzins, "Metropolitan Segregation," 197 *Scientific American* 33, at 38 (1957): "Negroes are over-represented in low-income jobs, in menial service, in unskilled factory labor and in 'dirty work' generally. . . . Aside from low income, movement into the unaccustomed city environment tends to break down whatever stability of attitude and habit the Negro brings with him from the rural South. Family disorganization among Negro city dwellers is high, as measured by such indices as broken marriages, families headed by females, and unrelated individuals living in the same household. How does a mother keep her teen-aged son off the streets if an entire family must eat, sleep and live in a single room? What opportunity for quiet or security is there in a tightly packed, restless neighborhood? The slum encourages rowdiness, casual and competitive sexuality, a readiness for combat; disease and crime rates soar."

among the major ethnic groupings, including the Negro,[22] while the incidence of detectable mental disease seems to be a correlative of economic status and family inheritance rather than of race.[23]

Lately there has been a revival of biological forebodings that in earlier days were relied on as justifications of segregation. Judge Tom P. Brady, a state court judge in Mississippi whose views have been widely disseminated, has declared, for example: "We don't know what happens to the brain of man, but we do know that the Negro's brain pan seals and hardens quicker than the white man's. We do know that the Negro has, in certain instances, elliptical blood cells, which cause disease. We do know that his skull is one-eighth inch thicker, and we do know he has to have two determiners to have his kinky black hair. We don't know what it takes to make his mind different from our mind. This Supreme Court seeks to set aside all the laws of eugenics and biology!" [24] Eugenicists and biologists have apparently not as yet discovered the laws the Court has thus been accused of abrogating. On the contrary, skin color seemingly has no effect on the components of the blood that flows beneath the skin; the endocrine glands may be influenced by environment (as, for example, by the presence or absence of chemical traces in the water supply), but not by the elusive factor of race; neither brain size nor brain growth has been found to be significantly different among the different races of men; and the sealing of the brain pan that caused Judge Brady concern has been found to occur at the same period of physical development, regardless of race.[25]

More encouraging, in a way, than the documented findings of the savants are the common-sense conclusions of the common man.

The National Opinion Research Center, at the University of Chicago, is one of the most highly respected of this country's interviewing organizations. Over a period of fourteen years its trained interviewers asked a true sample of the white population this question: "In general, do you think Negroes are as intelligent as white people—that is, can they learn things just as well if they are given the same education and training?" This question was first explored in 1942, at the behest of the federal government, which was then concerned with racial attitudes as they might affect the war effort. It was asked again in 1944 and 1946 and then, after a lapse of ten years, in 1956. The change in attitude is very striking. In 1942, 50 per cent of the white northern population, but only 21 per cent of the white southern population, believed that Negroes were as intelligent as white people. By 1956 these figures had risen to 82 per cent in the North and 58 per cent in the South.[26] While belief in the educability of Negroes does not in itself mean that integration will occur, it certainly undercuts the theory that segregation is justified by the Negro's inherent inferiority.

Moreover, experience changes attitudes. During a shortage of ground troops in France in 1945, Negro platoons were incorporated in regiments in eleven previously all-white combat divisions, two of which were manned chiefly by Southerners. For months the white and Negro soldiers fought and worked together. Then the Army sent interviewers to find out what the reactions had been. In the beginning, the interviewers learned, two out of every three of the white soldiers had objected to the idea of serving with colored men. After sharing the perils of combat, however, 75 per cent of the objectors had a change of heart. "When I heard about it," declared a platoon sergeant from South Carolina, "I said I'd be damned if I'd wear the same shoulder patch they did. After that first day when we saw how they fought I changed my mind. They're just like any of the other boys to us." His sentiments were echoed by most of those who were interviewed; eight out of ten of the white soldiers thought the Negroes had "done very well" and almost all the rest said they had "done fairly well."

Perhaps the most interesting aspect of the whole study was its showing that prejudice yields to direct knowledge. Four groups of servicemen were asked how they would feel if their outfit were to include Negroes. The first group had had actual contact with Negroes as fellow soldiers; the second were members of an unintegrated regiment in the same division, who had thus had some opportunity to see or hear about the biracial enterprise though not to share in it themselves; the third group had been farther away from the experiment; and the fourth group had had no experience of integration at all. "The conclusion," an official report tells us, "can be simply stated: the closer white infantrymen had been to the actual experience of working with Negroes in combat units the more willing they were to accept integrated Negro platoons in white companies as a good idea for the future. Moreover, the sharpest break was between groups which had even the slightest contact with the experience of integration, and those which had none at all." [27]

Similarly, a study of attitudes among white merchant seamen toward Negro shipmates showed, according to the President's Committee on Civil Rights, that neither the place of a man's birth nor the sort of work he had done before going to sea shaped his sentiments. "What determined whether a white man was prejudiced against Negroes was the kind and amount of experience he had had with them. Where there was contact with Negroes on an equal footing in a situation of mutual dependence and common effort prejudice declined." [28]

A GUESS ABOUT THE FUTURE

Social catastrophes like the disturbances in Little Rock and the intransigence elsewhere in the South may lead one to think that the Supreme Court's decisions about unconstitutionality mean very little. A second glance gives a different impression. In only five states— Alabama, Georgia, Louisiana, Mississippi, and South Carolina— have no steps been taken to desegregate elementary or high schools; and Louisiana, though laggard in other respects, has admitted Negroes to its state university. In all the other states a real beginning has been made. In Missouri and West Virginia and the District of Columbia, desegregation has been accomplished. In the remaining ten states affected by the 1954 ruling, advances toward compliance have been achieved, grudgingly in some (as in Arkansas and Virginia and Texas) and more positively in others. The Supreme Court from the first recognized that its decision would have an uneven impact, for the South is by no means all of one piece. For that reason the lower courts were left substantial discretion for tailoring the remedy to fit local needs;[29] and this is the process now apparent.*

This is not the place to attempt a thorough social or economic forecast. There is some reason to believe that the South, like the North, will soon have to take account of wasted manpower resources,[30] especially as the reservoir of Negro labor becomes more and more depleted by massive migration.[31] Increasing mechanization of agriculture, coupled with urban industrialization and a good deal of rural industrialization as well, may create demands for skills and intellectual powers that the South has until now not particularly desired.

Moreover, opinions do shift. Even the untutored now believe what the social psychologists have long known, that racial feelings are taught and are not inborn.[32] Education seems to have a benign influence on the chief teachers of a child's attitudes, for a recent careful and comprehensive study shows strongly that "The higher the level of mother's education, the more favorable are the attitudes of students toward attending school with people of other races."[33] This finding is supported by other inquiries, which have consistently shown a diminution of racial antagonism as the educational level rises. According to a recent survey, "In the U.S. as a whole 61 per cent of the college-educated white persons endorse school integration, but only 36 per cent of those with a grammar school education. In the South 28 per cent of the college-educated favor school integration, but only 5 per cent of those with eight years or less schooling."[34] Since the tendency all over the nation is in the direction of a higher school-leaving age and a more advanced achieve-

* The Civil Rights Commission stated in a report issued on September 8, 1959, that 154 school districts in southern and border states had ended segregation in the school year beginning September 1954; there were 297 additions to the list in 1955, 248 in 1956, 61 in 1957, and 37 in 1958. "Future progress," the Commission added, "will be at a much slower pace in the absence of events providing a new stimulus. Experience shows that this might arise from court orders, from the invalidation of state laws now preventing voluntary action, or from strong leadership."

ment in absorbing formal schooling, a gradual spread of enlightened sentiments may hopefully be anticipated.

Acceptance of constitutional precepts is not easy when they run counter to habit and deeply entrenched ways of thought. Calm discussion is unlikely to cool those who are heated by visions of "mongrelization" of the races if equality of educational opportunity becomes a reality. Bit by bit, however, the conviction gains ground that no part of the American population can decently or lawfully be denied equal opportunities for personal fulfillment and socially useful achievement. Gradually others in the South as well as elsewhere in the nation find wisdom in the words of John B. Orr, Jr., a brave young Florida legislator who, in 1956, stood alone in voting against bills that sought to circumvent the Supreme Court's desegregation decision:

"I believe that had we devoted as much energy, time, and talent to discovering means to live under the law instead of in defiance of it, we could have discovered a way. I believe segregation is morally wrong. . . . If we hope to maintain our leadership among the free peoples of the world, if we hope to give hope to those subjugated people behind the Iron and Bamboo Curtains, we must demonstrate by our acts as well as our words that our democratic form of government places no artificial barriers on the opportunity to live and work with our fellow men. . . .

"For us to set an example of hypocrisy and deceit—of disrespect for our laws—will surely do more harm to our children than will result from their being seated in a classroom next to one whose skin is of a different hue." [35]

Change in segregation patterns cannot be brought about by personal determinations alone. No one family or group of families can decide to have an integrated school. This must be the product of a social decision that relieves the individual of the burden of judging, each for himself, whether the time is ripe. To end the drawing of lines between citizens will require leadership of high purpose and firm resolve. The Constitution, as the Supreme Court has now declared, sheds light on the path true leaders must tread.

Chapter 9

"PRIVATE GOVERNMENT" AND THE CONSTITUTION

The preceding chapters of this book have dealt with various governmental impairments of freedom. The constitutional provisions of the United States are aimed at preventing overly oppressive actions by the many (acting through official organs) against the few. Preoccupation with governmental affairs should not, however, distort one's perception of the basic realities of modern life. Looming ever larger among those realities is the capacity of private power-aggregates to limit the very freedoms the Constitution has attempted to protect.

No elaborate demonstration of this point need be made, for it is obvious to the least observant. The Constitution forbids governmental interference with freedom of expression; but a handful of companies that control the nation's radio and television networks can in fact do what the government is forbidden to do. The Constitution forbids governmental discrimination on the ground of race or religion; but employers can grant or deny job opportunities on the basis of personnel policies that would be illegal if they had been formulated by public officials. The Constitution forbids an arbitrary legislative determination of wages and working conditions; but labor unions can establish requirements whose validity would be subject to attack if the legislature had embodied them in a statute. The Constitution forbids the state to extinguish a person's professional career because it disapproves of his ideas and sympathies; but advertising agencies can "blacklist" television and radio performers, and can thus destroy their hopes of future employment, because the advertisers do not wish to engage "controversial personalities."

Multiplication of examples is not necessary. Perhaps, however, a few comments upon matters of degree may be appropriate and useful.

Of course men and women in past generations have not been immune from nongovernmental interferences with their personal freedom. For example, until very recently the employer was often able to maintain a somewhat autocratic control not only over his own establishment, but also over the personal conduct (including the political activity) of those whom he employed. Moreover, at various times in the past, powerful religious organizations have exerted an extralegal but nonetheless effective superintendence of "morals" to a degree that few constitutional governments would nowadays attempt. So it would be wholly inaccurate to say that the framers of our Constitution concentrated their attention upon governmental oppressions because there was no awareness that private oppressions existed or might in future exist. Quantitative change may, however, become so great that it must be reckoned as a qualitative change. Perhaps that point has been closely approached, if not actually reached.

In generations past, the power of employers was great, but it was somewhat diffused. Today, by contrast, Adolf Berle has reckoned that 50 per cent of American manufacturing (that is, everything other than financial and transportation) is held by about one hundred and fifty corporations; two-thirds of the economically productive assets of the entire United States, excluding agriculture, are owned, he says, by not more than five hundred corporations, of which an even smaller number have the ultimate decision-making power.* Since almost a half of the world's manufacturing produc-

---

* Of course it is true that ownership of these corporations is diffused through share-holdings by the public at large. But ever since the pioneering work of A. A. Berle, Jr., and Gardiner C. Means, *The Modern Corporation and Private Property* (1932), it has been recognized that, in modern industry, ownership through shares is far less significant than control of corporate management.

tion comes out of the United States, the giant dimensions of this concentration of economic power can readily be sensed. In Professor Berle's words, "Many of these corporations have budgets, and some of them have payrolls, which, with their customers, affect a greater number of people than most of the ninety-odd sovereign countries of the world. American Telephone & Telegraph, for example, based on combined population and wealth, would be somewhere around the thirteenth state of the union in terms of budget, and certainly larger than many of the countries of South America. Some of these corporations are units which can be thought of only in somewhat the way we have heretofore thought of nations." [1]

In fact, as Wolfgang Friedmann has effectively shown, dominant corporations may themselves think that they are the equivalent of nations; at times they seemingly deem themselves empowered to enter international arrangements closely resembling the treaties made by independent sovereigns.[2]

No change in this pattern of concentrated power is likely to occur in America. Once upon a time a man might perhaps aspire to "be his own boss." He worked as an individual, saved his money, saw his chance, and became an employer himself. Perhaps that continues to be "the American dream"; but if the dream includes ownership of a factory, it will bear little relationship to the hard realities. Each year many new American businesses are begun—well over 300,000 in a typical year. But fully two-thirds of these are service, retail, and sales offices. Nobody can save his pennies until he can afford to start a new automobile company, or newspaper, or steel mill; there simply are not enough pennies. Hence, the old longing to be an independent owner and operator of a major enterprise must be reshaped. Now it must be expressed in terms of opportunities for employment and for a chance to rise to the top through the bureaucracy of business.

This does not inevitably mean that there has been an over-all loss of freedom. Even though the worker is increasingly separated from hope of personally owning the instruments of production, he has in fact made tremendous forward strides in his material well-being.

Karl Marx asserted that concentration of ownership in private hands would result in heightened exploitation of the workers. At least in America, the opposite has been true. From 1939 to 1957, for example, which was a period of large corporate growth, American industrial workers experienced a 79 per cent increase in their real income. Rising standards of living do not assure freedom, of course. But, as Samuel Johnson remarked, "Poverty makes all virtues difficult, and some impossible." Free minds are more likely than not to be found in bodies that are free from hunger. Hence the creation of a new and higher level of material satisfactions for all may be regarded as a positive contribution toward attainment of a free society.

Moreover, the very fact that so great power resides in a small segment of the business comunity tends to stimulate development of balances and offsets. The economist John Kenneth Galbraith, in his book on "American Capitalism," has fully expounded the theory of what he calls "countervailing power." Corporate power, in his view, does not function in unchallenged supremacy, but is checked by the power of organized labor; the power of a manufacturer's association may be challenged by the combined power of retailers and wholesalers; and so on. In times not so very far past, wages and working conditions were autocratically (though not necessarily whimsically) fixed by employers; in theory, the worker and the boss bargained and made a contract satisfactory to both, but in reality the disparity between the bargaining power of the boss and that of the worker was so acute that the theory usually bore little resemblance to the actuality. Now 300 unions with members in numerous establishments, organized in some 75,000 local branches, bargain collectively for about 18,000,000 workers. While it would be incorrect to assert that the United Automobile Workers can exactly balance the power of, say, the General Motors Corporation, nevertheless the former inequality of bargaining power has been greatly reduced even in the giant corporations. Indeed, in some occupations the inequality may now have been reversed; big unions may be able to overpower little employers.

Just as the bigness of business has not inevitably discouraged the creation of a free atmosphere, the bigness of unions has not inevitably stimulated it. The union may overpower its members as well as an occasional employer. Clyde Summers, Philip Taft, and other scholars have made valuable studies of labor union functioning; they have shown numerous unjust practices in organizations that control their members' economic destinies without any of the checks and balances commonly found in modern governments. The scholars' findings have been amply confirmed by recent Congressional investigations of some of the more malodorous unions. A few labor leaders have been shown to have been extortioners rather than bargainers; others have been found to have acted collusively with employers, with a view to mulcting the consumer or, perhaps more commonly, the workers whose interests the union was ostensibly safeguarding.

A moment ago we used the phrase "a free atmosphere." To some degree the very fact that persons are employed by and must work within a large organization may affect the prevailing atmospheric conditions. Without any volition on the part of a corporation, those who work for it may lose both the capacity and the desire to function as free individuals. Satisfactions come from the approbation of one's fellows; approbation is often dependent upon conformity to the patterns set by the group, and thus individuality, innovation, and eccentricity are discouraged. The regular office hours that are maintained simply as a matter of corporate efficiency prevent participation in public and political affairs, which do not respect the same time clocks as the corporation. Moreover, if important executives in a large corporation manifest a distaste for politics, junior employees in that corporation probably need no formal admonitions not to become political enthusiasts. As William Whyte has shown in his brilliant sociological study, *The Organization Man*, the same may be said of most other aspects of life; the governors of a corporation do not have to flex their muscles, for a wink or a nod will suffice to keep most organization men in the approved grooves.

Indeed, quite without reference to their own "immediate families,"

so to speak, the large, privately controlled enterprises have a sometimes subtle but nonetheless positive tendency to impose their attitudes (whatever they may be) upon the population at large. The
case of mass media of communication is plain. The television, the
newspapers, the movies, and the other opinion-shapers represent a
fairly narrow spectrum of choice. While nobody is compelled to
accept the values and the manners thus insistently reflected, diver-
gence from the norms set by the mass media requires a great deal
more effort than does conformity. Similarly, the large corporations
through their choice of activity, through their advertising, through
their stylistic preferences, and through their estimates of the sort
of accomplishment that deserves the largest monetary rewards, are
powerful shapers of the society in which they function. Businessmen
adhere to the dogma that competition forces them to give the public
what it wants; but there is much room to believe that business itself
often induces the wants it then proceeds to fill. In the area of styles—
whether of women's clothing or of automobile tailfins—this seems
clear enough. In a much broader sense, however, the same kind of
thing is true. When an industrial giant announces its decision to ex-
pand its production facilities, economic euphoria may sweep over the
entire community; when "retrenchment" is decided upon, previous
optimism may turn to pessimism and a chain reaction may lead
swiftly to a depression. Sometimes the decisions taken by corporate
officers seem to be made almost without consciousness that they do
have sweeping social implications. When the motorcar manufacturers concluded, for example, that what Americans really wanted
(whether or not they knew it) was automobiles overladen with
chrome, more crowded with gadgetry, and packed with greater
power than was needed for normal transportation in a crowded
country, they probably did not even think about some of the
consequences—such as, for example, the destruction of the useful-
ness of previously adequate one-car garages that were now too narrow to house the newly designed monsters of the road, or the need
of municipal spending for street widening instead of for more urgently needed public purposes such as water supply, schools, or

low-cost housing. An astute sociologist-economist, Peter Drucker, has said, after an analysis of the part played in America by the General Motors Corporation, that the large corporation is "the instrument which sets the standard for the way of life and mode of living of our citizens; which leads, molds and directs; which determines our perspective on our own society; around which crystallize our social problems and to which we look for their solution." [3] This may be an overstatement, because it fails fully to reflect the broad impact on society of large specialized organizations or, as they are sometimes called, special interest groups—such as, for example, the American Medical Association. This century-old association, with a membership of 160,000 doctors and an annual revenue of more than 9,000,000 dollars, has performed valuable work in raising and maintaining the standards of medical care in the United States; but it has also shaped public opinion about matters of economics and social organization concerning which a medical training gives no special competence.[4]

There is no need to belabor the obvious any further. The mid-twentieth century is a time of bigness, in which the individual voice has difficulty being heard. When the American Constitution was framed, industry was small and, in the main, family operated. Self-employment was general; employment in the service of others was relatively rare. Family-size farms constituted the bulk of economic activity. Only the government was big enough and pervasive enough in its influence to seem capable of dangerously limiting the liberties of free men and women. Now the story is different. Does the Constitution have relevance to preserving a free society against the non-governmental pressures that may be applied today?

II

At the outset, perhaps we should pause to articulate a few suppositions. A "free society" cannot mean one in which each individual lives in a self-centered way, without concern for his fellows' needs or opinions. The freedom of the individual cannot be exercised in so abandoned a manner that other individuals are deprived of theirs. At some point, inescapably, choices have to be made between one desire and another. The role of organized government is, precisely, to serve as a mechanism by which these necessary choices can be made, and can be made with binding effect. Laws are enacted because of a judgment, often imperfectly formed and sometimes consciously distorted, that controls must be placed upon some persons' conduct (or even ideas) in order to advance or protect the physical well-being, the convenience in life, the future opportunities, the chances for self-expression, in short the freedom, of others. We think of a free society as one in which means are preserved for the individual's participating in this continuous process of choice; and we think of "the rule of law" as existing in a society where fair procedures are utilized to give even-handed rather than capricious effect to the choices already made, while safeguarding the channels of opinion formation that might lead to different choices for the future. What we are now discussing is, in a sense, whether the power concentrates of modern times have unduly constricted the individual's ability (freedom, if you will) to make choices, either alone or through groups, including even "the government."

Let us put aside the tendency of human beings to resemble sheep, and to follow wherever they may be led. We need not concern ourselves with, for example, the readiness of women to bolster their bosoms into artificial protuberance during one year and then, when a couturier so decrees, to deflate them the next year; or their enthusiastic acceptance of the notion that the hem lines of their skirts should be at a preordained distance from the floor regardless of the shape of their legs. Choices such as these are not enforced; they are willingly embraced.

What shall we say, however, when the individual is given no real option, but is compelled to acquiesce in the choices others have made for him? Consider, for example, the elaborate structure of rules that govern workers in industrial establishments, usually as a result of agreement between management and union leaders, but sometimes by edict of the one or the other. Who will get what job, seniority provisions, hours of work, the content of the various jobs (that is, the demands that may properly be made upon a particular worker) must be fixed by somebody if chaos is to be avoided. That is inevitable in an industrialized society. These rules could be made by the state, in the form of statutes or administrative regulations. In some industries, in fact, they are so made; for instance, the permissible driving hours of locomotive engineers and bus operators, the types of safety equipment to be installed in coal mines, the allowable extent of night work for women, and the occupations in which children may be employed are defined by government. For the most part, however, the rules of industrial life are privately established though, as to the worker whom they affect, the rules are just as decisive as if they were fixed by law. What if those rules are unfair in content? Can the affected individual look to the Constitution for help, or must he quit his job and seek for one in which the governing rules are more palatable?

Consider the policies of the powerful institutions that lend money for new building purposes. They are to some degree controlled by law. The controls, however, are almost invariably negative; some sorts of loans may be forbidden as involving too great a risk to the solvency of financial institutions of great public importance. Suppose, now, that the institutions add some rules of their own. Suppose, for example, that they decide not to lend money in any circumstances to those who wish to erect multifamily apartment buildings for occupancy by Negroes as well as whites. As a consequence segregated housing will be encouraged, and a disadvantaged minority will be unequally treated contrary to the spirit of the Constitution. Does this raise constitutional questions, or does it mean merely that the disadvantaged group must seek a statutory prohibition of similarly unjust policies in the future?

A large automobile manufacturing corporation distributes cars through dealers who obtain from the corporation an exclusive franchise to sell that type of automobile in a particular territory. May the manufacturer summarily revoke the franchise if the manufacturer concludes that the dealer has disregarded the corporation's rules? If a public agency were to revoke a comparably valuable license, due process of law would probably require that the licensee be given a full and fair hearing before decision was made, and the reasons for revocation would afterward be subject to attack in court on the ground that they were arbitrary. May the corporation do unrestrainedly what the state is forbidden to do?

In a "laissez-faire" system, it has been supposed that matters like these are not the concern of anybody other than those who are immediately involved. Laissez faire has been defined as the principle of "hands off!" But, as one sardonic critic has remarked, this leaves unsolved the question, "Whose hands off whom?" The truth of the case is that when the state does not intervene in situations like those just instanced, it is making a choice just as surely as when it does intervene. It is, in essence, choosing not to prevent the exercise by others of a power that it itself could (if it wished) exercise directly or could modify in some manner.[5]

One may optimistically hope that these supposititious cases are unrelated to real life, but they are by no means wholly fabricated. Until 1935 an American employer could, for example, lay down with impunity a rule that anybody who joined a labor union (or, indeed, who expressed sentiments favorable to a union) would be instantly dismissed; a federal statute in that year prohibited as an "unfair labor practice" what had previously been an employer-enforced limitation upon freedom of speech and association. Lending institutions have in fact discouraged biracial housing in many cities. Even without this discouragement, landlords have often adopted discriminatory rental policies that have crowded Negroes into urban ghettoes that were just as real as though they had been created by law; only in recent years has New York, a state that is among the leaders in seeking decency for all rather than merely for some of its citizens, forbidden by law the further enforcement of these dangerously antisocial, privately created policies. Automobile manufacturers did in fact grow callous in relation to those who served as their retail distributors; a Congressional committee concluded in

1956 that "concentration of economic power has increased to the degree that traditional contractual concepts are no longer adequate to protect the automobile dealers under their franchises." [6] A federal statute was enacted in that year, supplementing the laws of nineteen states that deal with the same subject matter, seeking to assure the dealers "freedom from coercion, intimidation, or threats of coercion or intimidation." [7] The dealers who were thus found to be in need of protection had in the aggregate invested more than five billion dollars in their businesses (their average investment being 118,000 dollars), and they employed 668,000 persons; this is worth noting lest it be supposed that it is only the very lowly who are powerless against giants.[8]

No suggestion is made that existing power is always used, let alone abused. In 1947, for example, America suffered very acutely from a steel shortage; and in some types of heavy industry, shortages continued to be experienced until after the end of the war in Korea. Producers were in a position to direct the economy. Should steel be made available for structural work and, if so, should a preference be given to structures intended for one purpose or for another? Should the automobile or the refrigerator industry be given the steel with which to satisfy demand for consumer products? Interestingly enough, the steel corporations were eager to avoid responsibility for making the debatable choices such questions imply; they joined in urging enactment of new legislation which directly involved the government in the task of allocating the available supplies. This is not a phenomenal instance. Many of those who could wield power if they wished choose to avoid doing so—perhaps in realization that they who become identified as decision makers cannot escape responsibility for the results, and may in the end find themselves embroiled in damaging political controversy. They realize, in brief, that too nakedly exposed a use of power that affects "the public" may cause a demand for state intervention and tightened controls, to ensure a broader representation of interests in the decision-making process.[9]

III

The Fifth Amendment of the American Constitution provides that "No person shall . . . be deprived of life, liberty or property, without due process of law." This has long been understood as being a limitation solely upon action by the federal government, rather than by state governments or private parties.[10] The Fourteenth Amendment says that "No State shall make or enforce any law which shall abridge the privileges or immunities of citizens of the United States; nor shall any State deprive any person of life, liberty, or property, without due process of law; nor deny to any person within its jurisdiction the equal protection of the laws." This, too, is a limitation upon governmental rather than private action; it is directed against the states and any who act under its authority, such as counties, municipalities, and school districts.[11]

To state this differentiation between "public" and "private" action is much simpler than to apply it meaningfully.[12] If the government affirmatively endorses and supports private arrangements of economic and social affairs, no doubt "state action" has occurred and constitutional questions may be raised.[13] If government simply stands idly by, doing nothing while "fundamental human rights" are being impaired on a large scale by private powers, can its inaction be regarded as the equivalent of action? Can the Constitution stretch far enough to reach discriminations that the state does not initiate, but in which it seemingly acquiesces? Questions of this sort have been touched upon by a slowly evolving constitutional doctrine to which we now turn.

Government action, to begin with, must be understood as involving action taken by any branch of the government, whether that be the legislative, the executive, or the judicial.[14] More than twenty years ago Professor Robert L. Hale argued effectively that whenever a court enforced a private contract or gave effect to a private exclusionary practice (such, for example, as a theater owner's refusal to admit a Negro to his theater), the state was an active participant, and constitutional prohibitions therefore should become operative.[15]

This view received highly significant recognition by the United States Supreme Court when it decided the famous case of *Shelley v. Kraemer* in 1948.[16] The Court had before it for review a lower court decision involving a "restrictive covenant." This is an agreement, generally among the owners of contiguous private residential properties, by which the signatories bind themselves not to sell or rent any of their property, for a designated period of time, to specified racial, religious, or ethnic groups. In the present instance the restriction was directed against "any person not of the Caucasian Race." It was a private agreement, among private citizens, none of whom could be designated as agents of the state; and the agreement concerned itself exclusively with private property. Since, as we have already noted, the Constitution does not forbid private conduct of a discriminatory nature, the mere existence of the restrictive covenant, standing alone, raised no issue; it was as though two neighbors had told one another that they disliked, for example, persons of Irish ancestry and would therefore never sell their property to such persons. But in this case one of the parties to the covenant decided to disregard it, and to sell his property to a Negro. Then a suit was commenced in court by the other covenantor, to prevent violation of his contract. When a state court used its power at that stage to give effect to the "private agreement," the Supreme Court concluded that state action had occurred; it was "the active intervention of the state courts supported by the full panoply of state power" that made the discrimination possible, and this was not constitutionally tolerable.[17]

Next let us consider a cluster of cases where no affirmative state action appears, but where failure to exercise readily available power has made possible a constitutionally obnoxious discrimination. *Derrington v. Plummer* [18] is suggestive. The new courthouse for Harris County, Texas, included space for a restaurant, and was furnished and equipped by the county for that purpose. The county then leased the space to a private caterer. He excluded Negroes from the use of "his" restaurant. They sued to enjoin him from continuing this discriminatory practice, which they alleged should be regarded as "state action" even though the county government was not shown to have formulated or positively to have endorsed the discriminatory practice. The court granted the relief sought, saying that where a branch of the government has joined in a private enterprise or has reserved control over the way the enterprise is operated, it may not stand idle while its partner is engaging in acts that the state itself could not constitutionally commit.[19]

Another group of cases hinges upon the theory that government may not confer powers upon a private organization unless the grant of power is coupled with a correlative duty to conform to constitutional standards. *Steele* v. *Louisville and Nashville Railroad Company* [20] is a leading case of this type. It involved an organization of railway workers. In America, unlike some other countries, a union chosen by a majority of the employees within a "bargaining unit" serves as bargaining representative not merely for its own members, but for all the employees in that unit; this is prescribed by the Railway Labor Act and by other federal statutes.[21] A union and the employing railroad agreed upon a seniority system that discriminated against Negro employees. The complaints of the Negroes were brushed aside by the employer on the ground that the union, their bargaining representative, had on their behalf made the very agreement against which they were now protesting. Then the affected Negroes sought judicial assistance. The Supreme Court held that the union was bound by law to represent in a fair way all for whom it bargained, and that the statute which clothed the union with power might well be deemed unconstitutional if it failed to require this.[22]

The doctrine of the Steele case has been consistently and extensively applied by the Court. The minority's right to be properly represented under the Railway Labor Act "is a federal right implied from the statute and the policy which it has adopted." [23] It follows that bargaining agreements which exclude Negroes from certain jobs or limit their chances for promotion cannot be enforced; [24] nor can discriminatory contracts be made by a bargaining representative chosen under other federal labor laws.[25]

This whole group of decisions rests, at least verbally, on the proposition that labor unions have derived their power from federal legislation, and that thus they are, in a sense, extensions of the state. It must be recognized, however, that unions were performing their functions as bargaining representatives long before statutes were enacted to buttress their strength. Union activities are, it is perfectly true, more fully protected by law today than was formerly the case; legislatures have come to recognize the great significance of those activities in maintaining a healthy society. But it is wholly untrue to say that the functions and capacities of American labor unions were created by the government. The existence of labor relations laws may have provided an analytical peg on which the courts could hang their opinions in the cases just discussed; realistically, however, the decisions reflect a heightened recognition that the conduct of union affairs has large public consequences, and that the public policies outlined in the Constitution ought not to be overridden by a powerful private body.*

Now let us turn to another area of judicial development in which can be seen a gradual obliteration of the line between state action and state inaction.

Party nominees are chosen in most American states through a "direct primary election." When more than one person aspires to be nominated as his party's candidate for public office, the adherents of that party express their preference in the primary election; the one chosen in that election then becomes his party's nominee in the general election that occurs later. If a state itself conducts

---

* Compare the view expressed by the late Justice Robert H. Jackson in his Godkin lectures at Harvard, "The Supreme Court in the American System of Government" (1955), at p. 69: "It is my basic view that whenever any organization or combination of individuals, whether in a corporation, a labor union or other body obtains such economic or legal advantage that it can control or in effect govern the lives of other people, it is subject to the control of the Government, . . . for the Government can suffer no rivals in the field of coercion. Liberty requires that coercion be applied to the individual not by other individuals but by the Government. . . ."

the primary election, of course it must observe the requirement of the Fifteenth Amendment that "The right of citizens of the United States to vote shall not be denied or abridged by the United States or by any State on account of race, color, or previous condition of servitude." [26]

Political parties are, however, private organizations rather than state agencies. Suppose that a state simply leaves it to the party to prescribe who shall be allowed to vote in its primaries. Precisely that occurred in Texas. The Democratic Party, by far the most powerful in that state, decided to restrict its membership to white persons; and since only members could vote in the primaries, Negroes were barred from participating in the choice of Democratic nominees who were virtually certain of victory in the ensuing general election. The Supreme Court, after at first vacillating,[27] held squarely and definitively in 1944, in *Smith* v. *Allwright*,[28] that a qualified Negro voter could not thus be practically blocked from access to the ballot. Texas, the Court said, had delegated a "state function" to a private group, whose acts must be regarded as the acts of the state itself.

Thus far the matter seems somewhat similar to cases discussed earlier in this chapter, in which a governmental unit had placed some of its physical property in the hands of private operators, whose conduct was afterward regarded as state action. But now a further step was taken. Texas had by law required that there be a primary election, the political parties being allowed to choose how it was to be conducted. After the decision in *Smith* v. *Allwright*, the state of South Carolina entirely repealed all laws that bore in any way on primaries. Each party was left free to pick its candidates as it chose, for primary elections were no longer required. The state said, in effect, that it would conduct a general election at a given time, but would not concern itself with how the candidates were selected. The Democratic Party of South Carolina, a voluntary association, conducted its own poll to choose its nominees—and the party would not allow Negroes to participate in this "private" polling. The federal courts were quick to declare that this was a subterfuge. The primary election, said the courts, had become an integral part of the state's election machinery, no matter whether it was conducted by state officials or by party officials. And no matter who was in charge of the voting, "the fundamental principles laid down by the Constitution" must be fully observed.[29]

Finally, there came before the Supreme Court a case involving as attenuated a form of "state action" as can readily be imagined. A Texas county political organization, calling itself the Jaybird Democratic Association, excluded Negro voters from a privately conducted primary election, entirely financed by the association. The Jaybirds held their "election" in May, while the state primary election, conducted pursuant to statutory authority, took place in July; Negroes were permitted to vote in the state primary, but by that time everyone knew the Jaybirds' choice and he was not likely to encounter serious opposition in the July balloting. What was the "state action" of which complaint could be made in these circumstances? The Supreme Court, in *Terry* v. *Adams*, answered that question as follows: "For a state to permit such duplication of its election process is to permit a flagrant abuse of those processes to defeat the purposes of the Fifteenth Amendment." [30] What this amounts to is condemnation of state inaction, rather than of action. The state had power to forbid a duplicate primary election, in order to preserve its citizens' opportunity for an actual voice in selecting candidates; its failure to do so must be taken as the equivalent of an endorsement, a sanctioning, of the impropriety.*

---

* Justice Frankfurter, in a separate opinion in *Terry* v. *Adams*, asserted that "The vital requirement is State responsibility—that somewhere, somehow, to some extent, there be an infusion of conduct by officials, panoplied with state power, into any scheme by which colored citizens are denied voting rights merely because they are colored." In the present case it is difficult to see what constituted the required "infusion of conduct by officials." What the officials did was—nothing.

Compare *Catlette* v. *United States*, 132 F. 2d 902, 907 (4th Cir., 1943), involving a prosecution of a deputy sheriff, in part because of his failure to afford police protection to nine members of the Jehovah's Witnesses sect who were threatened with mob violence; he was proceeded against under a statute making it a crime to deny constitutional rights under color of official

The cases thus far discussed have had to do with disregard of the fundamental rights of a racial minority. The conclusions to be drawn from the decisions need not be narrowly confined to this particularly blatant and therefore readily identifiable sort of un-constitutionalism. Two cases are especially suggestive of the further reach of the applicable principles.

Public Utilities Commission v. *Pollak*,[31] decided by the Supreme Court in 1952, raised the question of whether the Constitution of the United States precluded a privately owned streetcar company from receiving and amplifying radio programs through loud-speakers in its passenger vehicles. One of the passengers contended that when he paid his streetcar fare, he wanted to ride in quiet, so that he could read or think or rest; instead, he said, he became part of a "captive audience" that was compelled to listen to radio messages, including advertisements. This, he said, invaded his freedom and deprived him of his liberty without due process. The Court concluded otherwise as to the merits of the case; before reaching the merits, however, the Court first had to consider whether any constitutional question was present at all, since the offender (if there was one) seemed to be not the government, but rather, the private company that operated the streetcars. As to this, the Court decided that the requisite governmental element did exist. The objecting passenger had protested to the public utilities commission, the administrative agency that regulated the street railways. The commission had considered his complaint against the radio program, but had decided to do nothing because unpersuaded that the com-

---

authority. The defendant asserted that his failure to preserve the peace had involved mere inaction, and therefore he could not be adjudged guilty of wrongdoing. The court answered: "It is true that a denial of equal protection has hitherto been largely confined to affirmative acts of discrimination. The Supreme Court, however, has already taken the position that a culpable official state inaction may also constitute a denial of equal protection." In this case, however, it should be noted that the deputy sheriff had been guilty of affirmative misdeeds in addition to his inaction.

See also *Lynch* v. *United States*, 189 F. 2d 476 (5th Cir., 1951), upholding the conviction of officers who had failed to protect prisoners in their custody from being beaten by a mob. The court declined to differentiate between official acts and official inaction.

pany was inconveniencing its passengers. It was the decision to do nothing that constituted the "state action." The Court treated the administrative noninterference as though it were an administrative authorization. The implications of this are very broad. Many private activities are subject to regulation. If one may conclude that non-exercise of regulatory power is the equivalent of an affirmative sanctioning by government of what has been done on private in-itiative, then the area of possible constitutional litigation may be widely extended. Once again, moreover, the question must be asked whether failure to exercise an administrative restraint is qualitatively different from any other inaction by government in the face of private conduct that has the effect of eliminating rights the Consti-tution seeks to preserve.

The second case to be especially noted is *Marsh* v. *Alabama*,[32] a 1946 decision. In that case Marsh was prosecuted under a statute making it a crime to remain on private property after having been directed to leave. He was a sectarian who had insisted upon dis-tributing religious tracts in a "company town"—that is, a residential settlement not organized as a municipality under state laws, but existing solely as the private property of a single corporation which owned all the streets, land, and structures within the town. The corporation had forbidden the kind of religious propagandizing in which Marsh was engaged; the state, which had had no share in formulating the corporation's policy in this respect, lent its aid by enforcing the criminal law that was intended to protect property owners against unwelcome invaders of their property. As we have seen, this constituted "state action" sufficient to raise constitutional issues. The question remains on the merits, however, whether a private corporation is not entirely at liberty to manage its affairs without reference to constitutional standards. As to this question, the Supreme Court commented as follows:

Ownership does not always mean absolute dominion. The more an owner, for his advantage, opens up his property for use by the public in general, the more do his rights become circumscribed by the statutory and constitutional rights of those who use it. . . .

Whether a corporation or a municipality owns or possesses the town, the public in either case has an identical interest in the functioning of the community in such a manner that the channels of communication remain free. . . .
Many people in the United States live in company owned towns. . . . There is no more reason for depriving these people of the liberties guaranteed by the First and Fourteenth Amendments than there is for curtailing these freedoms with respect to any other citizen.[33]

Words like these go far in the direction of an admonition to private rule-makers that, at least with respect to freedom of speech, they should be mindful of the limitations that would be operative if the rules were to be promulgated by a public body.

IV

In the examples thus far discussed, privately exercised power has been linked with the state in the sense that the state has actively lent its aid (as in the restrictive covenant and company town cases), or has conferred the power that has subsequently been abused (as in the operation of public facilities, or the collective bargaining cases) or has seemingly endorsed the objectionable action by declining to halt it (as in the streetcar-radio case) or has transferred one of its own regular functions to other hands (as in the primary election cases). Now let us examine an instance of private action which, while causing deprivations of a type with which the Constitution is concerned, may not be reachable as a matter of constitutional law.

Many private groups seemingly regard themselves as arbiters of manners and morals. Sometimes they throw their weight against representations offensive to them as a special element of the population—as, for instance, when Jewish groups caused difficulty for the motion picture *Oliver Twist* because the characterization of the unsavory Fagin might stimulate anti-Semitism, or when Catholic groups arrayed themselves against the film *Martin Luther* because it was ideologically objectionable to them, or when Negro groups sought to have Mark Twain's *Huckleberry Finn* withdrawn from school libraries because they thought that the character called "Nigger Jim" would warp children's understanding of the Negro as a fellow citizen. More often, censorial groups are concerned with what they regard as violations of immutable standards of morality.[34]

Of course it is proper for such groups to have and to express opinions; the constitutionally protected freedom of belief and expression indubitably safeguards their doing so. Sometimes, however, the groups go further. They seek to use economic pressures in order to force the community as a whole to accept their appraisal of the work in question.

A recent instance of this type of action can be extracted from the economic history of the motion picture *Baby Doll*.

On November 28, 1956, the National Legion of Decency, a Roman Catholic film viewing organization, reviewed *Baby Doll* and declared it wholly objectionable.[35] For the close to thirty million American Catholics this action by the National Legion of Decency represented an impressive condemnation of the film. One day prior to the New York premiere of the film, and without viewing the film himself, Cardinal Spellman, the leading Catholic religious leader in the United States, denounced *Baby Doll* from the pulpit of St. Patrick's Cathedral in New York City. He declared that Catholics would commit sin in seeing the film. Cardinal Spellman said that he condemned the film in the performance of his duties as "a loyal citizen" in defense of America, and as Archbishop of New York, "in solicitude for the welfare of souls entrusted to my care." [36]

Mr. Joseph P. Kennedy, a prominent member of the Catholic laity, former United States Ambassador to the Court of St. James's and owner of a chain of twenty motion picture houses in the New England states, approved the action taken by the manager of the chain in refusing to exhibit the film in those theaters, and stated, "I think it [*Baby Doll*] should be banned everywhere." [37]

At the same time, in Albany, New York, the management of the Strand Theatre, unconnected with the Kennedy chain, sought from the distributor a release from its commitment to show the film. The request that the film not be shown was made first by the Reverend T. H. Kay, the Albany diocese director of the Roman Catholic Legion of Decency. A few days later, the management of the Strand Theatre announced that the film would be shown as originally scheduled.[38] The following day the Most Reverend William A. Scully, Roman Catholic Bishop of Albany, forbade the Catholics of his diocese, on the pain of mortal sin, from attending *any* movie at the Strand Theatre for the next six months; not only were they to avoid *Baby Doll*, but they were to inflict punishment on the theater operator for showing it to anybody else. Following Bishop Scully's lead, the Roman Catholic Bishops of Connecticut issued a joint statement condemning *Baby Doll* and forbidding Catholics to see it.[39]

In Syracuse, New York, neither of the two daily newspapers, *The Post Standard* and *The Herald Journal*, would accept advertisements for the film. The Record Company of Troy, New York, which publishes a morning and afternoon newspaper in that city, also announced that it would not accept advertisements for *Baby Doll*.[40]

In Pennsylvania, three theaters in the metropolitan Philadelphia area cancelled plans to show the now controversial film. At the religious services of Roman Catholic churches in the neighborhood of those theaters, parishioners had been urged to "express themselves" against the film. It is reported that almost immediately the theaters were swamped with telephone calls protesting its showing. Acting on these complaints, the owner of the theaters withdrew the film.[41]

Mr. Elia Kazan, the distinguished director who had been responsible for producing the film, announced some time afterward that the picture would be a financial success, though the opposition of the Catholic Church had reduced the number of national bookings that the film otherwise would have had.[42] That the moral standards applied in condemning the film in the United States were not immutable, and that men of good faith and, indeed, of the very same faith might disagree about the film, is shown by the fact that Roman

Catholic religious authorities in England [43] and France [44] approved the film for exhibition to adults.

This recital of episodes in the campaign against *Baby Doll* suffices to reveal what would certainly have been deemed to be unconstitutional deprivations of property and liberty if they had been undertaken by governmental authorities.[45] Private action by religious leaders, supported by theater and newspaper owners who were influenced by them, caused severe economic loss to the film's producers and, by means of organized boycott, to some of its exhibitors, who lost not only the patronage of those who chose not to see *Baby Doll*, but the future patronage of movie-goers who were advised to take vengeance on the exhibitor because of his past "sin." Even more certainly, the rest of the movie-going public suffered a loss of freedom. Choice is the essence of freedom; when *Baby Doll* was withdrawn from exhibition because of one group's threats, persons who did not share that group's view were nevertheless bound by it without choice—unless they were to construct a theater of their own as a means of preserving their freedom against arbitrary limitations upon what performances they could see.

What, however, are the practical remedies? In the absence of a specifically applicable contract, the film's producer has no redress against the theater operator who decides, for good or bad reasons or none at all, not to exhibit the film. Newspapers are not compelled by law to accept advertisements; so the theater owner cannot complain that he was not given opportunity to publicize his current screen attraction. Perhaps, as to an actual boycott, a lawsuit of some sort might be maintainable against the religious leader who had urged his followers to become avengers. But even this is, in the circumstances, at least somewhat doubtful; and surely, in any event, a prudent lawyer would advise his client that success in legal proceedings would very probably prove to be a Pyrrhic victory. As for the individual movie-goer, his only recourse is to move elsewhere.

What is the difference between this case of private imposition and those we have discussed in the preceding section? The chief difference is that in the previously described cases the state could withhold its aid from, or could successfully restrain, the private invasions of constitutionally recognized values without itself invading a constitutionally recognized value. Here, by contrast, the state could not intervene to protect the film producer, exhibitor, and spectator without coming perilously close to interfering with other persons' freedom of conscience and speech, which rank near the top of the constitutional scale of interests to be safeguarded. Conceivably an antiboycott law could be framed to meet cases of this sort; conceivably newspaper advertising could be regulated in terms of what should be accepted, instead of merely (as now) in terms of what must be rejected. The validity of such laws would, however, be highly debatable, even if they seemed useful, which in itself is doubtful. Assuredly the state could not undertake to prevent a religious leader from expressing his belief that a given film is immoral, and that those who sought pleasure in its contemplation would commit a sin. Assuredly the state could not undertake to force newspaper owners to turn over their pages to be edited by other private persons (advertisers) in return for a fee. And even if these things were possible, of course the state could not compel individuals to attend a film showing they preferred not to witness. In short, however obnoxious the campaign against *Baby Doll* may have been in libertarian terms, publicly initiated countermeasures against the campaign might have been even less desirable. As Professor Hale has well said, "the freedom from private control is not always a more vital liberty than the freedom to exert that control." [46]

V

Another type of case that is possibly worth exploring in some depth involves membership groups—labor unions, trade associations, professional societies, and the like—whose determinations may have constitutional implications. Much has been written about the oppressive potentialities of labor unions, which have in fact much too often denied members the opportunity to participate effectively in governing their own affairs; so grave were the actual or possible abuses that federal legislation was enacted in 1959 in an effort to define what should be the substantive and procedural protections of union members. Less fully publicized are the potential dangers in highly respected and socially valuable organizations of professional rather than laboring men. The American Medical Association (A.M.A.) may serve for purposes of illustration.

The A.M.A. is composed of fifty-three state and territorial medical societies and 1,987 county societies. It has labored earnestly and for many years to raise the standards of medical education, hospital administration, and scientific knowledge. Its accomplishments have given it deserved recognition as a worth-while force in American life.

Theoretically all reputable doctors of medicine have been free to join the A.M.A. But since admission to membership in a local medical society was long regarded as a prerequisite step toward establishing good repute, A.M.A. membership has at times depended in fact upon a subsidiary society's exercise of discretion. In a number of southern states many (if not most) county medical societies are known to have denied membership to Negro physicians; in any event, a whimsical, mistaken, or vicious exclusion from county membership, and thus from A.M.A. membership, has not been subject to any correction through regularized appellate procedures.[47]

This means much more than mere nonelection to a social club. It means not only loss of professional and social contacts, but also a major source of scientific information. As the Supreme Court of one of the states has said:

Only through such membership may a doctor secure access to numerous technical papers, and obtain the right to attend meetings and conferences of doctors devoted to general and local medical problems. Perhaps more important than all of these other considerations, a non-member of the society is quite generally regarded as an outcast by his fellow practitioners, his patients, and members of the public, and suffers very real humiliation and embarrassment.[48]

It may be added that the nonmember may also be unable to obtain certification as a specialist; other physicians, fearing disapprobation by the society, may refuse to join him in consultation; he may find it impossible to gain admittance of his patients into private hospitals; and he may be refused insurance against malpractice actions.[49] Note that these are entirely the product of "private" actions; there has been no public participation in either the initial decision to withhold the "privilege" of membership or to impose the disabilities that flow from nonmembership.

Of course if the matter is examined in terms of the impact on the individual, one immediately perceives that the "private" action operates exactly as though the doctor's license had been revoked or limited. Each applicant for county medical society membership has been accredited by the state as competent to practice his profession. Nonmembership substantially reduces the significance and value of that accreditation. If the state itself were summarily to limit the license previously granted, without informing the practitioner of charges against him or giving him a chance to defend himself, the arbitrariness of the procedure would at once provide grounds for judicial review. Yet essentially the same action by a medical society has been regarded by a number of courts as involving no problems because, in the judges' view, membership was only a "privilege." [50]

In a few states the problem has been attacked indirectly by statutory prohibition of discrimination by hospitals against any licensed physician;[51] this eliminates one of the serious losses that may arise from nonmembership, but leaves others untouched. Suggestions have been advanced that all states should enact laws requiring medical societies to utilize fair procedures in passing upon admissions and expulsions.[52] The question sought to be raised by the present discussion is whether new statutes are really necessary, or whether, instead, the courts could hold directly that the medical societies must act in accord with constitutional principles rather than with their own "private" conceptions of sound policy.

That question cannot be answered categorically. A decision of the California Supreme Court in 1945 is, however, suggestive of one possible approach. *James* v. *Marinship Corporation* [53] involved an effort by Negro employees to enjoin the corporation from discharging them. The corporation had entered into a contract with a certain union by which it agreed to employ only members of that union. The union at that time did not grant full membership privileges to Negroes, who thus, by the terms of the contract, became ineligible for continued employment. Contracts of this type have since been illegalized by federal law, but the *Marinship* case arose before any statutory prohibition had become applicable. In the California courts the corporation's position was very simple: Neither James nor anybody else had a legal right to be employed by it; it could hire and fire employees as it saw fit; in this instance, it had seen fit to hire only union members; it was exclusively the union's affair to decide whom it would accept as members; no "state action" was involved at any point, since neither of the contracting parties had derived authority from the state and neither one was seeking the state's help to enforce the agreement. The court was not impressed. The contract could not be given effect, the court declared, because it offended against the legal and moral principles that had long been recognized in California. As Chief Justice Gibson put the matter, "The discriminatory practices involved in this case are . . . contrary to the public policy of the United States and this State. . . . Although the constitutional provisions have been said to apply to state action rather than to private action, they nevertheless evidence a definite national policy against discrimination because of race or color. . . ."

The upshot of the case is that California employers remain free to hire and fire whom they want—unless the policy they adopt is clearly in conflict with a strongly declared public policy. Significantly, however, the court felt itself capable of deducing the state's policy from constitutional provisions that were not in terms applicable to private employers. By a parity of reasoning in the medical society problem here under discussion, the courts might deduce the public policy that qualified doctors should not be arbitrarily deprived of any part of their capacity to contribute to health preservation.

VI

If it is true that the courts, given a strong enough desire, can find ways of applying constitutional standards to what may traditionally have been deemed "private" action, the problem must be faced of how and where to draw the line. In a sense, private individuals constantly intrude upon "constitutional rights" of others. Employees are dismissed summarily and for indefensible reasons, parents interfere with their children's choice of marriage partners, racial or religious prejudice infects a boarding school's selection of new students. Unless courts are to transmute great masses of petty disagreement into the much nobler stuff of constitutional controversy, they must somehow differentiate between what is really private and what is really public.

One differentiation is, of course, purely quantitative. In Professor Sutherland's words, "Private government stays private so long as it affects only a few people." *

Numbers alone, however, will not provide the answer. True, the courts are not likely to be impressed by petty tyrannies. *De minimis non curat lex*—the law does not concern itself with trifles. Even quite spectacularly big things, however, may not be appro-

---

* See Arthur E. Sutherland, "Private Government and Public Policy," 41 *Yale Review* 405, at 418–419 (1952). The quoted words appear in the following context: "Private lawmaking is only a rather new name for something as old as mankind. . . . Patriarchs, masters of apprentices and servants, faculties of colleges have been making standing rules and spot decisions for centuries. Such small rulers throughout the history of the race have been judges, legislators, and executives all in one, without awakening much philosophical speculation as to the nature of their functions, and without many limits on any but the grosser aspects of their rule. . . . Private government stays private so long as it affects only a few people. . . . Statute books and writs and sheriffs are clumsy. Habeas corpus is ill-suited to Junior, locked in his room for rudeness to his mother. But as soon as a few can control many in matters the many deem important, the many demand control of their few private rulers by the greater many called government."

priate for judicial governance in the absence of explicit statutory guidance. If, for example, the sole large employer in a particular city abruptly decides to move his factory elsewhere ostensibly because of economic advantage but perhaps actually because he dislikes his present employees, his employees may feel that he has deprived them of the right to life, liberty, and the pursuit of happiness. But can courts undertake to make the large policy choices that are implicit in the interplay between economics and humanitarianism?

The underlying theory in this country has been that business decisions, being shaped by competitive influences, were likely to be of a sort the public at large would approve. Poor decisions, as Professor Galbraith has pointed out, were thought to be harmful to the businessman, rather than the public, while the businessman's good decisions helped everybody. When that conception prevailed, "state interference with business decisions was either redundant or positively harmful." [54] But as the assumption of competition has become less and less plausible, justification for an uncontrolled business judgment has become less and less clear.* Even so, it does not follow that the courts should undertake to maintain a revisory power over all business or other group judgments because they have an impact on individuals. Ill equipped as they are to make the

---

* Incidentally, in the United States at least, corporate power is little checked by the formerly urgent need of conforming to public opinion prevailing in the capital markets. In 1953 the National City Bank calculated that during the eight years 1946–1953 some 150 billion dollars had been spent in the United States for capital expenditures. Of this tremendous amount, only 6 per cent was raised by the issue of stock, while 64 per cent came from accumulated corporate earnings not distributed as dividends. A. A. Berle, Jr. comments on this in his *The 20th Century Capitalist Revolution* (1954), at pp. 37–40: ". . . this is representative of the real pattern of the twentieth century capitalism. The capital is there; and so is capitalism. The waning factor is the capitalist. . . . Not the public opinion of the market place with all the economic world from which to choose, but the directoral opinion of corporate managers as to the line of greatest opportunity with their own concern, now chiefly determines the application of risk capital. Major corporations in most instances do not seek capital. They form it themselves." See also the same author's "The Developing Law of Corporate Concentration," 19 *Univ. of Chicago Law Rev.* 639 (1952).

more difficult choices among competing values, the courts should perhaps leave the issues to be investigated and debated by the people's direct representatives, the legislature.[55]

Some choices, on the other hand, have clearly been made already. The Constitution speaks plainly, even if its words are addressed to the state rather than to so-called private interests. Courts can understand and, if they want, they can at least sometimes apply the specific prohibitions of the Constitution in cases involving what used to be thought of as private action. If a formula consistent with the past is needed, courts must continue to evolve theories of "state action" that will, as it were, infuse a trace of public responsibility into seemingly private decisions.

In all truth, however, the element of "state action" seems at bottom less important than three other elements to which attention must always be directed:

1. The clarity of conflict between privately-adopted policies on the one hand, and publicly-declared policies on the other;
2. The gravity, from a public point of view, of allowing a private disregard of constitutional principles to go unchecked;
3. The extent to which judicial relief can effectively end such a disregard without creating a fresh area of conflict.

A few hypothetical illustrations will perhaps clarify the suggestion.

Suppose, first, that a restaurant concessionaire at a federally-owned airport requires all employees to share in Sunday work, by rotating the hours of duty in a way that causes an equal distribution of this unwelcome assignment. An employee whose religious scruples prevent his doing any work on Sunday now sues to compel the employer to abandon this method of work assignment. He contends that its being maintained runs afoul of the First Amendment, which says that no law shall be made prohibiting "the free exercise" of religion. The court should dismiss the proceeding. The applicability of the constitutional provision is by no means clear. Moreover, the court is incapable of entering a useful order in a case of this type, for it could not (even if it desired to do so) construct a suitable set of work schedules and employee regulations for all the myriad businesses that flourish in a complex society.

Second, suppose that a campaign has been launched to obtain signatures to a petition for the recall of an official, in a state where this method of removal from office has been established by the state constitution. The proprietor of a small machine shop engaged exclusively in repair of office equipment owned by the state, informs his employees that he is a strong supporter of the criticized official, and that he would not wish to continue in his employ anyone who signed the recall petition. One of the four or five employees in the shop nevertheless does sign. He is at once discharged. He now sues to be reinstated, arguing that there has been action by his employer that nullifies the constitutional creation of the right to petition peacefully for the removal of a public officer. Moreover, he says, his freedom of speech and thought has been all but destroyed if he can be dismissed for exercising it. Here, the conflict between the constitutional objective and the employer's will is perfectly clear. Moreover, the court can grant effective relief by ordering the employee's reinstatement. The question, then, is whether the gravity of the matter warrants judicial intercession, even if, by stretching the point, an element of "state action" could be imported into the case. As to that, the fact that only one man is involved in the particular episode need not be wholly decisive, though perhaps it is indicative. If the episode seems to be isolated, probably the court would not deem it important; the ousted employee can presumably find another job, and employers as well as employees are entitled to have passionate (and, indeed, irrational) political attitudes. If this particular employer simply felt he could not work happily with an employee of different convictions, no public policy is served by making him do so—and, in fact, to force him to do so might have the effect of invading *his* freedom of thought and expression. On the other hand, if there were a basis for finding that employers with close business connections with the state were as a group acting concertedly to discourage their employees' political independence, the case would have entirely different dimensions even though there were still only one plaintiff before the court.

Third, suppose that each of the financial institutions used by a state as depository of its funds and each of the banks chartered by state or federal law were to require every applicant for employment to present what might be described as a family pedigree, with the seeming purpose of excluding from positions in the financial community all persons whose background is not "acceptable." This policy, privately adopted, would defeat the hope embodied in the Fourteenth Amendment that inequalities based on social status or family origin would receive no governmental encouragement. Might not a court, if this were challenged in suitable proceedings, say with some confidence that the conflict did apparently exist, that the public interest warranted upsetting the private policy *unless the policy could be justified on a functional ground that overcame the first impression of naked discrimination,* and that suitable relief could be framed to end the criticized practice without imposing any improper restraints upon the employers?

Objection may be voiced that this provides no clear doctrine to guide decisions. Everything is left to pragmatic evaluation, case by case, instead of being governed by a fully articulated philosophy of what may and what may not permissibly be done by private pressures.

The statement just made is true, but it is merely a description rather than a criticism. There is no good reason why every problem of law and government should be settled on the basis of abstract doctrine. In this field we are meeting new situations, facing new needs. Perhaps it is wise to approach them gingerly, proceeding from one case to another until through successive experiences a matured pattern may emerge.

Of course this does not mean that the legislature should leave all to the courts. Whenever and wherever general formulations seem feasible, they should be made. Thus, for example, both federal and state statutes explicitly prohibit employers from curbing their em-

ployees' freedom of expression concerning the desirability of union-
ization; statutes in numerous states forbid discriminatory employment practices; in other states, places of public accommodation
such as hotels, restaurants, and theaters are told by law that they
must not exclude persons because of their religion or race. But
legislatures may not have the needed time, insight, or inclination
to reinforce the Constitution at every spot where it can be undermined by private acts. When undermining comes to light in ways
of which courts are capable of taking cognizance, they should suitably use their powers to protect the constitutional structure.

Discovery that the cases involve problems of degree should cause
no alarm. If the preceding chapters have demonstrated anything,
they have surely demonstrated that few constitutional issues can
be presented in black and white terms. Most things in life that are
worth talking about are found, in the end, to be matters of degree.
The great judges are those who are most capable of discerning which
of the gradations make a genuine difference.

EPILOGUE

If the Constitution had remained, as it began, a repository of words often dry and sometimes unrevealing, nobody would care about it very deeply today. But, as these pages have sought to show, constitutional verbiage has been translated time and again into action, vibrantly touching the life of our times as it has touched the lives of other generations. Every nation, regardless of its governmental form, must in one fashion or another juggle the same social desiderata that have been glimpsed in the preceding discussion. Hence American constitutional experience holds meaningful lessons for other peoples—and, indeed, for Americans yet to come.

Looming large among these lessons is the vagueness of the Constitution itself as a bulwark against oppression. Schoolchildren learn at teacher's knee of their supreme good fortune in living under the Constitution. The Constitution, they are told, will protect them against all manner of wrongdoing hobgoblins. Alas, the Constitution contains few positive weapons with which to defend the people. Its clear prohibitions are few.* For the most part it is composed of generally framed principles whose content may change with the times.

The Fourth Amendment declares, for example, that there shall

---

* Examples of explicit protections are Article III, which defines the crime of treason, and forbids a conviction "unless on the Testimony of two Witnesses to the same overt Act, or on Confession in open Court"—thus blocking tyrannical liquidation of political opposition by the simple expedient of a denunciation; the Fifth Amendment, which forbids causing a person "to be twice put in jeopardy of life or limb" for the same criminal offense—though even this seemingly explicit prohibition can generate subtle differentiations that laymen sometimes fail to grasp; and Article I, which forbids the enactment of *ex post facto* laws in language sufficiently absolute to block any blatant attempt to rewrite criminal laws retroactively.

be no "unreasonable searches and seizures"; but it cannot define in advance what should be deemed reasonable. The First Amendment tells Congress that it must not abridge "the freedom of speech, or of the press"; but it does not tell how to distinguish between "freedom" and, by contrast, an abuse of freedom, subject to legislative restraint. The Fourteenth Amendment says that no person shall be deprived of his liberty "without due process of law"; but the words are expressive of a sentiment rather than of a command formulated certainly. All we can say of them is that presumably they do not leave the Legislature "free to make any process 'due process of law' by its mere will." [1]

How, then, do the amorphous principles of the Constitution acquire solidity and significance? The preceding chapters have illustrated that they do so only through the erratic, sometimes conflicting currents of judicial decision, and that they have little independent vitality.

The states, we have seen, may not ignore a defendant's need for legal counsel. They may not extort confessions. They may not use violent means to draw evidence from the body of a prisoner. Nor may a state forbid itinerant preaching by imposing restrictive license requirements; nor prohibit the distribution of pamphlets and leaflets, lest discarded papers litter the streets; nor suppress dissidence under the guise of preventing disturbances of the peace. All of these extremely varied conclusions are drawn from the simple words, "due process of law." But surely no one of those conclusions can be discerned nestling amidst those words, like a jewel in its matrix. They are not so much derived from the Constitution as built upon it.

The master builders—the judges—drew inspiration for the building design elsewhere than from the simple language of the forefathers. Sometimes they had recourse to history, which lays bare a record of evils against which the Constitution-makers presumably sought to create a shield. Sometimes, perhaps more often, the inspiration came from the judges' own perception of values.

Whose values were thus perceived? The judges disclaim any intent to be uninhibited subjectivists when they apply soft words to hard facts. They purport to recognize not their own inner hopes and fears, but, rather, the aspirations of society at large. When the words of the Constitution are not given precision by context and usage or by history or by binding precedents, then the judges must "gather meaning not from reading the Constitution but from reading life." [2]

Obviously, it is no easy task to read life. Procedural steps, for example, are declared by the Supreme Court to be unacceptable if they violate a "principle of justice so rooted in the traditions and conscience of our people as to be ranked as fundamental." [3] No simple instrument has yet been devised for accurately measuring the conscience of the people. Again the Court has announced that within the scope of the due process clause are those protections which constitute "the very essence of a scheme of ordered liberty." [4] No known chemistry enables the isolation of the very essence; no calculus draws the line between a liberty that is ordered and a liberty that is confined. "Due process," another Justice has written, "is that which comports with the deepest notions of what is fair and right and just" [5]—a comforting assurance that would be even more comforting if the judges possessed a tool for gauging which notions are deepest. Inevitably, in applying such broad formulations, no judge can wholly escape the promptings of personal predispositions.

None the less, despite its imprecision, the judging process works reasonably well as a means of formulating not purely subjective opinions, but social views that would otherwise be incoherent and indecisive. When socially defensible considerations clash for supremacy, as they have done in the areas to which this book has been devoted, somebody must make a choice. Somebody must declare which set of competing values will be accorded primacy in the context of concrete controversies. The judges choose for society, and then declare the choice as though the Constitution had dictated it.

And yet the choice is not entirely the judges' own. The judges seek to speak for society, not to it. The point can be seen clearly in the Eighth Amendment, which, among other things, forbids "cruel and unusual punishments." Not long ago as historians measure time, cutting off a wrongdoer's ears or branding his cheek or drawing and quartering him or, if he were a child of less than twelve years, hanging him, was not thought cruel or unusual. If any such punishment were now sought to be imposed, the Constitution would no doubt be thought to prohibit it—not because the punishment would revolt a judge, but because the judge would suppose the community as a whole would be revolted. By contrast, electrocuting a man or strangling him or suffocating him with poison fumes will not be held by any judge in this generation to be unconstitutionally cruel, regardless of his own feelings about the coldly planned execution of a fellow man. The punishment is not "cruel" because capital punishment is sustained by a dominant opinion; and it is not "unusual" because the dominant opinion has long been acted upon. We may guess that judges in some future generation will look upon death sentences with horror akin to that we all now experience when we learn of our ancestors' gory penology. Meanwhile, the constitutional language is applied not according to the individual judge's taste, but according to the taste of the community at large.

Because they are an oligarchy of aristocrats, uncontrolled by popular ballot, the judges may perhaps at times seem to be free agents. By no means is this in fact true. If judges were persistently to make choices that evoked social opposition rather than accord, their authority would quickly wane. Power is derived from and not merely imposed upon the persons affected by its exercise. A man "cannot command unless another obeys. He cannot control unless the social organization invests him with the apparatus of control." [6] The Supreme Court, unlike Zeus, cannot hurl thunderbolts of judgment without taking heed of the pervasive social judgment.

To be sure, the Supreme Court finally decides the particular case that comes before it; but it rarely decides an issue with finality unless its judgment either reflects an existing belief or successfully generates an enlightened understanding among those who care at all. The rules by which men are in the end governed, Justice Oliver Wendell Holmes long ago noted, are shaped less by abstruse propositions than by "the felt necessities of the time, the prevalent moral and political theories, intuitions of public policy, avowed or unconscious, even the prejudices which judges share with their fellowmen." [7] The matter may have been oversimplified by Peter Finley Dunne when he asserted that the Supreme Court follows the election returns. Beyond a doubt, however, the judges do constantly strive to strike a balance between their own personal "intuitions of public policy" and the sentiments prevailing in the surrounding society. It is no accident that "courts love liberty most when it is under pressure least." [8]

America can remain a land in which majorities of the moment are forbidden to tyrannize political minorities, a land in which what happens to an individual is deemed important to the community as a whole, a land in which means as well as ends are matters of moral concern, only if Americans want this kind of land. The Supreme Court cannot decree its preservation. The Supreme Court can only reflect the expressed or latent convictions of all those who in the aggregate are America.* Charles Evans Hughes, in a widely quoted aphorism he no doubt regretted having uttered, once declared that the Constitution is what the Supreme Court says. So it is. Back of the Supreme Court, however, providing the ethical current that animates its decisions, is the massive though sometimes formless body of public sentiment. In the end, the Constitution always becomes what the People of America will it to be. That is why liberty is everybody's business.

---

* In this light, there is cause for considerable concern in the findings of the polls of teen-age opinion made for fifteen years by the Purdue University Division of Educational Reference. Among the startling conclusions reached by the Purdue sociologists are that 83 per cent of the teen-age population approve wire tapping; 58 per cent accept the third degree as permissible police practice; 60 per cent endorse censorship of books, newspapers, and magazines; 25 per cent believe it proper for police to search homes without first obtaining a warrant. See H. H. Remmers and D. H. Radler, *The American Teenager* (1957), at pp. 16–17, and chap. 8, *passim.*

ACKNOWLEDGMENTS

Tokyo University invited me to lecture in 1958 on various problems of constitutional law encountered in both Japan and the United States, with special emphasis upon what the Japanese aptly call "fundamental human rights." Not having found a non-technical and yet accurate explanation of the relevant American constitutional law to which I could refer my Japanese students, I felt it necessary to prepare a fresh analysis of the present realities. This volume embodies, though in revised form and without reference to comparable foreign materials, some of the lectures originally intended to be read in Japan, where they have been published under the somewhat overwhelming title, "Kihonteki Jinken—Nichibei Kempô no Hikakuhâeki Kenkyû no Tame ni" (which, I am told, means "Fundamental Human Rights—Towards a Comparative Study of Japanese and American Constitutional Law").

They have been transformed into American Rights *in the hope that they may, for Americans, increase understanding of the content and the method of our own constitutional law. This understanding is not easily obtained. Many writings in this field, directed toward a professional audience, are necessarily complex and detailed. Some others, intended for laymen, are perhaps too simplified and generalized.*

I am particularly grateful to my colleague Professor Gerald Gunther, of Columbia Law School, who read much of the manuscript and made many valuable suggestions. I owe a great deal to his encouragement. Of course he is in no degree responsible for remaining shortcomings. I am also indebted to Professor Nobushige Ukai of Tokyo University, Professor Takeo Hayakawa of Kobe

University, and other former colleagues in Japan whose penetrating comments and questions clarified my own thinking and presentation.

Norman Holmes, of the New York Bar, a former student and present friend, assisted me in preparing Chapter 9. I am glad to acknowledge his help.

Walter Gellhorn

October 1959

NOTES

INTRODUCTION

[1] *Marbury* v. *Madison*, 1 Cranch 137 (U.S., 1803).

[2] For a useful discussion of the various types and theories of judicial review, as well as of the tribunals to which constitutional questions are referred, see Karl Loewenstein, *Political Power and the Governmental Process* (1958), Chap. VIII.

[3] Hand, *The Bill of Rights* (1958), at p. 11.

[4] Compare the statement of Justice Roberts in *United States* v. *Butler*, 297 U.S. 1 (1936): "When an act of Congress is appropriately challenged in the courts as not conforming to the constitutional mandate the judicial branch of the Government has only one duty,—to lay the article of the Constitution which is invoked beside the statute which is challenged and to decide whether the latter squares with the former."

CHAPTER 1

HABEAS CORPUS AND JUST PROCEDURES

[1] Zechariah Chafee, Jr., *How Human Rights Got into the Constitution* (1952), p. 51.

[2] See H. M. Hart, Jr. and H. Wechsler, *The Federal Courts and the Federal System* (1953), at p. 1238. And see Application of Yamashita, 327 U.S. 340 (1946).

[3] *Ex parte Milligan*, 4 Wall. 2 (U.S., 1866).

[4] *Sterling* v. *Constantin*, 287 U.S. 378, 397, 401 (1932). Cf. *Moyer* v. *Peabody*, 212 U.S. 78, 85 (1909).

[5] Charles Fairman, *Law of Martial Rule* (2d ed., 1943), p. 104; see also Frederick Wiener, *Martial Law: A Practical Manual* (1940), p. 19.

[6] *Hirabayashi* v. *United States*, 320 U.S. 81, 95 (1943).

[7] *Dow* v. *Johnson*, 100 U.S. 158, 169 (1879).

[8] *Duncan* v. *Kahanamoku*, 327 U.S. 304, at 330 (1946).

[9] *McNabb* v. *United States*, 318 U.S. 332, 347 (1943).

[10] Walter V. Schaefer, "Federalism and State Criminal Procedure," 70 *Harvard Law Rev.* 1, 26 (1956).

[11] For brief descriptions of habeas corpus, see Pendleton Howard, "Habeas Corpus," 7 *Encyclopedia of the Social Sciences* (1932) 233; Note, "Remedies Against the United States and Its Officials," 70 *Harvard Law Rev.* 827, 864 *et seq.* (1957). And see Note, "The Freedom Writ—The Expanding Use of Federal Habeas Corpus," 61 *Harvard Law Rev.* 657, at 662 (1948): "In de-

termining whether it must issue a writ of habeas corpus which will bring the petitioner before it or whether it may dismiss the petition as not affording grounds for habeas corpus relief, the court must take all allegations in the petition as true, however they may 'tax credulity,' except to the extent that, in the judgment of the court, they conflict with the records before it."

[12] *Sunal* v. *Large*, 332 U.S. 174 (1947).

[13] Act of February 5, 1867, c. 28, Sec. 1, 14 Stat. 385, 28 U.S.C. Sec. 2241 (c) (3)(1952).

[14] *Frank* v. *Mangum*, 237 U.S. 309, 331 (1915).

[15] *Louisiana ex rel. Francis* v. *Resweber*, 329 U.S. 459 (1947). Francis was in fact later executed.

[16] *Smith* v. *O'Grady*, 312 U.S. 321 (1941).

[17] Louis H. Pollak, "Proposals to Curtail Federal Habeas Corpus for State Prisoners: Collateral Attack on the Great Writ," 66 *Yale Law Journal* 50, 53 (1956). For other judicial statistics bearing on habeas corpus proceedings, see Walter V. Schaefer, "Federalism and State Criminal Procedure," 70 *Harvard Law Rev.* 1, 19, 23 (1956).

[18] Louis E. Goodman, "Use and Abuse of the Writ of Habeas Corpus," 7 Federal Rules Decisions 313, 316 (1947). And see also *Johnson* v. *United States,* 267 F. 2d 813 (9th Cir. 1959), in which Judge Pope objected to the burdens of hearing "outrageously frivolous appeals."

[19] Walter V. Schaefer, "Federalism and State Criminal Procedure," 70 *Harvard Law Rev.* 1, 22 (1956).

CHAPTER 2

SOME ASPECTS OF FAIRNESS IN CRIMINAL PROCEDURES

[1] 304 U.S. 458 (1938).

[2] Jerome N. Frank, "Today's Problems in the Administration of Criminal Justice," 15 Federal Rules Decisions 93, 101 (1953).

[3] "Aid for Indigent Litigants in the Federal Courts," 58 *Columbia Law Rev.* 832 (1958). And see also *Ellis* v. *United States*, 356 U.S. 674 (1958).

[4] *Powell* v. *Alabama*, 287 U.S. 45, 68–69 (1932).

[5] *Betts* v. *Brady*, 316 U.S. 455 (1942). And see also *Moore* v. *Michigan,* 355 U.S. 155 (1957). For a more extended treatment, see William M. Beaney, *The Right to Counsel in American Courts* (1955); and see also "The Indigent's Right to Counsel and the Rule of Prejudicial Error," 97 *Univ. of Pennsylvania Law Rev.* 855 (1949).

[6] The present scope of these ameliorative measures is described in *Equal Justice for the Accused,* a study published in 1959 by the Association of the Bar of the City of New York and the National Legal Aid and Defender Association.

[7] See *Griffin* v. *Illinois*, 351 U.S. 12 (1956); *Burns* v. *Ohio*, 360 U.S. 252 (1959). But compare *People* v. *Breslin*, 4 N.Y. 2d 73, 149 N.E. 2d 85 (1958), holding that the state is not required to furnish counsel to handle an appeal by indigents who had been convicted after a trial in which they had had legal representation. The case is criticized in 1959 *Duke Law Journal* 484.

[8] These suspicions were fully confirmed by a "Report on Lawlessness in Law Enforcement" made in 1931 as the fourth volume of the report of the National

Commission on Law Observance and Enforcement. This commission was appointed by President Hoover; its chairman was former Attorney General Wickersham. For a recent comprehensive discussion of the tangled motives that lead to confessions and that may render them unreliable, see O. John Rogge, *Why Men Confess* (1959).

[9] *Brown* v. *Mississippi*, 297 U.S. 278 (1936).

[10] Glanville Williams, *The Proof of Guilt* (1955), p. 13.

[11] *Watts* v. *Indiana*, 338 U.S. 49, 52 (1949). In that same case the Court remarked (p. 55): "Protracted, systematic and uncontrolled subjection of an accused to interrogation by the police for the purpose of eliciting disclosures or confessions is subversive of the accusatorial system. It is the inquisitorial system without its safeguards. For while under that system the accused is subjected to judicial interrogation, he is protected by the disinterestedness of the judge in the presence of counsel."

[12] *People* v. *Leyra*, 302 N.Y. 353, 98 N.E. 2d 553 (1951); *Leyra* v. *Denno*, 347 U.S. 556 (1954). Upon a later retrial that led to a finding of guilty, the appellate court set aside the conviction and ordered the prisoner's release because it felt that "the prosecution has produced not a single trustworthy bit of affirmative, independent evidence connecting defendant with the crime. . . ." *People* v. *Leyra*, 1 N.Y. 2d 199, 210, 134 N.E. 2d 475, 481 (1956). And see also *Spano* v. *New York*, 360 U.S. 315 (1959), setting aside as involuntary a confession obtained through "official pressure, fatigue and sympathy," without any use of physical force or threats.

[13] *McNabb* v. *United States*, 318 U.S. 332 (1943).

[14] The *McNabb* rule has been reinforced by later decisions, including one as recent as 1957. See *Upshaw* v. *United States*, 335 U.S. 410 (1948); *United States* v. *Carignan*, 342 U.S. 36 (1951); *Rettig* v. *United States*, 239 F. 2d 916 (D.C. Cir. 1956); *Mallory* v. *United States*, 354 U.S. 449 (1957). The last of these cases involved a detention of nine or ten hours before the accused was taken before a judicial officer as the Federal Rules of Criminal Procedure (Rule 5-a) require to be done "without unnecessary delay." The Court said (pp. 455–456): "We cannot sanction this extended delay, resulting in confession, without subordinating the general rule of prompt arraignment to the discretion of arresting officers in finding exceptional circumstances for its disregard. In every case where the police resort to interrogation of an arrested person and secure a confession, they may well claim, and quite sincerely, that they were merely trying to check on the information given by him. Against such a claim and the evil potentialities of the practice for which it is urged stands Rule 5-a as a barrier. Nor is there an escape from the constraint laid upon the police by that Rule in that two other suspects were involved for the same crime. Presumably, whomever the police arrest they must arrest on 'probable cause.' It is not the function of the police to arrest, as it were, at large and to use an interrogating process at police headquarters in order to determine whom they should charge before a committing magistrate on 'probable cause.'" For pertinent discussion, for and against the Supreme Court's position, see James F. Coakley, "Restrictions in the Law of Arrest," 52 *Northwestern Law Rev.* 2 (1957); Caleb Foote, "Safeguards in the Law of Arrest," *id.* at p. 16; Fred E. Inbau, "Restrictions in the Law of Interrogation and Confessions, *id.* at p. 77; Samuel S. Leibowitz, "Safeguards in the Law of Interrogation and Confessions," *id.* at p. 86. And see also Fred E. Inbau, "The Confession

Dilemma in the United States Supreme Court," 43 *Illinois Law Rev.* 442 (1948).

[15] *Brown* v. *Allen*, 344 U.S. 443 (1953); *Gallegos* v. *Nebraska*, 342 U.S. 55 (1951). And see also *People* v. *Alex*, 265 N.Y. 192, 192 N.E. 289 (1934) (delay in arraignment is simply one factor to take into account in deciding whether confession was voluntary).

[16] *Fikes* v. *Alabama*, 352 U.S. 191 (1957). And compare *Malinski* v. *New York*, 324 U.S. 401 (1945).

[17] James E. Hogan and Joseph M. Snee, S.J., "The McNabb-Mallory Rule: Its Rise, Rationale and Rescue," 47 *Georgetown Law Journal* 1, 32 (1958).

[18] *Carroll* v. *United States*, 267 U.S. 132 (1924); *Brinegar* v. *United States*, 338 U.S. 160 (1929) ("This does not mean . . . that every traveler along the public highways may be stopped and searched at the officers' whim, caprice or mere suspicion"). And see *United States* v. *DiRe*, 332 U.S. 581, 595 (1948) (A person was arrested on mere suspicion and without good cause. When he was searched, evidence of crime was found. But the Court refused to allow the evidence to be used. "We have had frequent occasion to point out that a search is not made legal by what it turns up. In law it is good or bad when it starts and does not change character from its success.")

[19] *McDonald* v. *United States*, 335 U.S. 451, 455 (1948).

[20] Monrad G. Paulsen, "Safeguards in the Law of Search and Seizure," 52 *Northwestern Univ. Law Rev.* 65 (1957).

[21] *United States* v. *Rabinowitz*, 339 U.S. 56 (1950), discussed in 36 *Cornell Law Quarterly* 125 (1950). Compare, however, *Harris* v. *United States*, 331 U.S. 145 (1945): Defendant was arrested while in his apartment, charged with having obtained money as a result of having sent a forged check through the mails. The officers searched all of his rooms for genuine checks which had presumably furnished the model for the forgery. While searching, they found some government documents that the defendant illegally possessed. He was prosecuted for this illegal possession, and the discovered evidence was used against him. The Court said that the search and seizure were not invalid.

[22] *Kremen* v. *United States*, 353 U.S. 346 (1957).

[23] See *Weeks* v. *United States*, 232 U.S. 383 (1914); *Silverthorne Lumber Co.* v. *United States*, 251 U.S. 385, 392 (1919). Note, however, that the exclusionary rule is not operative if the evidence was seized by persons not officials of the federal government, and not in league with it. The present rule requires, in effect, that there be an agency relationship between searcher and government. But compare *Benanti* v. *United States*, 355 U.S. 96 (1957). This view has been effectively criticized in Note, "Judicial Control of Illegal Search and Seizure," 58 *Yale Law Journal* 144, 159–160 (1948). But see also *Rea* v. *United States*, 350 U.S. 214 (1956): The defendant was charged with violation of a *state* law concerning narcotics possession. The evidence had been acquired by a *federal* agent acting under an invalid search warrant. The defendant succeeded in enjoining the federal agent from turning over the evidence to the state, or testifying about it. The Federal rules governing searches and seizures, said the Court, "are drawn for innocent and guilty alike. They prescribe standards for law enforcement. They are designed to protect the privacy of the citizen, unless the strict standards set for searches and seizures are satisfied. That policy is defeated if the federal agent can flout them and use the fruits of his unlawful act either in federal or state proceedings."

[24] *Wolf* v. *Colorado*, 338 U.S. 25 (1949). See Francis A. Allen, "The Wolf

Case: Search and Seizure, Federalism, and the Civil Liberties," 45 *Illinois Law Rev.* 1 (1950).

[25] For an example of a large award of damages, see *Bucher* v. *Krause*, 200 F. 2d 576 (7th Cir. 1952), certiorari denied, 345 U.S. 997 (1953). For further discussion of the general ineffectiveness of penal and tort sanctions in this area, see Monrad G. Paulsen, "Safeguards in the Law of Search and Seizure," 52 *Northwestern Univ. Law Rev.* 65, at 72–76 (1957), and references there given.

[26] *People* v. *Cahan*, 44 Cal. 2d 434 (1955). The court said (p. 434): "We have been compelled to reach the conclusion because other remedies have completely failed to secure compliance with the constitutional provisions on the part of the police with the attendant result that the courts under the old rule have been constantly required to participate in and in effect condone, the lawless activities of law enforcement officers." See also E. L. Barrett, "Exclusion of Evidence Obtained by Illegal Searches—A Comment on *People* v. *Cahan*," 43 *California Law Rev.* 565 (1955). For criticism of the exclusionary rule, see Virgil W. Peterson, "Restrictions in the Law of Search and Seizure," 52 *Northwestern Law Rev.* 46 (1957).

[27] This view was forcefully expressed by Justice Jackson in his dissenting opinion in *Brinegar* v. *United States*, 338 U.S. 160 (1949).

[28] *Rochin* v. *California*, 342 U.S. 165 (1952).

[29] 352 U.S. 432 (1957).

[30] The California Supreme Court has subsequently held that tests of blood taken in a medically approved manner from an accused person without his consent while he is conscious and protesting, may be received in evidence. The taking "did not constitute brutality or shock the conscience"; hence, *Rochin* v. *California* was not applicable. The compulsory blood sampling did not violate the constitutional privilege against self-incrimination, which relates only to testimonial compulsion and not to objective evidence. *People* v. *Duroncelay*, 48 California 2d 766, 312 Pacific 2d 690 (1957).

[31] Dissenting in *Olmstead* v. *United States*, 277 U.S. 438, 478 (1928).

[32] *Olmstead* v. *United States*, note 31 above.

[33] See *Nardone* v. *United States*, 302 U.S. 379 (1937); *Nardone* v. *United States*, 308 U.S. 338 (1939). Some states, however, permit wire tapping in limited circumstances. Evidence obtained in that fashion has been admitted in state criminal proceedings, and its use has been sustained. See *Schwartz* v. *Texas*, 344 U.S. 199 (1952); *People* v. *Stemmer*, 298 N.Y. 728, affirmed by an equally divided court, 336 U.S. 963 (1949). Compare, however, *Benanti* v. *United States*, 355 U.S. 96 (1957).

[34] See *Goldman* v. *United States*, 316 U.S. 129 (1942).

[35] See *On Lee* v. *United States*, 343 U.S. 747 (1952).

[36] *Irvine* v. *California*, 347 U.S. 128 (1954).

[37] *Brinegar* v. *United States*, 338 U.S. 160, at pp. 180–181 (1949) (dissenting).

[38] Quoted by Sir James Fitzjames Stephen, in *A History of the Criminal Law of England* (1883), vol. 1, p. 442 note.

[39] For an extensive and very effective treatment of this matter, see Frederick J. Ludwig, "The Role of the Prosecutor in a Fair Trial," 41 *Minnesota Law Rev.* 602 (1957).

[40] Robert H. Jackson, in an address before a conference of United States Attorneys, reported in 24 *Journal of American Judicature Society* 18, 19 (1940).

[41] The comment is quoted from a letter by the Attorney-in-Charge, Criminal Courts Branch of New York Legal Aid Society. See Note, "The Right to a Speedy Criminal Trial," 57 *Columbia Law Rev.* 846, 867 (1957).

[42] Cockburn, C. J., quoted more extensively in Professor Ludwig's article, cited in note 39 above, at p. 613.

[43] *Berger* v. *United States*, 295 U.S. 78 (1935). See also *People* v. *Stroble*, 36 Cal. 2d. 615, 226 P. 2d 330 (1951), affirmed 343 U.S. 181 (1952). For a fuller treatment of this matter, see "The Nature and Consequences of Forensic Misconduct in the Prosecution of a Criminal Case," 54 *Columbia Law Rev.* 946 (1954).

[44] See Arthur L. Goodhart, "Newspapers and Contempt of Court in the English Law," 48 *Harvard Law Rev.* 885 (1935). And see also *Rex* v. *Bolam*, 93 Sol. J. 220 (1949).

[45] A leading case, invalidating a state attempt to copy the British approach, is *Baltimore Radio Show, Inc.* v. *State*, 193 Maryland 300 (1949), certiorari denied 338 U.S. 912 (1950). And see "Free Speech versus Fair Trial in the English and American Law of Contempt by Publication," 17 *Univ. of Chicago Law Rev.* 540 (1950); "Controlling Press and Radio Influence on Trials," 63 *Harvard Law Rev.* 840 (1950); "Free Press and Fair Trial—A Conflict," 39 *Minnesota Law Rev.* 431 (1955); "Due Process for Whom—Newspaper or Defendant?" 4 *Stanford Law Rev.* 105 (1951); Frederick J. Ludwig, "Journalism and Justice in Criminal Law," 28 *St. John's Law Rev.* 197 (1954).

CHAPTER 3

THE FREEDOM TO SPEAK FREELY

[1] The quoted words come from a famous dissenting opinion of Justice Holmes, in *Abrams* v. *United States*, 250 U.S. 616, at 630 (1919).

[2] *Thomas* v. *Collins*, 323 U.S. 516, at 545 (1945). And see *Staub* v. *City of Baxley*, 355 U.S. 313 (1958). See also "Validity of Statutes and Ordinances Requiring the Licensing of Union Organizers," 70 *Harvard Law Rev.* 1271 (1957).

[3] *Poulos* v. *New Hampshire*, 345 U.S. 395, at 405 (1953).

[4] *Niemotko* v. *Maryland*, 340 U.S. 268 (1951).

[5] That was essentially the holding in *Cox* v. *New Hampshire*, 312 U.S. 569 (1940), sustaining the validity of a license (for street or park meetings) that could be denied only for "considerations of time, place and manner so as to conserve the public convenience."

[6] *Hague* v. *Congress of Industrial Organizations*, 307 U.S. 496 (1939).

[7] *Saia* v. *New York*, 334 U.S. 558 (1948). But compare *Kovacs* v. *Cooper*, 336 U.S. 77 (1949), which held valid an ordinance that permitted a conviction for operation of a sound truck emitting "loud and raucous" noises.

[8] *Lovell* v. *Griffin*, 303 U.S. 444 (1938).

[9] *Kunz* v. *New York*, 340 U.S. 290 (1951).

[10] *Boyd* v. *United States*, 116 U.S. 616, 635 (1885).

[11] *Chaplinsky* v. *New Hampshire*, 315 U.S. 568, 571–572 (1942).

[12] *Cantwell* v. *Connecticut*, 310 U.S. 296, 310 (1940).

[13] *Lovell* v. *Griffin*, 303 U.S. 444 (1938); *Jamison* v. *Texas*, 318 U.S. 413 (1942);

Schneider v. State, 308 U.S. 147 (1939). Compare *Valentine* v. *Chrestenson*, 316 U.S. 52 (1942).

[14] *Martin* v. *Struthers*, 319 U.S. 141 (1943).

[15] Zechariah Chafee, Jr., *Free Speech in the United States* (1946), at p. 406. Recently the Supreme Court has upheld an ordinance that forbade the distribution of *commercial* information (as distinct from religious or political ideas) on a door-to-door basis. *Breard* v. *Alexandria*, 341 U.S. 622 (1951).

[16] *Whitney* v. *California*, 274 U.S. 357, at 377 (1927). And see also Paul A. Freund, *On Understanding the Supreme Court* (1949), at pp. 27–28.

[17] See *Fowler* v. *Rhode Island*, 345 U.S. 67 (1953).

[18] Compare *DeJonge* v. *Oregon*, 299 U.S. 353 (1937).

[19] *Feiner* v. *New York*, 340 U.S. 315 (1951).

[20] *Sellers* v. *Johnson*, 163 F. 2d 877 (8th Cir., 1947), certiorari denied, 332 U.S. 851 (1948).

[21] *Terminiello* v. *Chicago*, 337 U.S. 1, 4 (1949).

[22] Bertrand Russell, *Authority and the Individual* (1949), at p. 25.

[23] *Selected Literary and Political Papers and Addresses of Woodrow Wilson* (1926), Vol. II, p. 333.

[24] For discussion of these matters, see Karl Loewenstein, "Legislative Control of Political Extremism in European Democracies," 38 *Columbia Law Rev.* 725, 752–755 (1938); "Freedom of Speech and Assembly: The Problem of the Hostile Audience," 49 *Columbia Law Rev.* 1118 (1949).

[25] Jay Murphy, "Free Speech and the Interest in Local Law and Order," 1 *Journal of Public Law* 40, 69 (1952).

[26] See Report of the Commission on Freedom of the Press, *A Free and Responsible Press* (1947), at p. 37.

[27] *Thornhill* v. *Alabama*, 310 U.S. 88 (1940).

[28] For useful discussions, see Joseph Tanenhaus, "Picketing—Free Speech," 38 *Cornell Law Quarterly* 1 (1952); Archibald Cox, "Strikes, Picketing and the Constitution," 4 *Vanderbilt Law Rev.* 574 (1951); "Picketing and Free Speech," 26 *New York Univ. Law Rev.* 183 (1951).

[29] *Milk Wagon Drivers* v. *Meadowmoor Dairies*, 312 U.S. 287 (1941). And see also *Youngdahl* v. *Rainfair, Inc.*, 355 U.S. 131 (1957).

[30] *Carpenters and Joiners Union* v. *Ritter's Cafe*, 315 U.S. 722 (1942). Compare *Bakery and Pastry Drivers Union* v. *Wohl*, 315 U.S. 769 (1942), holding that picketing was constitutionally protected so long as the union members were simply following the subject matter of their dispute, and were not seeking to embroil a noncombatant in their controversy. Mr. Tanenhaus, in the article cited in note 28 above, says (at p. 19) that these two cases reflect the Court's feeling that a state does have power "to prevent pickets from levelling economic pressure against third parties having no close relationship to a particular controversy. At the same time [the Court] denied the power to draw the circle of economic competition so narrowly as to insulate parties vitally associated with a labor controversy from the pressures of the picket line."

[31] *Giboney* v. *Empire Storage & Ice Co.*, 336 U.S. 490 (1949).

[32] *International Brotherhood of Teamsters* v. *Vogt, Inc.*, 354 U.S. 284 (1957).

[33] Public Law 86-257, 73 Stat. 519 (1959).

[34] Learned Hand, *The Spirit of Liberty* (1952), at pp. 189–190.

CHAPTER 4

FREE SPEECH AND THE COMMUNIST CONSPIRACY

[1] The quoted words are from the opinion of Judge Learned Hand, in *United States* v. *Associated Press*, 52 F. Supp. 362, 372 (S.D. N.Y., 1943).

[2] For a description of the massive body of American federal legislation that deals in one way or another with actual or supposed threats to national security, see Arthur E. Sutherland, Jr., "Freedom and Internal Security," 64 *Harvard Law Rev.* 383, 386–388 (1951); Robert E. Cushman, *Civil Liberties in the United States* (1956), at pp. 393–440. For material on legislation in the several states, see Walter Gellhorn, *The States and Subversion* (1952), at pp. 393–440. Some of the state laws have been rendered inoperative by *Pennsylvania* v. *Nelson*, 350 U.S. 497 (1956), which held that federal anti-sedition legislation precludes the enforcement of a state statute dealing with acts of sedition against the federal government. Compare, however, *Uphaus* v. *Wyman*, 360 U.S. 72 (1959), in which the Court made clear that a state still could proceed with prosecutions for sedition against the state itself.

Excellent general discussions in brief compass will be found in Jack W. Peltason, "Constitutional Liberty and Seditious Activity" (Freedom Agenda Pamphlet, 1954); Walter Millis, "Individual Freedom and the Common Defense" (Fund for the Republic Pamphlet, 1957).

[3] See *Weiman* v. *Updegraff*, 344 U.S. 183 (1952): "There can be no doubt about the consequences visited upon a person excluded from public employment on disloyalty grounds. In the view of the community the stain is a deep one; indeed it has become a badge of infamy."

[4] See, e.g., *Peters* v. *Hobby*, 349 U.S. 331 (1955); *Cole* v. *Young*, 351 U.S. 536 (1956); *Service* v. *Dulles*, 354 U.S. 363 (1957); *Schware* v. *Board of Bar Examiners*, 353 U.S. 232 (1957); *Konigsberg* v. *State Bar of California*, 353 U.S. 252 (1957); *Harmon* v. *Brucker*, 355 U.S. 579 (1958); *Greene* v. *McElroy*, 360 U.S. 474 (1959); *Parker* v. *Lester*, 227 F. 2d 708 (9th Cir., 1955). The *Cole* case, above, involved a minor inspector in the employ of the Food and Drug Administration; the Court held that the loyalty program was not suitably applied to him under then existing statutes, because his position was not of a "sensitive" character and had nothing to do with the nation's security. The chairman of the House Committee on Un-American Activities promptly declared that this decision would open up the entire government "to the infiltration of our mortal enemies." But now, several years after the decision was announced, no such dire result has yet appeared, and Congress has not acted on legislative proposals to revitalize the program the Supreme Court had limited.

For extensive studies of these matters see Ralph S. Brown, Jr., *Loyalty and Security* (1958); Eleanor Bontecou, *The Federal Loyalty-Security Program* (1953); *Report of the Special Committee on the Federal Loyalty-Security Program, Association of the Bar of the City of New York* (1956); *Commission on Government Security*, Report (Loyd Wright, ch., 1957). And see also Alan Westin, "The Constitution and Loyalty Programs" (Freedom Agenda Pamphlet, 1954).

[5] 54 Stat. 671, 18 U.S.C.A. sec. 2385.

⁶ The case against eighteen members of the Socialist Workers Party (popularly known as "Trotskyites") resulted in their convictions; but the Supreme Court declined to review the case. *Dunne* v. *United States*, 138 F. 2d 137 (8th Cir., 1943), certiorari denied, 320 U.S. 790 (1943). The trial of the alleged pro-Nazis lasted for nearly eight months during 1944. Then, before decision, the trial judge died. No retrial occurred, and the indictment was later dismissed for failure to prosecute. *United States* v. *McWilliams*, 163 F. 2d 695 (D.C. Cir., 1947).

⁷ 341 U.S. 494 (1951).

⁸ *Schenck* v. *United States*, 249 U.S. 47 (1919).

⁹ *Whitney* v. *California*, 274 U.S. 357 (1927).

¹⁰ In *Dennis* v. *United States*, 341 U.S. 494, at 507 (1951), Chief Justice Vinson said: "Although no case subsequent to Whitney and Gitlow has expressly overruled the majority opinion in those cases, there is little doubt that subsequent opinions have inclined toward the Holmes-Brandeis rationale." He cited nine examples, to which others could readily be added.

¹¹ Thus, for example, as a perceptive writer has suggested, advocacy of walking on the grass in violation of an ordinance intended to protect the beauty of the public parks, would require a higher degree of probability of occurrence of the evil than would be needed when the evil apprehended is a very grave one, like overthrow of the government. Elliot L. Richardson, "Freedom of Expression and the Function of Courts," 65 *Harvard Law Rev.* 1, 19 (1951).

¹² There were five separate opinions in that case. Chief Justice Vinson wrote the main opinion, in which Justices Reed, Burton, and Minton joined—one less than a majority of the entire Court. Justices Frankfurter and Jackson wrote separate concurring opinions, while Justices Black and Douglas wrote separate dissenting opinions. Justice Clark did not participate in the decision because he had been Attorney General when the case had been initiated.

¹³ See *Herndon* v. *Lowry*, 301 U.S. 242 (1937), reversing 182 Ga. 582 (1936). And compare L. Hand, C.J., in *United States* v. *Dennis*, 138 F. 2d 201, 212 (2d Cir., 1950): "We can never forecast with certainty; all prophecy is a guess, but the reliability of a guess decreases with the length of the future which it seeks to penetrate."

¹⁴ For criticism of the "bad tendency" test in speech cases, see Zechariah Chafee, Jr., *Free Speech in the United States* (1946), pp. 388–398; and see also Richardson, cited note 11 above, at pp. 14–15.

¹⁵ 354 U.S. 298 (1957).

¹⁶ *Gitlow* v. *New York*, 268 U.S. 652, 673 (1925) (dissenting opinion).

¹⁷ Information about these matters is derived from *American Civil Liberties Union Weekly Bulletin* No. 1927, December 9, 1957, p. 1. But compare *Bary* v. *United States*, 248 F. 2d 201 (10th Cir., 1957), a case in which the appellate court felt the evidence against seven Colorado leaders of the Communist Party did meet the tests laid down in *Yates*. Somewhat similar holdings occurred in *Wellman* v. *United States*, 253 F. 2d 601 (6th Cir. 1958), and *Sentner* v. *United States*, 253 F. 2d 310 (8th Cir. 1958). Prosecutions were found to be groundless, however, in *United States* v. *Jackson*, 257 F. 2d 830 (2d Cir. 1958), *United States* v. *Kuzma*, 249 F. 2d 619 (3d Cir. 1957), and *Fujimoto* v. *United States*, 251 F. 2d. 342 (9th Cir. 1958).

See also Benjamin Ginzburg, *Rededication to Freedom* (1959).

¹⁸ But cf. Learned Hand, *The Bill of Rights* (1958), at p. 59, expressing "doubt

that the [clear and present danger] doctrine will persist"—or deserves to do so.
Supreme Court Justice William O. Douglas, in his book *The Right of the People* (1958), reflects a very strongly opposed view. He declares that "The First Amendment does not say there is freedom of expression provided the talk is not 'dangerous.' It does not say there is freedom of expression provided an utterance has no tendency to subvert. It does not put free speech and freedom of the press in the category of housing, sanitation, hours of work, factory conditions and the like. . . . All notions of regulations and restraint by government are absent from the First Amendment. For it says in words that are unambiguous, 'Congress shall make no law . . . abridging freedom of speech, or of the press.'"

[19] 64 Stat. 987, 50 U.S.C.A. sec. 781. The statute is discussed in Arthur E. Sutherland, Jr., "Freedom and Internal Security," 64 *Harvard Law Rev.* 383 (1951). Perhaps the most detailed examination of the legal problems raised by this enactment appears in "The Internal Security Act of 1950," 51 *Columbia Law Rev.* 606 (1951).

[20] *Winters* v. *New York*, 333 U.S. 507 (1948); and see also *Connally* v. *General Construction Co.*, 269 U.S. 385, 391 (1925); *United States* v. *L. Cohen Grocery Co.*, 255 U.S. 81 (1921). And see "Due Process Requirements of Definiteness in Statutes," 62 *Harvard Law Rev.* 77 (1948).

[21] *Musser* v. *Utah*, 333 U.S. 95 (1948).

[22] *Communist Party U.S.A.* v. *Subversive Activities Control Board*, 351 U.S. (1956). The problem of "professional witnesses" who have made a sort of career out of testifying before legislative committees, administrative bodies, and courts in matters involving Communists, has occasioned much discussion. Law enforcement officials have stanchly defended the use of paid informers, though there are many historic reasons for placing somewhat less than complete reliance upon their testimony. In some instances courts have felt it necessary to upset convictions because of the dubious quality of the witnesses. See, e.g., *Mesarosh* v. *United States*, 352 U.S. 1 (1956); and see also, for an example from a somewhat earlier period, *Colyer* v. *Skeffington*, 265 Fed. 17 (D. Mass., 1920). That the problem is by no means a new one is shown by Austin P. Evans, "Hunting Subversion in the Middle Ages," 33 Speculum (*Journal of Medieval Studies*) 1 (1958).

[23] *Communist Party* v. *Subversive Activities Control Board*, reported in 87 Wash. Law. Rep. 785 (Aug. 3, 1959).

[24] The President's views are set forth in his Veto Message, printed in the *Congressional Record*, 81st Congress, 2d Session, September 22, 1950, pp. 15629–31.

[25] 68 Stat. 775, ch. 886.

[26] See *Calder* v. *Bull*, 3 Dallas 386 (U.S., 1798).

[27] See *United States* v. *Lovett*, 328 U.S. 303 (1946). And see also *Cummings* v. *Missouri*, 4 Wall. 277, 323 (U.S., 1867): "A bill of attainder is a legislative act which inflicts punishment without judicial trial."

[28] See W. Gellhorn, *The States and Subversion* (1952), at pp. 404–405. For a further compilation, see Senate Document No. 97, 85th Congress, 2d Session, p. 149.

[29] The California statute, aimed at Communists specifically and other revolutionary parties generically, was held to be unconstitutional in *Communist*

Party v. *Peek*, 20 Cal. 2d 536, 127 P. 2d 889 (1942). A somewhat similar statute was, however, sustained as valid in Arkansas. *Field* v. *Hall*, 201 Ark. 77, 143 S.W. 2d 567 (1940). For discussion of the questions raised, see "May the States, by Statute, Bar Subversive Groups from the Ballot?" 25 *Notre Dame Lawyer* 319 (1950), and "The Communist Party and the Ballot," 1 Bill of Rights Review 286 (1941). See also *Washington ex rel. Huff* v. *Reeves*, 5 Wash. 2d 637, 106 P. 2d 729, 130 A.L.R. 1465 (1940).

³⁰ *Dennis* v. *United States*, 341 U.S. 494 (1951).

CHAPTER 5

THE FREEDOM NOT TO SPEAK

¹ Leo Pfeffer, *The Liberties of an American* (1956), p. 88.

² *West Virginia State Board of Education* v. *Barnette*, 319 U.S. 624 (1943).

³ *Minersville District* v. *Gobitis*, 310 U.S. 586 (1940).

⁴ *American Communications Association* v. *Douds*, 339 U.S. 382 (1950).

⁵ *Garner* v. *Los Angeles Board*, 341 U.S. 716 (1951).

⁶ *Wieman* v. *Updegraff*, 344 U.S. 183 (1952).

⁷ See W. Gellhorn, *The States and Subversion* (1952), at pp. 408, 410 for description of these statutes.

⁸ *Ibid.*, at p. 363.

⁹ For discussion of these licensing matters, see W. Gellhorn, *Individual Freedom and Governmental Restraints* (1956), at pp. 129 ff.

¹⁰ In two recent cases the Supreme Court has held, by 5-to-4 votes, that specific questions addressed to public employees (a schoolteacher and a subway conductor, respectively) were relevant to inquiries into their fitness. See *Beilan* v. *Board of Education*, 357 U.S. 399 (1958), and *Lerner* v. *Casey*, 357 U.S. 468 (1958). In both instances the questions had to do with the employees' alleged Communist connections. The Court was extremely careful, however, to point out that the questions in the particular setting in which they were asked were relevant to a suitably conducted inquiry into an employee's qualifications. The cases did not sanction a "dragnet" requirement that everybody disclose his political views.

¹¹ Lord Chancellor Hardwicke, 1742, quoted in *Wigmore on Evidence*, vol. 8, sec. 2192 (3d ed., 1940).

¹² *Ullman* v. *United States*, 350 U.S. 422, at 439n (1956).

¹³ Erwin N. Griswold, *The Fifth Amendment Today* (1955), p. 7.

¹⁴ *Ullmann* v. *United States*, 350 U.S. 422, 428 (1956). And see *Feldman* v. *United States*, 322 U.S. 487, 489 (1944): The guarantee against testimonial compulsion "was added to the original Constitution in the conviction that too high a price may be paid even for the unhampered enforcement of the criminal law and that, in its attainment, other social objectives of a free society should not be sacrificed."

¹⁵ *Wigmore on Evidence*, vol. 8, sec. 2251, at 309 (3d ed., 1940). Dean Wigmore also remarks that "The real objection is that any system of administration which permits the prosecution to trust habitually to compulsory self-disclosure as a source of proof must itself suffer morally thereby. The inclina-

tion develops to rely mainly upon such evidence, and to be satisfied with an incomplete investigation of other sources. The exercise of the power to extract answers begets a forgetfulness of the just limitations of the power."

Prof. Bernard D. Meltzer, in "Required Records, the McCarran Act, and the Privilege against Self-Incrimination," 18 *Univ. of Chicago Law Rev.* 687, 692–693 (1951), subscribes to a more sporting theory than Dean Wigmore's. He says, in effect, that we simply do not think it fair to make a man join in producing his own ruination. Thus, he expresses belief that the rule against self-incrimination is "perhaps a reflection of a humane attitude which saves even the guilty from a harsh choice among perjury, recalcitrance, or confession. . . ."

[16] See, e.g., *Twining* v. *New Jersey*, 211 U.S. 78, 91 (1908): the privilege is "a protection to the innocent though a shelter to the guilty, and a safeguard against heedless, unfounded or tyrannical prosecutions."

[17] *Slochower* v. *Board of Higher Education*, 350 U.S. 551, 557–558 (1956). In another case, *Halperin* v. *United States*, 353 U.S. 391 (1957), the Court suggested (at p. 422) that "the nature of the tribunal which subjects the witness to questioning bears heavily on what inferences can be drawn from the plea of the Fifth Amendment. Innocent men are more likely to plead the privilege in secret proceedings, where they testify without advice of counsel and without opportunity for cross-examination, than in open court proceedings, where cross-examination and judicially supervised procedure provide safeguards for the establishing of the whole, as against the possibility of merely partial, truth." The same suggestion was made earlier by Dean Griswold in *The Fifth Amendment Today* (1955), at p. 62.

With the Slochower case may be compared *Beilan* v. *Board of Education*, 357 U.S. 399 (1958), and *Lerner* v. *Casey*, 357 U.S. 468 (1958), where the court sustained dismissals of employees who had refused to answer questions. In those instances, however, the questions were deemed to be relevant to the issue of the employee's fitness to occupy his post; and refusal to answer was regarded as exhibiting a lack of candor that bore on his qualifications for employment.

A recent study by Professor Daniel H. Pollitt of cases involving so-called "Fifth Amendment Communists" has shown persuasively that in a large percentage of instances persons who claimed the privilege against self-incrimination were not in fact hiding guilt. See Pollitt, "The Fifth Amendment Plea before Congressional Committees Investigating Subversion," 106 *Univ. of Pennsylvania Law Rev.* 1117 (1958).

[18] *Blau* v. *United States*, 340 U.S. 159 (1953).

[19] *Hoffman* v. *United States*, 341 U.S. 479, 486–487 (1951). For discussion of the lower federal courts' liberality in applying the quoted proposition, see "The Privilege against Self-Incrimination in the Federal Courts," 71 *Harvard Law Rev.* 1454 (1957).

[20] *Hale* v. *Henkel*, 201 U.S. 43 (1905); *United States* v. *White*, 322 U.S. 694 (1944).

[21] *Wilson* v. *United States*, 221 U.S. 361 (1910); *Essgee Co.* v. *United States*, 262 U.S. 151 (1922).

[22] *United States* v. *White*, 322 U.S. 694 (1944). Compare, however, *Curcio* v. *United States*, 354 U.S. 118 (1957); *Nilva* v. *United States*, 352 U.S. 385 (1956).

[23] *United States* v. *Murdock*, 284 U.S. 141, 148 (1931); *Emspak* v. *United States*, 349 U.S. 190 (1955); *Bart* v. *United States*, 349 U.S. 219 (1955).

[24] *Rogers* v. *United States*, 340 U.S. 367 (1951).

[25] Erwin N. Griswold, *The Fifth Amendment Today* (1955), p. 23.

[26] For discussion of the statutory developments, see Robert G. Dixon, Jr., "The Fifth Amendment and Federal Immunity Statutes," 22 *George Washington Law Rev.* 447 (1954). One of the earlier immunity statutes was declared invalid because it "would not prevent the use of his testimony to search out other testimony to be used in evidence against him or his property in a criminal proceeding. . . ." *Counselman* v. *Hitchcock*, 142 U.S. 547 (1892). This defect was cured by later statutes that foreclosed any prosecution whatsoever, no matter what might be the source of the evidence the prosecutor might later be able to dig up, for any offense concerning which the witness had testified. *Brown* v. *Walker*, 161 U.S. 591 (1896).

[27] *Ullmann* v. *United States*, 350 U.S. 422 (1956). The holding is consistent with the earlier case of *Brown* v. *Walker*, 161 U.S. 591 (1896), which had brushed aside a suggestion that an unwilling witness might be disgraced even though not prosecuted.

CHAPTER 6

LEGISLATIVE INVESTIGATIONS

[1] For an excellent account of the developing history of legislative investigations, see Telford Taylor, *Grand Inquest* (1954).

[2] Compare, however, John J. Mitchell, "Government Secrecy in Theory and Practice: 'Rules and Regulations' as an Autonomous Screen," 58 *Columbia Law Rev.* 199 (1958).

[3] *Anderson* v. *Dunn*, 6 Wheat. 204 (U.S., 1821); *Jurney* v. *MacCracken*, 294 U.S. 125 (1935). But compare *Marshall* v. *Dunn*, 243 U.S. 521, 541 (1917): A committee of the House of Representatives was inquiring into alleged wrongdoing by a government lawyer. He wrote a highly insulting letter to the committee. The House of Representatives directed that he be arrested. The courts, however, ordered that he be released from detention. The Supreme Court declared that his insulting conduct, offensive though it was, did not obstruct Congress in performing its functions. The purpose of the contempt power is self-preservation rather than punishment. Hence, Congress may exercise its authority only in terms of employing "the least possible power adequate to the end proposed."

[4] *In re Chapman*, 166 U.S. 661 (1897).

[5] See concurring opinion by Bazelon, J., in *Quinn* v. *United States*, 203 F. 2d 20, at 37n (D.C. Cir. 1952).

[6] The figures in the text are derived from George Galloway, "The Investigative Function of Congress," 21 *Am. Pol. Sci. Rev.* 47 (1927), and from Will Maslow, "Fair Procedure in Congressional Investigations," 54 *Columbia Law Rev.* 839 (1954), where figures may also be found that show a similar growth in state legislative investigating activity.

[7] *Quinn* v. *United States*, 349 U.S. 155, 160 (1955).

[8] *United States* v. *Rumely*, 345 U.S. 41, 46 (1953).

[9] See "Applicability of Privilege against Self-Incrimination to Legislative Investigations," 49 *Columbia Law Rev.* 87 (1949); "The Power of Congress to Investigate and to Compel Testimony," 71 *Harvard Law Rev.* 671 (1957). In a broad dictum (that is, in a remark that was not directly related to the precise decision that was made), Chief Justice Warren recently declared: "It is unquestionably the duty of all citizens to cooperate with the Congress in its efforts to obtain facts needed for intelligent legislative action. It is their unremitting obligation to respond to subpoenas, to respect the dignity of the Congress and its committees and to testify fully with respect to matters within the province of proper investigation. This, of course, assumes that the constitutional rights of witnesses will be respected by the Congress as they are in a court of justice. The Bill of Rights is applicable to investigations as to all forms of governmental action. Witnesses cannot be compelled to give evidence against themselves. They cannot be subjected to unreasonable search and seizure. Nor can the First Amendment freedoms of speech, press, religion, or political belief and association be abridged." *Watkins* v. *United States*, 354 U.S. 178 (1957).

[10] *Sinclair* v. *United States*, 279 U.S. 263, 293 (1929).

[11] 354 U.S. 178 (1957).

[12] A concurring opinion by Justice Frankfurter summarized the decision in this way: "Prosecution for contempt of Congress presupposes an adequate opportunity for the defendant to have awareness of the pertinency of the information that he has denied to Congress. And the basis of such awareness must be contemporaneous with the witness' refusal to answer and not at the trial for it. Accordingly, the actual scope of the inquiry that the Committee was authorized to conduct and the relevance of the questions to that inquiry must be shown to have been luminous at the time when asked and not left, at best, in cloudiness. The circumstances of this case were wanting in these essentials."

[13] 360 U.S. 109 (1959).

[14] *Scull* v. *Virginia*, 359 U.S. 344 (1959).

[15] H. Rep. No. 57, 84th Congress, 1st Session, p. 15.

[16] Compare *Uphaus* v. *Wyman*, 360 U.S. 72 (1959), which held that "exposure" as incidental to an authorized investigation was permissible, with *National Association for the Advancement of Colored People* v. *Alabama*, 357 U.S. 449 (1958), which held that an organization could not be compelled to produce its membership lists where to do so would expose its members to economic reprisal, loss of employment, threat of physical coercion, and other manifestations of public hostility, and where the state had demonstrated no substantial interest in obtaining the members' names.

CHAPTER 7

THE FREEDOM OF MOVEMENT

[1] See Zechariah Chafee, Jr., *Three Human Rights in the Constitution* (1956) 163–166.

[2] *Crandall* v. *Nevada*, 6 Wall. (U.S.) 35 (1867).

³ *Edwards* v. *California,* 314 U.S. 160 (1941). For a good general discussion, see Ivan C. Rutledge, "Regulation of the Movement of Workers: Freedom of Passage Within the United States," [1953] *Washington Univ. Law Rev.* 270.

⁴ *Williams* v. *Fears,* 179 U.S. 270, 274 (1900).

⁵ The whole matter is considered more extensively in Allan D. Vestal, "Freedom of Movement," 41 *Iowa Law Rev.* 6 (1955).

⁶ *Truax* v. *Raich,* 239 U.S. 33 (1915).

⁷ Eugene V. Rostow, "The Japanese American Cases—A Disaster," 54 *Yale Law Journal* 489 (1945).

⁸ See *Hirabayashi* v. *United States,* 320 U.S. 81 (1943); *Korematsu* v. *United States,* 323 U.S. 214 (1944). Compare, however, *Ex Parte Endo,* 323 U.S. 283 (1944), holding that once an individual had been "cleared," he could no longer be detained.

⁹ *Korematsu* v. *United States,* 323 U.S. 214, at 246 (1944). Compare Rostow, note 7 above, at p. 530: "The war power is the power to wage war successfully, as Chief Justice Hughes once remarked. But it is the power to wage war, not a license to do unnecessary and dictatorial things in the name of the war power." And see Walter F. Murphy, "Civil Liberties and the Japanese American Cases: A Study in the Uses of *Stare Decisis,*" 11 *Western Political Quarterly* 3 (1958).

¹⁰ For discussion of the early freedom (or lack of it) to go to America from Spain, France, and England, see Chafee, note 1 above, at pp. 167–176.

¹¹ A full and useful account of American immigration laws and policies up to 1953 can be found in the final report of the President's Commission on Immigration and Naturalization, "Whom We Shall Welcome" (1953). The title of the report comes from an address of George Washington, delivered at New York on December 2, 1783: "The bosom of America is open to receive not only the Opulent and Respectable Stranger, but the oppressed and persecuted of all Nations and Religions; *Whom we shall welcome* to a participation of all our rights and privileges, if by decency and propriety of conduct they appear to merit the enjoyment."

¹² Head Money Cases, 112 U.S. 580 (1884); *Nishimura Ekiu* v. *United States,* 142 U.S. 651 (1892).

¹³ *United States ex rel. Knauff* v. *Shaughnessy,* 338 U.S. 537 (1950); *Shaughnessy* v. *United States ex rel. Mezei,* 345 U.S. 206 (1953).

¹⁴ Leo Pfeffer, *The Liberties of an American* (1956), at 223.

¹⁵ 8 United States Code sec. 1185.

¹⁶ *Urtetiqui* v. *D'Arbel,* 9 Pet. 692, 698 (U.S., 1835). A great deal of historical material is cited in the various opinions in *Briehl* v. *Dulles,* 248 F. 2d 561 (D.C. Cir., 1957).

¹⁷ Hackworth, *Digest of International Law,* vol. III, p. 435.

¹⁸ Reginald Parker, "The Right to Go Abroad," 40 *Virginia Law Rev.* 853, 865 (1954).

¹⁹ See Parker, cited above note 18, at p. 864.

²⁰ This thesis is more fully developed in Murray Cohen and Robert F. Fuchs, "Communism's Challenge and the Constitution," 34 *Cornell Law Quarterly* 182 (1948), where the following conclusion is stated at p. 189: "The slight indirect deterrent on the freedom of speech of those who seek to further the world communist movement by use of the privilege to travel to and from the United States would not seem to outweigh the taking of an effective step to prohibit such travel."

[21] *Schachtman* v. *Dulles,* 225 F. 2d 29 (D.C. Cir., 1955).
[22] *Kent* v. *Dulles, Briehl* v. *Dulles, Dayton* v. *Dulles,* 357 U.S. 116 (1958).

CHAPTER 8

DESEGREGATING THE SCHOOLS

[1] Robert D. Cross, *The Emergence of Liberal Catholicism in America* (1958), at p. 23.
[2] See *Dominion Hotel* v. *Arizona,* 249 U.S. 265, 268 (1919); *Lindsley* v. *Natural Carbonic Gas Co.,* 220 U.S. 61, 78–79 (1911); *Strauder* v. *West Virginia,* 100 U.S. 303 (1880).
[3] 347 U.S. 483 (1954).
[4] In *Oyama* v. *California,* 332 U.S. 633 (1948), an attempted restraint upon land ownership was blocked. And see *Takahashi* v. *Fish Commission,* 334 U.S. 410 (1948) (exclusion of Japanese from fishing held to be invalid). For earlier and more successful discriminations, see *Terrace* v. *Thompson,* 263 U.S. 197 (1923); *Cockrill* v. *California,* 268 U.S. 258 (1924). See, generally, Milton R. Konvitz, *The Alien and the Asiatic in American Law* (1946).
[5] *Plessy* v. *Ferguson,* 163 U.S. 537 (1896).
[6] Quoted in Albert P. Blaustein and Clarence C. Ferguson, Jr., *Desegregation and the Law* (1956), at p. 105.
[7] See *Cumming* v. *County Board of Education,* 175 U.S. 28 (1899); *Gong Lum* v. *Rice,* 275 U.S. 78 (1927). And see also *Berea College* v. *Kentucky,* 211 U.S. 45 (1908).
[8] See *Missouri ex rel. Gaines* v. *Canada,* 305 U.S. 337 (1938); *Sipuel* v. *Board of Education,* 332 U.S. 631 (1948); *Sweatt* v. *Painter,* 339 U.S. 629 (1950); *McLaurin* v. *Board of Regents,* 339 U.S. 637 (1950). And see Robert A. Leflar and Wylie H. Davis, "Segregation in the Public Schools—1953," 67 *Harvard Law Rev.* 377 (1954), for material showing how little equality was in fact achieved in the separate educational facilities provided for Negroes.
[9] For a more temperate denunciation than many that have become popular, see James F. Byrnes, "The Supreme Court Must Be Curbed," *U.S. News and World Report,* May 18, 1956, p. 52.
[10] *Hertz* v. *Woodman,* 218 U.S. 205, at 212 (1910).
[11] *Burnet* v. *Coronado Oil & Gas Co.,* 285 U.S. 393, at 407–408 (1932) (dissenting opinion). Justice Brandeis cited more than thirty instances of overruling or qualifying earlier constitutional decisions. And see also Malcolm P. Sharp, "Movement in Supreme Court Adjudication—A Study of Modified and Overruled Decisions," 46 *Harvard Law Rev.* 361, 593, 795 (1933).
[12] William O. Douglas, "Stare Decisis," 49 *Columbia Law Rev.* 735, at 747 (1949). Justice Douglas observed (p. 743) that between 1937 and 1949 the Court had in thirty cases overruled earlier decisions. Twenty-one of these reversals were on constitutional grounds.
[13] *Farmers Loan & Trust Co.* v. *Minnesota,* 280 U.S. 204 (1930), in an opinion by Mr. Justice McReynolds, overruled *Blackstone* v. *Miller,* 188 U.S. 189 (1903), which had been cited approvingly by the Supreme Court fifteen times during the twenty-seven years between its appearance and its overruling.
[14] See Williams S. Jenkins, *Pro-Slavery Thought in the Old South* (1935),

at p. 243; Charles Johnson, *The Negro in American Civilization* (1930), at pp. 5–15.

[15] See John Hope Franklin, *The Free Negro in North Carolina, 1790–1860* (1943), at pp. 59–120; Stephen B. Weeks, "History of Negro Suffrage in the South," 9 *Political Science Quarterly* 671, 673–686 (1894); Jenkins, *op. cit.* note 14 above, at p. 246.

[16] See Willis D. Weatherford and Charles Johnson, *Race Relations: Adjustment of Whites and Negroes in the United States* (1934), at pp. 56–60.

[17] See C. Vann Woodward, *The Strange Career of Jim Crow* (1955), at pp. 63–64; and see also John Dollard, *Frustration and Aggression* (1939), at pp. 152, 153.

[18] For a compact résumé of socioeconomic factors that have affected current developments, see Robert B. McKay, "With All Deliberate Speed: A Study of School Desegregation," 31 *N.Y.U. Law Rev.* 991, 993 ff. (1956).

[19] The quoted phrase comes from a very perceptive analysis by W. J. Cash, *The Mind of the South* (1941), at p. 38.

[20] See John Dollard, *Caste and Class in a Southern Town* (1937), at p. 98. The stratification affects attitudes on both sides. See Eugene L. Horowitz, *Race Attitudes*, Part IV, "Characteristics of the American Negro" (1944), at p. 184; Samuel Stouffer, *Studies in Social Psychology in World War II* (1949), vol. I, p. 566. And see Dudley O. McGovney, "Racial Residential Segregation," 33 *Calif. Law Rev.* 5, at 27 (1945): ". . . it is fallacious to say . . . that the intention and effect [of segregation] is not to impose any badge of inferiority. . . . When a Negro workingman or woman is seated in the third seat of a street car on St. Charles Avenue in New Orleans and when a white man and woman is seated on the fourth seat, separated only by a bit of wire mesh ten inches high on the back of the third seat this is a 'separation' that is merely a symbolic assertion of social superiority, a 'ceremonial' celebration."

[21] See Otto Klineberg, *Negro Intelligence and Selective Migration* (1935), at p. 59, reviewing the outcome of school tests, New York City groups tests, investigation by the Chicago Commission on Race Relations, the National Intelligence Tests, and Stanford-Binet tests. See also the same author's *Social Psychology* (1954), at p. 259, and his "Race and Psychology," in *The Race Question in Modern Science* (UNESCO, 1956), at pp. 55–84, and Stuart Chase, *Proper Study of Mankind* (1948), at p. 103. Compare, however, Audrey M. Shuey, *The Testing of Negro Intelligence* (1958), which (at p. 318) concludes that intelligence tests have established "the presence of some native differences between Negroes and whites."

[22] See, e.g., F. C. Summer, "Mental Health Statistics of Negro College Freshmen," 33 *School and Society* 574, 576 (1931); H. M. Bond, "An Investigation of the Non-Intellectual Traits of a Group of Negro Adults," 21 *Journal of Abnormal and Social Psychology* 276, 286 (1931); Otto Klineberg, *Characteristics of the American Negro* (1944), at p. 138.

[23] See Benjamin Malzberg, "Mental Disease Among American Negroes," in *Characteristics of the American Negro* (Klineberg, ed., 1944), at pp. 373–395.

[24] Tom P. Brady, "A Review of 'Black Monday,'" being an address delivered before the Indianola, Mississippi, Citizens' Council on October 28, 1954, and published by the Association of Citizens Councils of Mississippi (Winona, Miss.), at p. 16; quoted in Albert P. Blaustein and Clarence C. Ferguson, Jr.,

Desegregation and the Law (1957), at p. 141. Somewhat similar "scientific" findings concerning Negro physiology were popular in the South a century ago in order to prove that the Negro was indeed inferior and should be servile. See, e.g., John H. Van Evrie, *Negroes and Negro Slavery* (1861), at pp. 120 ff., 214 ff., and *White Supremacy and Negro Subordination: or Negroes a Subordinate Race, and (So-called) Slavery Its Normal Condition* (1853); Samuel A. Cartwright, "Diseases and Peculiarities of the Negro Races," 9 *DeBow's Rev.* 64 (1851).

[25] For a brief but thorough review of extensive scholarly investigations of these matters see Otto Klineberg, *Race Differences* (1935), chaps. III, IV, V; M. F. Ashley-Montagu, *Man's Most Dangerous Myth* (3d ed. 1952), ch. 14. As to the brain pan, see T. W. Todd, "Entrenched Negro Physical Features," 1 *Human Biology* (1929), at pp. 57–69. And see also L. C. Dunn, "Race and Biology," in *The Race Question in Modern Science* (UNESCO, 1956), at pp. 245–284; and, in the same volume at pp. 285–322, G. M. Morant, "The Significance of Racial Differences."

As to the matter of blood, the blood of Negroes and whites is wholly compatible for purposes of transfusion. It appears to be the fact, however, that one type of anemia—sickle-cell anemia—occurs peculiarly among Negroes, being attributable to genetic factors in some Negro family lines. Pernicious anemia and haemophilia are, by contrast, more likely to be among the inheritance of white families than of Negro. These statements are based on interviews with medical authorities and are supported by Blaustein and Ferguson, *op. cit.* note 24 above, at p. 142, citing Herman Lewis, Biology of the Negro (1942), at pp. 139, 227, 249.

[26] See H. H. Hyman and P. B. Sheatsley, "Attitudes Toward Desegregation," 195 *Scientific American* 35 (Dec., 1956).

[27] The study in question is recorded in Report No. ETO-82 of the Research Branch, Information and Education Division, in the European Theater of Operations of the Army. It is described in "To Secure These Rights," The Report of the President's Committee on Civil Rights (1947), at pp. 83–84. The same report, at p. 140, makes this significant observation: "Practically all white officers and enlisted men in all branches of service [during World War II] saw Negro military personnel performing only the most menial functions. They saw Negroes recruited for the common defense as men apart and distinct from themselves. As a result, men who might otherwise have maintained the equalitarian morality of their forbears were given reason to look down on their fellow citizens. This has been sharply illustrated by the Army study discussed previously, in which white servicemen expressed great surprise at the excellent performance of Negroes who joined them in the firing line. Even now, very few people know of the successful experiment with integrated combat units."

In 1955 the Defense Department, reporting on integration in the Army, Navy, Air Force, and Marine Corps, asserted that "Thorough evaluation of the battle-tested results to date indicates a marked increase in overall combat effectiveness through integration. Economies in manpower, material, and money have resulted from the elimination of racially duplicated facilities and operations." Office of Assistant Secretary of Defense (Manpower and Personnel), "Integration in the Armed Services: A Progress Report" (1955), at p. 9.

²⁸ The study in question is Ira N. Brophy, "The Luxury of Anti-Negro Prejudice," 9 *Public Opinion Quarterly* 456 (1945). It is summarized in the report of the President's Committee, cited in the preceding note, at p. 85.

²⁹ See the second *Brown* v. *Board of Education*, 349 U.S. 294 (1955), in which the Court directed that integration was to be achieved with "all deliberate speed," in the light of variant circumstances. For discussion of progress toward compliance, see Theodore Leskes, "The Civil Rights Story—1958," in *American Jewish Year Book*, vol. 60, 1959; and see also Professor McKay's article, cited in note 18 above, at pp. 100 ff., and the same author's " 'With All Deliberate Speed': Legislative Reaction and Judicial Development 1956–1957," 43 *Virginia Law Rev.* 1205 (1957); H. C. Fleming and John Constable, "What's Happening in School Integration?" Public Affairs Pamphlet No. 244 (1956).

³⁰ See Eli Ginzberg, *The Negro Potential* (1956), at pp. 121–124. In this study, prepared for the Conservation of Human Resources Project launched at Columbia University by President Eisenhower, Professor Ginzberg declares (p. 122): "The time is near when the South will have to make a major decision. Negroes represent approximately one fourth of the population of the South. It is indeed questionable whether the South will be able to keep pace with the rest of the country if it continues to lose its most competent and best-trained Negroes. At present, a young Negro who has acquired skills in the armed services and comes back even to such a metropolitan center as Atlanta finds it difficult to obtain a job which uses his skills. Before long his availability is made known to employment exchanges north of the Mason-Dixon Line, and he is likely to be on his way, lost to the South forever. Other costs are also implicit in the maintenance and operation of a segregated system of employment. Such a system inevitably results in excessive overhead and faulty utilization practices since men must be assigned primarily according to their color rather than the needs of the plant. The South will have to give up the luxury of maintaining segregation in the work place and begin to make progressive moves to abandon it, if it is to strengthen its position in the never-ceasing competition for new plants."

³¹ See Ernest W. Swanson and John A. Griffin, *Public Education in the South* (1955), at p. 19. In 1900, 34.5 per cent of the Southern population was Negro. By 1950 the percentage had declined to only 22.5.

³² See H. H. Remmers and D. H. Radler, *The American Teenager* (1957), at p. 205, showing responses of a scientifically determined cross section of the youthful population to the following question: "Do you think we are born with our feelings toward persons of other races, or do we learn those feelings?" Six per cent of the respondents thought they were born with their feelings; but 88 per cent thought their feelings had been learned. The other 8 per cent were undecided or uncommunicative.

³³ See the work of Remmers and Radler, cited in the preceding note, at p. 204.

³⁴ H. H. Hyman and P. B. Sheatsley, cited in note 26 above. The impact of education on attitude is suggested by responses to questions carefully propounded in the two state universities of Florida: "Would you admit Negroes to higher public education in Florida either now or after a reasonable period of preparation?" Answering *yes* were Faculty Members, 82.30 per cent; Students, 63.65 per cent; Alumni, 43.48 per cent; Parents of Enrolled Students, 30.24 per cent. For these and further data concerning Florida opinion con-

cerning various aspects of educational integration, see *Study on Desegregation,* Florida Board of Control for State Institutions of Higher Learning (1956), vol. I.
    [35] Quoted in Wilma Dykeman and James Stokely, *Neither Black Nor White* (1957), at p. 358. And see also William Peters, *The Southern Temper* (1959), an especially perceptive analysis of the past and future of segregation. Compare Harold H. Quint, *Profile in Black and White* (1958), a study of retrogression in South Carolina, one of the "die hard" states.

CHAPTER 9

"PRIVATE GOVERNMENT" AND THE CONSTITUTION

[1] A. A. Berle, Jr., "Economic Power and the Free Society," pp. 14, 15 (Fund for the Republic Pamphlet, 1958). See also Professor Berle's *The 20th Century Capitalist Revolution* (1954), p. 25, referring to M. A. Adelman, "The Measurement of Industrial Concentration," *The Review of Economics and Statistics,* Nov., 1951, vol. 33, no. 4. Compare J. K. Galbraith, *American Capitalism* (1952), at pp. 6–7: ". . . the heads of the corporations that produce between a third and a half of the national product of the United States could be seated comfortably in almost any neighborhood motion-picture theater."
    [2] See Wolfgang G. Friedmann, "Corporate Power, Government by Private Groups, and the Law," 57 *Columbia Law Rev.* 155, at 172–176 (1957).
    [3] Peter Drucker, *The Concept of the Corporation* (1946), at pp. 6–7.
    [4] There is a growing literature concerning the important role of special interest groups in forming "public policy" as expressed in legislation, but perhaps not enough has been written concerning their more subtle impact on public attitudes. As to the American Medical Association, see Note, "The American Medical Association: Power, Purpose and Politics in Organized Medicine," 63 *Yale Law Journal* 938 (1954). More broadly, see, e.g., Earl Latham, *The Group Basis of Politics* (1952); Fred Riggs, *Pressures on Congress* (1950); E. Pendleton Herring, *Group Representation Before Congress* (1929); Donald C. Blaisdell, "Economic Power and Political Pressures" (*TNEC* Monograph 26, 1941); David B. Truman, *The Governmental Process* (1951); Arthur Bentley, *The Process of Government* (1935); Stephen Bailey, *Congress Makes a Law* (1950). As to the administrative process, see, e.g., W. Gellhorn, *Federal Administrative Proceedings* (1941), chap. IV.
    It is worth noting that a "group" rarely has a single view. Within any group there is likely to be a minority that may be overriden and, indeed, oppressed or virtually destroyed by the rest. Thus, for example, in a businessmen's organization, high-cost producers may succeed in gaining the group's support of price-fixing programs or tariff programs that may shatter the competitive position of those who can undersell them. For a brilliant discussion, see E. E. Schattschneider, *Politics, Pressures, and the Tariff* (1935).
    [5] Compare Morris R. Cohen, "Property and Sovereignty," 13 *Cornell Law Quarterly* 8 (1927). As Professor Cohen there observed, the state itself once upon a time fixed most wages and most prices. Then, under the influence of laissez-faire philosophy, it allowed this sort of economic regulation to be done instead by the individual property owner, who thus acquired (by default, as

it were) some of the "sovereign" power of prescribing the rules by which society is governed.

[6] House Report No. 250, 84th Congress, 2d Session; *U.S. Code Congressional and Administrative News* 4596 (1956).

[7] Public Law No. 1026, 84th Congress, 2d Session (Aug. 8, 1956). As to state laws, see Brown and Convill, "Automobile Manufacturer-Dealer Legislation," 57 *Columbia Law Rev.* 219 (1957).

[8] The figures about the dealers' investments are derived from the House Report cited in note 6 above, at pp. 4597, 4599. The same report discloses how very gigantic the giants are. General Motors Company in 1956 produced 55 per cent of all automobiles manufactured in America. In 1955 it had assets of 6,344,722,000 dollars, far more than any other corporation in the country. Its sales, amounting to nearly 12½ billion dollars, accounted for approximately 3 per cent of the gross national product of the United States. The Ford and Chrysler corporations, the other two members of the Big Three of the automobile industry, were, respectively, the third and fifth largest corporations in the country. The assets of the three corporations were approximately 10.2 billion dollars. Through the control they exercised over their franchised dealers (with assets of five billion dollars), their economic power might be said to have been increased by 50 per cent.

[9] Compare W. W. Wirtz, "Government by Private Groups," 13 *Louisiana Law Rev.* 440, 450–451 (1953); A. A. Berle, Jr., *The 20th Century Capitalist Revolution* (1954), pp. 54–59.

[10] See, e.g., *Corrigan* v. *Buckley*, 271 U.S. 323 (1926).

[11] See, e.g., Civil Rights Cases, 109 U.S. 3 (1883).

[12] For helpful discussion, see W. W. Wirtz, "Government by Private Groups," 13 *Louisiana Law Rev.* 440 (1953). And see also Arthur S. Miller, "The Constitutional Law of the 'Security State,'" 10 *Stanford Law Rev.* 620 (1958); Alexander Pekelis, *Law and Social Action* (1950), pp. 91–128.

[13] See, e.g., *Carter* v. *Carter Coal Co.*, 298 U.S. 238 (1936). And see especially the luminous study by Louis L. Jaffe, "Law Making by Private Groups," 51 *Harvard Law Rev.* 201 (1937).

[14] *Ex parte Virginia*, 100 U.S. 339, 347 (1880); *Shelley* v. *Kraemer*, 334 U.S. 1, 14 (1948).

[15] See R. L. Hale, "Force and the State: A Comparison of 'Political' and 'Economic' Compulsion," 35 *Columbia Law Rev.* 149 (1935); and see generally Professor Hale's masterwork, *Freedom Through Law* (1952).

[16] Cited in note 14 above.

[17] In the later case of *Barrows* v. *Jackson*, 346 U.S. 249 (1953), the Court applied the reasoning of *Shelley* v. *Kraemer* when a suit for damages was brought by one covenantor against another who had allegedly disregarded a restrictive covenant. The Court enunciated its position as follows (at p. 258): "This Court will not permit or require California to coerce respondent to respond in damages for failure to observe a restrictive covenant that this Court would deny California the right to enforce in equity . . . ; or that this Court would deny California the right to incorporate in a statute; . . . or that could not be enforced in a federal jurisdiction because such a covenant would be contrary to public policy. . . ." For other examples of finding "state action" in discrimination that was incidentally effectuated rather than initially planned by the state,

see *Pennsylvania* v. *Board of Directors of the Philadelphia City Trusts,* 353 U.S. 230 (1957); *Kerr* v. *Enoch Pratt Free Library,* 149 F. 2d 212 (4th Cir., 1945), certiorari denied, 326 U.S. 721 (1945).

This approach is not invariably adopted. Compare, for example, *State* v. *Clyburn,* 247 N.C. 455, 101 S.E. 2d 295 (1958): Negroes, led by a minister, took seats in a Durham, North Carolina, ice cream and sandwich shop in a section reserved for "White," and they refused to move to the section marked "Colored." They were prosecuted for "unlawfully refusing to leave that portion of [private] premises reserved for members of the White Race, knowing or having reason to know that [they] had no license therefor." The court rejected the defendants' contention that "state action" was involved in enforcing the shop owner's segregation policy. Convictions were upheld, the court citing many other state cases which had recognized "the right of an operator of a private enterprise to select the clientele he will serve, and to make such selection based on color, if he so desires."

[18] 240 F. 2d 922 (5th Cir., 1956), certiorari denied, 353 U.S. 924 (1957).

[19] In the somewhat similar case of *Lawrence* v. *Hancock,* 76 F. Supp. 1004 (S.D. W.Va. 1948), the federal district court held that a city could not escape its constitutional obligations by leasing a publicly-constructed swimming pool to a private operator, who then denied Negroes the use of the pool. Judge Moore wrote: "It is not conceivable that a city can provide the ways and means for a private individual or corporation to discriminate against its own citizens. Having set up the swimming pool by the authority of the legislature, the city, if the pool is operated, must operate it itself, or if leased, must see that it is operated without any such discrimination." For comparable holdings as to operation of a golf course and a theatrical amphitheater, see *Simkins* v. *City of Greensboro,* 149 F. Supp. 562 (W.D.N.C. 1957); *Muir* v. *Louisville Park Theatrical Association,* 347 U.S. 971 (1954); *Holmes* v. *City of Atlanta,* 223 F. 2d 93 (5th Cir., 1955), affirmed 350 U.S. 879 (1955).

The holdings have not been uniform, some courts not having been able to find the degree of state involvement necessary to constitute "state action." See, e.g., *Norris* v. *Baltimore,* 78 F. Supp. 451 (D.Md., 1948); *Dorsey* v. *Stuyvesant Town Corp.,* 299 N.Y. 512, 87 N.E. 2d 541 (1949), certiorari denied, 339 U.S. 981 (1950).

[20] 323 U.S. 192 (1944).

[21] The Railway Labor Act, 45 U.S.C.A. 152 (1934) provides, for example, that "the majority of any craft or class of employees shall have the right to determine who shall be the representative of the craft or class. . . ."

[22] Note especially the language of Justice Murphy's concurring opinion (at p. 208): "While such a union is essentially a private organization, its power to represent and bind all members of a class or craft is derived solely from Congress . . . it cannot be assumed that Congress meant to authorize the representative to act so as to ignore rights guaranteed by the Constitution. Otherwise the Act would bear the stigma of unconstitutionality under the Fifth Amendment in this respect. The Constitution voices its disapproval whenever economic discrimination is applied under authority of law against any race, creed or color."

In *American Communication Association* v. *Douds,* 339 U.S. 382, at 401 (1950), Chief Justice Vinson remarked that "power is never without responsibility. When authority derives in part from Government's thumb on the scales, the exercise of that power becomes closely akin, in some respects, to its exercise by Government itself."

[23] *Tunstall* v. *Brotherhood of Locomotive Firemen,* 323 U.S. 210 (1944). And see also *Brotherhood of Railroad Trainmen* v. *Howard,* 343 U.S. 768 (1952), where the reasoning of the earlier cases was extended to a situation in which there was no bargaining relationship at all between the union and the affected employees.

[24] *Central of Georgia Railway Co.* v. *Jones,* 229 F. 2d 648 (5th Cir., 1956); *Graham* v. *Brotherhood of Locomotive Firemen,* 338 U.S. 232 (1949). And see also *Betts* v. *Easley,* 161 Kans. 459, 169 P. 2d 831, 166 A.L.R. 342 (1946), in which the Kansas Supreme Court invalidated a union rule that Negro members should be organized in "separate lodges" which were "under the jurisdiction of and represented by the delegate of the nearest white local." The union argued that the manner of its internal organization was nobody's business, because the union was merely a private association, like a club. But the court thought otherwise, saying: "When the Negro workmen . . . are not permitted to participate in meetings where 'delegates may be seated,' they are denied rights and privileges accorded to white workmen in vital matters subject to negotiation and adjustment under the [Railway Labor] Act. . . . This Court cannot be blind to present-day realities affecting labor in large industrial plants. The individual workman cannot 'go it alone.' Every person with an understanding of mass production and other features of modern industry long ago recognized the necessity of collective bargaining by labor representatives freely chosen, if human rights are to be adequately safeguarded. In the Railway Labor Act, Congress gave clear and firm recognition to this necessity. . . . The petition alleges not only that Negro employees are denied the right to take part in such local affairs of the union as the election of officers and the fixing of dues, but are denied the right to participate in determining the position to be taken by the union, as bargaining agent for all employees, as to wages, hours, working conditions, and other such matters vitally affecting their economic welfare. . . . The acts complained of are in violation of the Fifth Amendment."

[25] *Syres* v. *Oil Workers International Union,* 350 U.S. 892 (1955).

[26] See *Nixon* v. *Herndon,* 273 U.S. 536 (1927).

[27] Compare *Nixon* v. *Condon,* 286 U.S. 73 (1932), with *Grovey* v. *Townsend,* 295 U.S. 45 (1935).

[28] 321 U.S. 649 (1944).

[29] *Rice* v. *Elmore,* 165 F. 2d 387 (4th Cir., 1947). And see also *Baskin* v. *Brown,* 174 F. 2d 891 (4th Cir., 1949).

[30] 345 U.S. 461, at 469 (1953).

[31] 343 U.S. 451 (1952).

[32] 326 U.S. 501 (1946).

[33] 326 U.S. at pp. 506, 507, 508–509.

[34] For discussion of censorship problems in connection with books, see W. Gellhorn, *Individual Freedom and Governmental Restraints* (1956), chap. 2.

[35] *New York Times,* Nov. 28, 1956, p. 32, col. 2.

[36] *New York Times,* Dec. 17, 1956, p. 28, col. 1.

[37] *New York Times,* Dec. 27, 1956, p. 21, col. 3.

[38] *New York Times,* Dec. 29, 1956, p. 8, col. 6.

[39] *New York Times,* Dec. 30, 1956, p. 24, col. 4.

⁴⁰ *New York Times*, Jan. 1, 1957, p. 19, col. 2.

⁴¹ *New York Times*, Mar. 19, 1957, p. 76, col. 6.

⁴² *New York Times*, May 25, 1957, p. 25, col. 4.

⁴³ *New York Times*, Dec. 21, 1956, p. 18, col. 6.

⁴⁴ *New York Times*, Jan. 7, 1957, p. 29, col. 2.

⁴⁵ In fact some such suppressive actions were attempted by public officials in scattered cities. See *New York Times*, Jan. 24, 1957, p. 34, col. 7; Jan. 30, 1957, p. 33, col. 3. In one such city, a courageous owner of a chain of theaters refused to comply with a "request" by city officials that he cancel the booking of this film. "It is one thing," he said, "for a group not to want to see a movie, but it is another to force opinions on a whole city." So far as is known, no steps were taken against him to enforce the "request." If they had been, state action would clearly have been present and constitutional issues could have been raised.

⁴⁶ Robert L. Hale, *Freedom Through Law* (1952), at viii.

⁴⁷ Hearings before the Committee on Education and Labor on S. 1606, 79th Congress, 2d Session 2637 (1946), referred to in Note, "The American Medical Association: Power, Purpose and Politics in Organized Medicine," 63 *Yale Law Journal* 938 (1954).

⁴⁸ *Group Health Cooperative of Puget Sound* v. *King County Medical Society*, 39 Wash. 2d 586, 626, 237 P. 2d. 737, 759 (1951).

⁴⁹ *Id.*, at 601, 619, 636; *Walker* v. *Medical Society of Mobile County*, 247 Ala. 169, 22 So. 2d 715 (1945); *American Medical Association* v. *United States*, 130 F. 2d 233 (App. D.C., 1942), affirmed 317 U.S. 519 (1942).

⁵⁰ See, e.g., *Brown* v. *Harris County Medical Society*, 194 S.W. 1179 (Tex. Civ. App., 1917); *Weyrens* v. *Scotts Bluff County Medical Society*, 133 Neb. 814, 277 N.W. 378 (1938) (a case of expulsion from membership, rather than denial of admission); *Smith* v. *Kern County Medical Association*, 19 Cal. 2d 263, 120 P. 2d 874 (1942). Compare, however, *Alpert* v. *Board of Governors of City Hospital*, 145 N.Y.S. 2d 534 (App. Div. 4th Dept., 1955) (where expulsion from membership led to denial of hospital privileges or staff position in a publicly-administered hospital, due process requirements were held to be applicable).

⁵¹ E.g., Montana Rev. Code, Sec. 69–2917 (1947).

⁵² See Note, "Legal Limitations on Right of Unincorporated Medical Association to Expel Members," 41 *Minnesota Law Rev.* 212, 214 (1957).

⁵³ 25 Cal. 2d 721, 155 P. 2d 329, 160 A.L.R. 900 (1945).

⁵⁴ John Kenneth Galbraith, *American Capitalism* (1952), at 171–172. And see also W. W. Wirtz, "Government by Private Groups," 13 *Louisiana Law Rev.* 440, 450, 451 (1953).

⁵⁵ Compare *Miller* v. *Schoene*, 276 U.S. 272 (1928): A Virginia statute directed a state official to order the destruction of ornamental red cedar trees infected with a fungus that was harmless to the cedars but destructive of apple orchards, when the cedar trees were found within two miles of the orchards. Previously, the property of the orchard owners had been subject to destruction by the property of the owners of infected cedar trees. But the orchard owners had been without recourse. Now the state legislature, regarding orchards as of great economic importance to the state, decided to come to the rescue. Said Justice Stone (pp. 279–280): ". . . the state was under the necessity of making a choice between the preservation of one class of property and that of the

other whenever both existed in dangerous proximity. It would have been none the less a choice if, instead of enacting the present statute, the state, by doing nothing, had permitted serious injury to the apple orchards . . . to go unchecked. . . ."

EPILOGUE

[1] *Den ex dem. Murray* v. *Hoboken Land & Improvement Co.*, 18 How. 272, 276 (U.S., 1876).

[2] Felix Frankfurter & James M. Landis, *The Business of the Supreme Court* (1928), p. 310.

[3] *Snyder* v. *Massachusetts*, 291 U.S. 97, 105 (1934).

[4] *Palko* v. *Connecticut*, 302 U.S. 319 (1937).

[5] *Solesbee* v. *Balkcom*, 339 U.S. 9, 16 (1950).

[6] Robert M. MacIver, *The Web of Government* (1947), 107–108.

[7] O. W. Holmes, Jr., *The Common Law* (1881), at p. 1.

[8] John P. Frank, in *Supreme Court and Supreme Law* (Edmond Cahn ed., 1954), at p. 114. Mr. Frank remarks that "Neither the spirit of liberty nor the spirit of repression is ever totally absent from the American scene." We have our cycles. When repression is dominant, we experience "an intense spasm of social fury in which a commonly latent impulse to destroy opposition without regard to the norms of democratic behavior becomes a dominantly conspicuous element in the American scene." With two very minor exceptions, "Congress has never yet passed a statute in a fit of repression which the Supreme Court has invalidated. . . . The dominant lesson of our history in the relation of the judiciary to repressions is that courts love liberty most when it is under pressure least."

INDEX

Aliens, control over entry, 72, 85
American Communications Association v. *Douds*, 101
American Medical Association, 169, 187

Baby Doll, efforts to suppress, 183–186
Barenblatt v. *United States*, 123–130
Berle, Adolf A., Jr., on concentration of economic power, 164–165; on twentieth century capitalism, 191
Betts v. *Brady*, 22
Black, Justice Hugo L., on search of the person, 34; on unions' picketing rights, 66; on *Dennis* case, 79; on penalizing unorthodoxy, 104; on legislative investigating powers, 124, 126–130
Brady, Tom P., on eugenics and biology, 158
Brandeis, Justice Louis D., on the right of privacy, 35; on regulation of speech, 53; on speech as a social corrective, 60; on clear and present danger, 76; on *stare decisis*, 154
Breithaupt v. *Abram*, 33
Brown v. *Board of Education*, 151, 153
Brownell, Herbert, Jr., on counsel for indigents, 21

Censorship, by private pressures, 182–186
Chafee, Zechariah, Jr., on habeas corpus, 7–8; on freedom of the home, 53
Chessman v. *Teets*, 16–17
Clark, Justice Tom, on Yates decision, 80; on public employees' qualifications, 103

Communist Control Act of 1954. *See* Subversion, control of
Confessions, reliance on, 24–25; pressing the accused, 25–26; psychological pressures, 26; delayed arraignment, 26–27; delayed trial, 38
Congressional investigation. *See* Investigating committees
Constitution, Article I, 7; Article VI, 2; First Amendment, 41, 97, 192, 197; Fourth Amendment, 28, 196–197; Fifth Amendment, 4, 108, 174; Sixth Amendment, 20; Eighth Amendment, 199; Fourteenth Amendment, 4, 16, 22, 41, 159; Fifteenth Amendment, 178, 179, 197
Control of subversion. *See* Subversion, control of
Counsel, right to, for indigents, 20; federal practice, 20–21; British practice, 21; state practice, 21–24; Scandinavian practice, 38

Dennis v. *United States*, 75–79, 95
Derrington v. *Plummer*, 175
Douglas, Justice William O., on search of the person, 34; on unions' picketing rights, 66; on Smith Act prosecutions, 78; on freedom to travel, 147
Drucker, Peter, on corporation as social force, 169

Emigration. *See* Passports
Ex Parte Milligan, 10

Feiner v. *New York*, 56–58
Flag salute cases, 98–99
Frank, Jerome N., on justice for indigents, 21

229